FREUD:
A GUIDE FOR THE PERPLEXED

Continuum *Guides for the Perplexed*

Continuum's Guides for the Perplexed are clear, concise and accessible introductions to thinkers, writers and subjects that students and readers can find especially challenging. Concentrating specifically on what it is that makes the subject difficult to grasp, these books explain and explore key themes and ideas, guiding the reader towards a thorough understanding of demanding material.

Guides for the Perplexed available from Continuum:

Adorno: A Guide for the Perplexed, Alex Thomson
Deleuze: A Guide for the Perplexed, Claire Colebrook
Derrida: A Guide for the Perplexed, Julian Wolfreys
Descartes: A Guide for the Perplexed, Justin Skirry
Existentialism: A Guide for the Perplexed, Stephen Earnshaw
Freud: A Guide for the Perplexed, Céline Surprenant
Gadamer: A Guide for the Perplexed, Chris Lawn
Habermas: A Guide for the Perplexed, Eduardo Mendieta
Hegel: A Guide for the Perplexed, David James
Hobbes: A Guide for the Perplexed, Stephen J. Finn
Hume: A Guide for the Perplexed, Angela Coventry
Husserl: A Guide for the Perplexed, Matheson Russell
Kant: A Guide for the Perplexed, TK Seung
Kierkegaard: A Guide for the Perplexed, Clare Carlisle
Leibniz: A Guide for the Perplexed, Franklin Perkins
Levinas: A Guide for the Perplexed, B. C. Hutchens
Merleau-Ponty: A Guide for the Perplexed, Eric Matthews
Nietzsche: A Guide for the Perplexed, R. Kevin Hill
Plato: A Guide for the Perplexed, Gerald A. Press
Quine: A Guide for the Perplexed, Gary Kemp
Ricoeur: A Guide for the Perplexed, David Pellauer
Rousseau: A Guide for the Perplexed, Matthew Simpson
Sartre: A Guide for the Perplexed, Gary Cox
Spinoza: A Guide for the Perplexed, Charles Jarrett
Wittgenstein: A Guide for the Perplexed, Mark Addis

FREUD: A GUIDE FOR THE PERPLEXED

CÉLINE SURPRENANT

continuum

Continuum International Publishing Group
The Tower Building   80 Maiden Lane
11 York Road   Suite 704
London SE1 7NX   New York NY 10038

www.continuumbooks.com

First published 2008

British Library Cataloguing-in-Publication Data
A catalogue record for this book is available from the British Library.

ISBN-10: HB: 0-8264-9277-0
PB: 0-8264-9278-9
ISBN-13: HB: 978-0-8264-9277-7
PB: 978-0-8264-9278-4

Library of Congress Cataloging-in-Publication Data
Surprenant, Céline, 1961–
    Freud : a guide for the perplexed / Céline Surprenant.
      p. cm.
    Includes bibliographical references and index.
    ISBN 978-0-8264-9277-7 — ISBN 978-0-8264-9278-4
    1. Freud, Sigmund, 1856–1939. I. Title.

    BF173.F85S795 2008
    150.19′52092—dc22

                               2007034515

Typeset by Servis Filmsetting Ltd, Manchester
Printed and bound in Great Britain by Cromwell Press Ltd,
Trowbridge, Wiltshire

For Jean, Pierre and Émile

CONTENTS

ACKNOWLEDGEMENTS

I am very grateful to friends for their support while writing this book, in particular to Nicholas Royle, who encouraged me to write it, to Brian Cummings, Darrow Schecter, to Kate Briggs and Tanja Staehler, who read parts of it, and to Thamy Ayouch for his discussions and writings on Freud. I am also grateful to Tom Roberts from Sigmud Freud Copyrights for granting me permission to reproduce figures and texts from *The Standard Edition of the Complete Psychological Works of Sigmund Freud*.

INTRODUCTION

EVIL LOOKS

Laughter, Sigmund Freud writes, 'arises if a quota of psychical energy which has earlier been used for the cathexis of particular psychical paths has become unusable so that it can find free discharge' (SE 8: 147).[1] Instead of the physical, noisy and ravishing burst that laughter provokes, it apparently consists in the useful discharge of a certain quantity of psychical energy. Freud was proposing a stark theoretical account of a common, pleasurable experience. However, he was well aware of the forbidding nature of his explanation and amusingly anticipated what 'evil looks' it was likely to invite. In *Jokes and their Relation to the Unconscious* (1905), where he put forward that definition of laughter, he did not specify whom the hypothesis about quotas and discharge would so displease. Did he have in mind nineteenth-century writers on aesthetics, whom he quoted throughout the study on jokes? Was he suspecting that the non-scientific reading public might be interested in exploring the comic but not necessarily in approaching it as a scientific topic? Or else, was he anticipating the phenomenological critique of his work, developed in the vein of Edmund Husserl's critical outlook on late-nineteenth-century psychology and natural sciences?[2] Whatever the case, and judging by the reception of that aspect of Freudian psychoanalysis, Freud was right to imagine that such explanations could invite 'evil looks'. For once, he was not here reacting against the accusation of bringing everything back to genital sexuality or of pan-sexualism, or against that of reducing works of art and literary texts to Oedipal dramas (that is, to the staging the instinctual attraction that an individual has for the parent of the opposite sex in the course of his

1

sexual development). Rather, he was seemingly calling our attention to the discrepancy between a fragile object of inquiry, such as laughter, and a crushing theoretical quantitative explanation. What indeed can we gain by replacing an everyday social experience, and a pleasurable one at that, with such an abstract account?

One might expect to find such explanations in a scientific paper, as, for example, in Freud's 1890s papers on the aetiology of hysteria. However, psychoanalysis was not limited to explaining scientifically mental illness. Rather, the study of mental illnesses became a means of obtaining knowledge of 'normal' unconscious mental life, according to a notion of the unconscious that emerged through clinical practice during the 1890s. The disturbing contrast between laughter and the psychoanalytic account of it may be striking. But there is no less striking a contrast between many other phenomena and the theory of the unconscious to which Freud referred them. 'Discharge', 'quotas' and 'psychical energy', among other concepts, formed an integral part of that theory, which he elaborated in Vienna from the 1890s up until 1938, and in exile in London from 1938 until his death in 1939.

In the following *Guide for the Perplexed*, the discrepancy between phenomena and explanations as what particularly characterizes Freudian psychoanalysis will provide a guiding thread for introducing some of Freud's main ideas. However, we will not consider the latter as a negative feature, but as a result of Freud's following the idea of unconscious mental activity through. It is not that he 'invented' the concept of the unconscious. Rather, he appropriated the term unconscious, and transformed it into an unusually influential concept, and a complete theory of the mind.[3] By 1923, twenty-seven years after its appearances in a paper on 'Heredity and the Aetiology of the Neuroses' (1896) and in 'The Neuro-Psychoses of Defence' (1894), psychoanalysis had acquired two meanings. On the one hand, it referred to 'a particular method of treating nervous disorders', and on the other, to 'the science of unconscious mental processes' (SE 20: 264).[4] Freud predicted that, in the future, the latter meaning would become more important than the first, even though psychoanalytic views 'are bound to seem very strange to ordinary modes of thought and [. . .] fundamentally contradict current views' (1940 [1938] SE 23: 282). What sort of intellectual and practical object does psychoanalysis indeed constitute?

One of Freud's recurrent themes is that there are unconscious mental processes whose activity late-nineteenth-century philosophers and psychologists were not willing to admit.[5] Most of Freud's contemporaries believed that everything that is mental is conscious. Psychoanalysis put forward the hypothesis that a representation could be both mental (psychical) and unconscious. A representation could be unconscious, in so far as it could disappear, reappear, and persist in the interval. At first, the term unconscious was a 'purely descriptive term' pointing to the thought or representation of which the person concerned knows nothing (SE 9: 48). It was meant to be an 'easily understandable description' pointing to the thought as being 'concealed' or 'inaccessible' (SE 15: 113). However, it was not only that a thought could be 'unconscious' in that descriptive sense. Unconscious acquired a dynamic sense: what is unconscious is not static and latent, but is active even when, or perhaps because, it is prevented from becoming conscious. For example, one of my childhood impressions could 'produce' effects without my knowledge of that mental activity (or of the memory of the childhood impression). There are 'psychical acts which lack consciousness' (SE 14: 170). The term unconscious finally came also to stand for the name of a system, where specific processes operate, and which the theory of mental functioning (to which the quantitative account of laughter belongs) presents. The strangeness of psychoanalysis, then, lay, among other factors, in its challenge to received ideas about consciousness (recent commentators would say ideas about the *subject* or subjectivity, although Freud himself did not speak about the subject in that sense: he referred to patients, individuals, children and adults, family members, professionals, or else to the psychical apparatus: the Ego, the Id, the Super-Ego. It is uncontroversial that he did propose a 'science of subjectivity' as Lear suggests [1990: 3]).[6]

Today, many philosophers and intellectual historians believe that Freud's theory of the unconscious has enlarged our conception of the mind, notably 'by developing new *forms* of explanations' (Wollheim 1991: xxviii), and that to take some of Freud's ideas seriously could transform our view of the world (Lear 1990: 3). This positive approach to Freud is at variance with the considerable number of criticisms that psychoanalytic theories have provoked. That a general climate of objections surrounds Freud's work is perhaps one of the most well-known facts about it. Some of these objections have sought to show that psychoanalysis is quackery, and lacks legitimacy as a therapeutic method (See 'The Question of Lay-Analysis' (1926; SE 20: 183–258) for Freud's response to that accusation).[7] We will not elaborate on these endeavours to discredit Freud's thinking and therapy. Dismissals of Freud are readily available in daily conversation, in printed and visual media or fictional works, and in learned journals and books.[8]

However, some of the very commentators who endorse Freudian ideas on pathological and normal unconscious mental processes, still formulate criticisms against them. For example, one might ask whether it is true that '*a dream is a (disguised) fulfilment of a (suppressed or repressed) wish*' (Freud's emphasis, SE 4: 160), as Freud proposed in *The Interpretation of Dreams* (1900). Admitting that it is, does it follow that one needs the 'fiction' of the psychical apparatus, which is constructed according to a reflex arc, in order to explain the function of dreams, as Freud did in the last chapter of the book (SE 5: 538; 551; 565, but also in all of Chapter VII)? In other words, does one need such a causal story? Freud's theory of the unconscious did not lack a scientific character. Quite the reverse: for many philosophers, Freud relied too heavily on nineteenth-century scientific concepts for explaining the peculiarities of human behaviour. Freudian psychoanalysis rightly perceived the importance of some puzzling events and realized that all human actions, even the most trivial, deserve critical attention (Lear 2006: 28). Nevertheless, it would seem misguided to deal with them and with other problems such as self-knowledge, irrationality, freedom, love, happiness, life and death, within the framework of the natural sciences.

FREUD AND NATURAL SCIENCES

The idea that it is essential to disentangle Freud's valuable descriptions of phenomena from his scientific explanations has inspired many philosophical criticisms of his work. That critical position assumes, in various forms, that Freud's theory of the unconscious can extend our knowledge of the mind provided that one discards some of its problematic components. In fact, one could go so far as to state that such a 'diagnostic' position condenses to a large extent the philosophical reception of Freud's work.[9] The psychiatrist and philosopher Ludwig Binswanger, with whom Freud corresponded between 1908 and 1938, formulated some of these criticisms exemplarily. It is worth turning briefly to some of his reflections on Freud's work, because they clarify the contrast between phenomena and explanations that we identified above. Binswanger devoted a great part of his research to exploring what sort of instrument of knowledge psychoanalysis constituted in relation to psychology and psychiatry, notably in 'The Freudian Conception of Man from an Anthropological Point of View [Freuds Auffassung des Menschen im Lichte der Anthropologie]' (1936). Phenomenology informed his analyses, and his project of 'existential psychoanalysis', with which we will not, however, deal here.[10]

For Binswanger, Freud constructed a theoretical model of the human as a natural being (1970 [1936]: 202), because he believed that one could know about human existence through scientific experimental work. Freud expressed that belief in *The Future of an Illusion* (1930), among other places. The latter went together with his intuition of what Binswanger called a 'monstrous invisible', that is, an intuition connected with the foundation of life and death (1970 [1936]: 202). In Binswanger's account, *homo natura*, on which Freud's research rests, represents the 'requirement of naturalist research' rather than connects with a living human being (1970 [1936]: 206). It is a *tabula rasa*, from which Freud reconstituted the history of the individual and of humanity. Natural sciences, and Freud in their vein, posit their constructed model at the beginning of their inquiry. Freud first established the nature of man as *homo natura*, and then sought to explain history, myth and religion with reference to it, as though he had not elaborated it in the first place. The latter situates human beings between the drives and illusion, between a biological foundation and a 'superstructure', which determines it (1970 [1936]: 207).[11] The model rested on the hypothesis that human beings are determined by the drives, one of the fundamental elements of Freudian psychoanalysis, which we will consider below. Freud conceived of the drives (the sexual and component drives) in terms of necessities and needs, and with reference to their various modes of satisfaction or of renunciation. *Homo natura* therefore is founded on *physicality*: in so far as the human is reduced to needs and necessities, his/her multifarious essence becomes uniform (1970 [1936]: 212). On that view, the human becomes a 'unilateral' being, since the only real, human experience is that of *man* as a 'body', which the drives represent. Everything else, according to Binswanger, becomes 'refinement and illusion' (1970 [1936]: 213).

How is the model elaborated? Freud proceeded through what Binswanger called a 'dialectical reduction', which consisted in a number of operations. There is the reduction of the dissimilar to the similar, in so far as the essence of human beings lies in the drives, which are common to all. For Freud the same processes underlie various linguistic and social situations. There is also the reduction of qualitative differences between psychical productions to quantitative changes in their combination, as in chemistry. The above description of laughter as a release of a certain quota of psychical energy is an example of such a reduction. Another type of reduction is the introduction of scientific, abstract constructions, to aid scientific understanding (SE 22: 81). The fiction of the psychical apparatus is one such construction. For Binswanger, however, the most important process of reduction finally consists in the way in which 'the phenomena that are perceived must yield in importance to trends which are only hypothetical' (SE 15: 67, quoted in Binswanger 1970 [1936]: 209). In *Introductory Lectures on Psycho-Analysis*, which Binswanger was here quoting, Freud was discussing his approach to bungled actions and forgetting. Confronted with a man who says 'close' rather than 'open' for opening an important meeting, what mattered was not only 'to describe and to classify phenomena, but to understand them as signs of an interplay of forces in the mind, as a manifestation of purposeful intentions working concurrently or in mutual opposition'. Rather than being concerned directly with the disturbing error, Freud added, 'we are concerned with a dynamic view of mental phenomena' (SE 15: 67). For Binswanger, this admission precisely demonstrated that Freud approached phenomena essentially by divesting them of their phenomenality (Binswanger 1970 [1936]: 209–10). One finds a stronger statement of Freud's interest and preference for underlying mechanisms in 'A Disturbance of Memory on the Acropolis' (1936). Adopting a retrospective outlook on his work, he wrote: 'the aim of my scientific work was to throw light upon unusual, abnormal or pathological manifestations of the mind – that is to say, to trace them back to the psychical forces operating behind them and to indicate the mechanisms at work' (SE 22: 239). This is a pointed statement of just what Binswanger reproached Freud for. However, for our purpose it invites us to reflect on what it means for forces and mechanisms to be operating 'behind' our actions, without our knowledge, apparently 'hidden'.

Binswanger, moreover, underlined Freud's idea that the only source of knowledge of the world is the reasonings one builds from observations. That form of knowledge problematically implies that the observer is detached from the object of knowledge. The 'knowledge of the world' is replaced by the 'ideas' constructed by natural sciences. One therefore acquires the knowledge of one's own representations rather than of the world. One is not dealing with particular experiences, but with the condensation of multiples, changing ones into a model.

The strict determinism of mental life, which Freudian psychoanalysis upheld, by sending human actions back to physico-chemical and biological determinations is the object of repeated critical comments (SE 11: 52). Binswanger and subsequent philosophers such as Maurice Merleau-Ponty nevertheless aimed to retrieve something of Freud – his intuition, his insight of 'something' that cannot be grasped by natural sciences – and to criticize his inability to preserve that 'something' from natural sciences.[12] However, in criticizing that aspect of Freud's theory of the unconscious, commentators are exaggerating Freud's reliance on natural sciences, and neglecting the respects in which Freud did not simply adopt their methodology and attitude. Binswanger's account of the exclusive physical character of the drives, for example, is not as nuanced as it should be, as we will see below when turning to Freud's theory of the drives. For as some more generous reflections on Freud show, his scientific positions, his lack of conceptual clarity are not failures, feebleness or lack of philosophical culture and training on Freud's part. We will here send the reader back to these more generous reflections, such as those of Jonathan Lear (1990 and 2006) and Richard Wollheim (1971).

In this *Guide for the Perplexed*, we will not elaborate directly on Binswanger's criticisms. However, the latter will motivate our presentation of Freud's main ideas. In particular, instead of taking for granted that Freud's preference for underlying mechanisms over phenomena is damning, we will suggest that the founder of psychoanalysis might have sought to articulate together heterogeneous, but interdependent levels of realities (that of affect and thought, of affect and the body), by resorting to no less heterogeneous sets of concepts. Whatever the case, his work invites us to reflect on mechanisms and on the 'hidden' character of unconscious activity. Freud's work raises the question as to what sort of dualism the pairing of mechanisms and actions constitutes. Almost everyone agrees that Freud was a dualist in so far as he conceived of the mind in terms of a conflict. But his dualism was unconventional, as we will see in Chapter 2, where we speak of the juxtaposition of 'stories and mechanisms' to point generally to that perplexing feature of Freud (Bergo 2004: 344-3).

Although we do not discuss at length philosophical reflections on Freud's work, the elements we single out from it should encourage the reader to engage with the philosophical reception of Freud. Given the magnitude of Freud's work, it is inevitable that we say little about certain well-known and also controversial aspects of his thought. For example, we do not enter into the problem which feminine sexuality posed for Freud, as is shown by the 1932 lecture on 'Femininity', among other places on which the literary reception of Freud has focused. Nor will we deal in any detail with the changes in the concept of anxiety, even though anxiety is an important quantitative concept, or with primal phantasies or fetishism, among other notions. We also do not discuss at any length Freud's texts on culture. This is not because it is possible to know Freud's work without exploring these important debates and areas of interest. Rather, the questions we raise around a few elements of Freud's thinking should be relevant to an examination of other dimensions of the theory of the unconscious.

Freud: A Guide for the Perplexed is divided into five chapters. Our presentation is not consistently chronological. We begin with the emergence of psychoanalysis from the treatment of hysterical patients, which Freud carried out in collaboration with Josef Breuer during the 1890s. In so far as we follow the development of the cure, we adopt a historical approach in that chapter. However, in the last chapter, we turn to the metapsychological points of view formalized in 1915, to *Jokes and their Relation to the Unconscious* from 1905, and conclude with *The Future of an Illusion* (1927). One of the greatest difficulties when approaching Freud is that no concepts are ever established once and for all. Freud elaborated a systematic theory of the mind, but the elements of the system kept mutating and were only provisional. This might partly explain why Freud wrote many expository works and recapitulations, and justify the amount of repetition one finds in his work. For example, he stated more than once that the difference between health and neurosis 'is of a quantitative not of a qualitative nature' (SE 16: 457), or presented the various meanings of the term 'unconscious' more than once, as we saw above. However, each statement depends on different states of the theory. Readers will note, moreover, that, apart from mentioning or discussing Josef Breuer, Wilhelm Fliess, Wilhelm Stekel, Carl Gustav Jung, Jean-Martin Charcot and Binswanger among others we do not explore the history of the psychoanalytic movement or discuss contributions to Freud's ideas by his contemporaries. Our approach to Freud through the contrast between phenomena and explanations, however, should allow readers to pursue such further study from a fresh angle.

Even though the distinction between phenomena and explanations or 'things themselves' and explanations is not a rigorous one in Freud's thinking, the themes of the book should remind the reader of its importance. Binswanger's criticism of Freud's neglect of phenomenality will serve as a distant point of reference throughout the book. With respect to that criticism, we will put forward the idea that what philosophers (and beyond philosophers, readers of Freud in general) find most objectionable is the mechanistic, quantitative dimension of his work. Such a negative judgement is not directed at Freud's work alone. It participates in the modern critique of scientific objectivism that is initiated during Freud's lifetime, most particularly at the end of the nineteenth century. However, given his optimistic pronouncements on science, Freud would seem to have been oblivious to that concern. He indeed openly proclaimed psychoanalysis to be a science of the psychical unconscious; just as he provocatively placed science above religion as a means to overcome our primary mode of mental functioning, in *The Future of an Illusion*.

Because of the suspicion towards the scientific aspects of his work, the latter is also one of its least well-known features. That level of Freudian thought, commentators believe, 'obscures' Freud's more valuable contributions, which therefore need to be transposed into another register. The following guide aims to introduce some of these cumbersome conceptual elements, into which details one usually 'does not need to enter'. In particular, taking up Binswanger's suggestion, we will raise the question as to whether mechanisms are indeed 'hidden', and whether they indeed come to take the place of phenomena. That question potentially extends beyond Freud's thinking to all explanatory endeavours in science or in literature.

The first chapter introduces readers to the development of the psychoanalytic cure, from which the theory of the unconscious emerged. Freud repeatedly underlined the reliance of the theory of the unconscious on empirical, clinical observations. A question arises as to the kind of observation it is possible to make in psychoanalysis. What does one see, if at all, during the treatment? Hysterical patients display visible symptoms, but their cure gradually rested on 'an interchange of words', and on the handling of material emerging from the unconscious. As the treatment developed, it became increasingly dominantly a matter of 'interpretation' or of the 'analysis' of meanings. The development of the cure, from the cathartic method to the process of construction, attracts our attention to the particular status of 'psychical processes': they give rise to 'unconscious formations', and act so to speak in the background, but are not for all that 'hidden', or entirely inaccessible.

Chapter 2 sharpens the distinction between 'things themselves' and 'underlying mechanisms' by presenting the process of defence and repression, and the theory of sexuality. Freud noted early on that the formation of hysterical symptoms had to do with the repression of sexual ideas. It was only in 1905 that he systematized his observations and hypotheses on sexuality. Freud introduced the concept of the drive (the sexual drive and the component drives) in the *Three Essays on the Theory of Sexuality* (1905) on which we will focus in that chapter.

In Chapter 3 we continue to explore the move toward interpretation that emerged in the early days of the cure, by considering Freud's theory of dreams. The dream is not simply an 'unconscious formation' among others. It gives us the most direct access to unconscious processes. Chapter 1 alerted us to the problematic status of observation in Freud's theory of the unconscious. Dreams render psychoanalytic observation even more peculiar. They consist in mis-remembered fragments of illogical trains of thought and stories, contingently collected by the dreamer (Freud described such unconscious productions as resembling 'a piece of malicious treachery' (SE 9: 35). Yet it is precisely these characteristics that make of the dream an invaluable point of entry into the 'dream-work', the fundamental element of the theory, through some of Freud's dreams. It is the mode of functioning of the psychical apparatus, which Freud systematized for the first time in *The Interpretation of Dreams* (1900).

In Chapter 4, we consider how for Freud mental acts are composed of two components: a representation or an affect and a certain quota of energy. This double constitution underlies the whole of psychoanalysis, and has many ramifications. Here, we will concentrate on the theory of the drives, and on the changes in it (it is through the concept of the drive that Freud introduced the notion of the Ego). Whereas with the dream, it was possible to stay connected with the 'stories' of everyday life (dreams make use of day-residues), with the theory of the drives we are apparently dealing with abstract, scientific constructions. In fact, one of the first systematizations was the 'Project for a Scientific Psychology' (1895), where Freud introduced the notion of quantity in psychoanalysis. That work provides the reader with a sample of Freud's most difficult thinking (and, for that matter, most unwieldy prose).

Chapter 5 considers the metapsychology, the name Freud gave to the theory of psychoanalysis that a series of papers was to constitute in 1915. We began by drawing attention to the quantitative dimension of Freud's work. In Chapter 5, we suggest how the latter can point toward aesthetics and ethics, provided that one does not first discard what we described as Freud's 'crushing' explanations. We first present the three metapsychological points of view, and emphasize the 'imperative of quantification' that motivates Freud's early research. Rather than moving chronologically toward Freud's last work, we turn to *Jokes and their Relation to the Unconscious*, where the economical point of view dominates the account of jokes and the production of the comic. We conclude by arguing that one cannot relegate economy and quantification to Freud's adoption of the methods of natural sciences, as *The Future of an Illusion* suggests.

CHAPTER 1

THE PSYCHOANALYTIC CURE

Freud's work comprises different kinds of writings: there are the case studies, where he reported his treatment of the patients thanks to whom he elaborated the psychoanalytic cure; there are the meta-psychological works from 1915 to 1916, which provide the theory underlying the technique of psychoanalysis; and there are the works in which Freud applies psychoanalysis beyond the strictly therapeutic framework (for example, in *Totem and taboo* [1912–13], *Moses and Monotheism: Three Essays* (1939 [1937–39]) and *Civilization and its Discontents* (1930 [1929]), the works on literary texts such as the analysis of Wilhelm Jensen's *Gradiva* in *Delusions and Dreams in Jensen's* Gradiva (1907 [1906]), or in E. T. A. Hoffmann's *The Sandman* in 'The "Uncanny"' [1919]). Finally there are Freud's introductory and circumstantial pieces of writing, which, together with his voluminous correspondence, document the development of the theory, the practice and of the psychoanalytic movement. Freud was in constant dialogue with a host of interlocutors, who became disciples and also dissidents. Within that ensemble, it is possible to make a distinction between what relates to the therapeutic method of treatment and the theories that explain its power, the 'assumptions', postulates, and hypotheses on which they rest. For we are alternatively confronted with the description of various symptoms and illnesses – the 'mental phenomena' – with the explanations about unconscious mental functioning and that of psychical processes, and with their alteration through the employment of a certain therapeutic method.

In this chapter, we will examine how it might be possible to distinguish between 'things themselves' or 'mental phenomena' and the 'explanations' dealing with their causes in Freud's account of the psychoanalytic cure. This will allow us to begin to descry narrative, practical and theoretical concerns in Freud. We will focus on the foundations of the psychoanalytic cure, which are discovered during the late 1890s, but which are set up in a number of Freud's didactic papers from 1904 to 1914. We are obliged to leave many technical aspects aside, such as the duration and the ending of the cure. Although Freud does not separate rigidly 'things themselves' and 'explanations', it is helpful to do so when approaching the philosophical reception of psychoanalysis. For what has appeared most problematic to philosophers is the theories, the particular 'explanations' Freud produced to justify the effects of unconscious mental processes on our lives.

'THINGS' AND 'EXPLANATIONS'

Concerning his approach to the objects of study, Freud described his habit of 'always studying things themselves before looking for information about them in books' (SE 14: 19). What does that mean in psychoanalysis, given that we are dealing with the unconscious, which is not directly accessible to observations? Freud could have been referring to the recommendation made by the French neuropathologist Jean-Martin Charcot (1826–93), with whom he studied in 1885–6 and whose work he translated, that one should look 'at the same phenomenon, till [one's] repeated and unbiased efforts allowed [one] to reach a correct view of its meaning'.[1] Following such a method is a way of restraining 'speculative tendencies' (SE 14: 22). Freud wrote that Charcot

> used to look again and again at the things he did not understand, to deepen his impression of them day by day, till suddenly an understanding of them dawned on him. In his *mind's eye* the apparent chaos presented by the continual repetition of the same symptoms then gave way to order: the new nosological pictures emerged, characterized by the constant combination of certain groups of symptoms. ('Charcot', SE 3: 12; our emphasis)

In the passage from which the statement about 'things themselves' is extracted, Freud is referring to his study of dreams, and to the way in which he embarked upon the self-observation of his own dreams before turning to Karl Albert Scherner's *Das Leben des Traumes*

(1861), one of the sources of *The Interpretation of Dreams*. The 'things themselves' are in that case 'dreams'. However, even though it is possible to recall and narrate dreams, they cannot exactly be observed if by observations, we have in mind the sustained looking recommended by Charcot. The advice has to be considerably adapted to apply to unconscious mental processes that essentially escape direct observation.

As we saw, and according to Binswanger, what mattered for Freud was apparently less the symptomatic manifestations than the unconscious processes underlying them (which 'cannot be a subject of direct observation' [SE 20: 32]).[2] The existence of the latter could be inferred by observing the various disturbances occurring in everyday life, from neurotic symptoms, bungled actions, to forgetting, among other unconscious formations. Freud often spoke of these disturbances as 'gaps'. Even though symptoms such as washing one's hands a hundred times a day may be more easily perceptible than, say, forgetting, it was not a matter of being more or less perceptible, spatially extended or not.[3] For, as Freud's analysis of forgetfulness in everyday life showed first in 'The Psychical Mechanism of Forgetfulness' (1898) and, more extensively, in *The Psychopathology of Everyday Life* (1901), the gaps were not empty spaces, but rather signalled the presence of thoughts, which are active in me without my knowledge. In order to make this clearer, let us consider Freud's description of the experience of forgetting a proper name and of having it on the tip of one's tongue. Everything begins when one realizes being unable to recall a name in the midst of a conversation. One then develops an 'unmistakable feeling of irritation' (SE 3: 289) and makes pointless conscious efforts at remembering the name. Other names than the one for which one is looking then keep appearing. Finally one comes up with a single letter, which one mistakenly thinks is the first letter of the forgotten name. In brief, the conscious efforts at remembering reveal how far forgetting is from blankness. Faced with forgetfulness, one unconsciously summons up a host of thoughts, of reflections on the formation and rhythm of words (as we will see, a whole art of interpretation is deployed):

One day I found it impossible to recall the name of the small country of which *Monte Carlo* is the chief town. The substitute names for it ran: *Piedmont*, *Albania*, *Montevideo*, *Colico*. *Albania* was soon replaced in my mind by *Montenegro*; and it then occurred to me that the syllable 'Mont' (pronounced 'Mon') was found in all the substitute names except the last. Thus it was easy for me, starting from the name of Prince Albert [the ruling Prince], to find the forgotten name *Monaco*. *Colico* gives a pretty close imitation of the sequence of syllables and the rhythm of the forgotten. (SE 6: 55)

It is as though the name occurred by itself: after noticing the common syllable 'Mont', 'then suddenly, [he] had the forgotten word and exclaimed aloud: "Monaco!" ' (SE 15: 111). Under Freud's analytic approach the anodyne forgetting of a name – 'What *is* his name?' (SE 3: 289) – involves a reflection about language. However, psychoanalysis does not stop there. It seeks to understand by what unconscious functioning our mind sometimes plays with language through making us produce substitutes, replace a name by another, and so on.

Observation is central to the elaboration of psychoanalysis. However, as the example of forgetting shows, observation is not strictly 'visual' as it was in Charcot (it pertains to a large extent to language, and to the way in which thoughts inadvertently occur to one). The experimental encounter with symptoms is further mediated by the application of hypotheses and abstract constructions.[4] Freud insisted on the empirical character of psychoanalysis: 'it is . . . either a direct expression of observations or the outcome of a process of working them over' (SE 16: 244). It did not emerge from 'merely subjectively determined notions to which someone else might oppose others of his own choice' (SE 16: 244). The richness of Freud's work, according to Richard Wollheim, lies in the way in which 'the clinical and theoretical sources flow together' (Wollheim 1971: 21). Jonathan Lear pointedly suggested that 'much of the criticism of psychoanalysis as extravagant . . . occurs because theoretical terms are invoked in isolation, cut off from clinical reality' (Lear 2006: 9).

Nevertheless, Freud himself often distinguished the two dimensions. For example, in 'On Psychotherapy' (1904), he noted how the concepts elaborated jointly with Breuer in *Studies on Hysteria* (1893–95) were then generally known and understood at least in German-speaking countries, while the therapeutic procedure was 'still struggling for recognition' (SE 7: 257). At another level, the theory and practice remained interdependent: 'every advance in our knowledge means an increase in our therapeutic power' (SE 11: 141). If, however, psychoanalysis were found to be merely 'a particularly well-disguised and particularly effective form of suggestive treatment', as it had sometimes been suspected to be, the value of its views on the dynamics of the mind or the unconscious would be greatly diminished (SE 16: 452).

Observations obtained during clinical practice and their working over required different methods of exposition, and modes of transmission, adapted to diverse scientific and non-scientific audiences. Freud addressed this problem, for example, in a letter to Breuer dated 29 May 1892 concerning the theoretical sketch of the *Studies on Hysteria*. Faced with the task of presenting a two-dimensional picture of 'so much of a solid as our theory of hysteria', should one begin, Freud asked, with case histories or by 'dogmatically stating the theories' (SE 1: 147)? Freud returned to the alternative between the *genetic* and *dogmatic* methods in 'Some Elementary Lessons in Psycho-Analysis' (1940 [1938]). Should one make the reader follow 'the path along which the investigator himself has travelled earlier', and make him/her watch something 'coming into existence and passing through a slow and difficult period of growth' (SE 23: 281)? Or should one 'begi[n] straight away by stating its conclusions', a method which is likely to make a stronger impression, but which is also more likely to prompt scepticism on the part of the reader? The idea of a 'difficult period of growth' cannot be both more trivial and more appropriate for describing the contents of Freud's writings, where he constantly reformulated the theoretical foundations of psychoanalysis. In 'An Outline of Psycho-Analysis' (1940 [1938]) – Freud's last published work – he adopted the dogmatic method. However, the latter was not aimed at convincing anyone, for 'the teachings of psycho-analysis are based on an incalculable number of observations and experiences' (SE 23: 144), which alone can allow someone to make a judgement. Psychoanalysis made it impossible to choose between the genetic or the dogmatic method: it proceeded by putting forward 'conclusions', and made us see why they can only be provisional.

THE PSYCHOANALYTIC CURE

The distinction between 'experience' and 'theoretical considerations' loses its relevance when approaching psychoanalysis through

Freud's writings rather than through psychoanalytic training or treatment. Everything would seem to become theoretical from the moment that one leaves the analyst's room. It has often been said that unless one is involved, whether as a patient or as an analyst, in a psychoanalytic treatment, one cannot know psychoanalysis. Or conversely, that the intellectual knowledge of psychoanalysis is of no use to the progress of the cure. Theory and practice would seem to be as dependent on one another, as we saw above, as to be sometimes mutually exclusive. Freud noted in 'Analysis of a Phobia in a Five-Year-Old Boy' (1909): 'It is a regrettable fact that no account of a psychoanalysis can reproduce the impressions received by the analyst as he conducts it, and that a final sense of conviction can never be obtained from reading about it but only from directly experiencing it' (SE 10: 103).

Nevertheless, when it is a matter of presenting for didactic purposes the method of treatment, 'experience' can be distinguished from 'theoretical considerations' (SE 16: 448). Freud described the experience of the cure in the *Introductory Lectures on Psycho-Analysis* (1916–17 [1915–17]), which were addressed to medical students at the University of Vienna. On that occasion, he made the rather baffling admission: 'in the strictest sense of the word, it is only by hearsay that you will get to know psycho-analysis' (SE 15: 18). Whereas medical science offers students things to *see*, such as for example, an 'anatomical preparation, the precipitate of a chemical reaction, the shortening of a muscle as a result of the stimulation of its nerves' (SE 15: 16), in psychoanalysis there is nothing to see: 'nothing takes place during the psycho-analytic treatment but *an interchange of words* between the patient and the analyst' (SE 15: 17 [our emphasis]). Nothing visible and tangible – nothing that can be observed in the usual scientific sense of the word – can be presented to the expectant relatives of the patient. The latter are anyway only impressed 'by actions of the sort that are to be witnessed at the cinema', Freud added, probably referring to the expressivity which characterizes actions performed in silent films. However, it is not only that there is nothing to see because all that takes place is talking, but also that what it would be possible to hear from the therapeutic conversation 'brooks no listener' (SE 15: 17). Freud could have specified 'brooks no *extra* listener', for the expression would seem to imply that words spoken during the cure are not addressed to anyone. One might imagine a family member standing on the other side of the padded door unable to 'hear' what is taking place. There is nothing unusual in the way in which a medical treatment should take place behind closed doors. But the fact that listening is an essential feature of the treatment emphasizes its excluding procedure.

Nevertheless, treatments could be recounted in 'Case Histories', the record and stories of some of the treatments which Freud conducted between 1899 and 1920. In addition to the many 'cases' reported in *Studies on Hysteria* and in early writings on hypnotism and suggestion, Freud published the 'Case History' [*Krankengeschichte*] of his patients establishing the clinical data of various afflictions: the 'Dora case' or 'Fragment of an Analysis of a Case of Hysteria' (1905 [1901]); the 'Analysis of a Phobia in a Five-Year-Old Boy' (1909) or 'Little Hans'; 'Note upon a Case of Obsessional Neurosis' (1909) or 'the Rat Man'. Another case entitled 'Psycho-analytic Notes on an Autobiographical Account of a Case of Paranoia (Dementia Paranoides)' (1911) was not the story of one of Freud's treatments, but the result of his analysis of Daniel Paul Schreber's *Memoirs of My Nervous Illness* (1903 [1955]). In 1918, Freud published 'From the History of an Infantile Neurosis' or the story of the 'Wolf Man', before 'The Psychogenesis of a Case of Homosexuality in a Woman' (1920). There are throughout Freud's writings shorter notes on clinical experiences, as we will see. However, each of the main case histories introduces new problems. For example, the 'Wolf Man' allows Freud to discuss the role of the 'primal scene' in the formation of the individual. Through it, Freud discovered that the witnessing by infants of their copulating parents could have pathological effects later in life, but that it was an essential step in the development of the subject's ability to phantasize.

Even so, case histories did not give a full account of the history of the patient's symptoms and forgotten memories; some details needed to be omitted to respect the privacy of the patient. They took a narrative form, and read like detective novels. They recounted the story of the patient's illness, through Freud's interpretations and constructions of what the patient told him and the unfolding of the treatment as the analyst communicated his interpretations to the patient. For example, Freud reports his patients' reactions when he initiated them into the treatment – '[The 'Rat Man'] was much agitated at [being told that fears are former wishes] and very incredulous. He wondered how he could possibly have had such a wish . . .' – as one would report the thoughts of a character in a novel (SE 10: 180).

It is not simply details about the private life of his patients that were left out of the Case Histories. In the 'Postscript' to the 'Dora Case', Freud attempted to justify and rectify his failure to address not personal but technical concerns in his presentation of the case (SE 7: 112). He therefore inserted a discussion of the working of 'transferences', which we will consider below. For psychoanalytic therapy entailed a number of procedures, thanks to which narratives about traumatic events and phantasies could be constructed. Freud's writings (including in some of the case histories) give instructions for the practice of the cure, from the *Studies on Hysteria*, where the therapy was not yet the psychoanalytic one as such, up to 'An Outline of Psycho-Analysis' (1940 [1938]), where the basic elements of the technique were well established. Freud had planned to write a 'General Methodology of Psychoanalysis', on which he began work in 1908, but he never completed it. Instead, from 1911, he published separate 'Papers on Technique' (1911–15 [1914]). Up until then, Freud considered *The Interpretation of Dreams* as the 'forerunner' of an initiation into psychoanalytic technique.[5]

The other omission from the 'Dora Case', which Freud signalled in the 'Postscript', was that of the psychological postulates, which underlie his 'descriptions of mental phenomena' (SE 7: 112). For the technical means employed during the treatment were linked with ideas about the 'hypothetical trends', the underlying psychical mechanisms, which were forged by observing symptoms and the effects of the treatment on them. Other case histories included some of these postulates. Focusing on the therapeutic procedure, including the notations about it in Case Histories, then, allows us to consider the distinction between on the one hand, 'things themselves', that is, the symptoms, and the stories to which they belong, and on the other, 'explanations' of the functioning of unconscious psychical processes. (For Richard Wollheim, this would amount to a distinction between human actions and their physico-chemical determinations: see Wollheim 1971: 151.) For they alert us to the 'layers' that constitute Freudian thought – narrative, historical, technical and theoretical. We cannot experience the treatment through reading Freud. However, what we do experience is the heterogeneous points of view that Freud strikingly puts together. Considering some of the steps that Freud took for elaborating the method of treatment and the concepts that went with it will make this clearer.

The Cathartic Method

In 'Remembering, Repeating and Working-Through' (1914), Freud identified *three phases* of development of the psychoanalytic technique, without giving precise dates concerning the various changes affecting the therapeutic tasks. The first phase – that of Breuer's catharsis – is the most spectacular: it involved hypnosis, and called upon the theatrical idea of *catharsis*, which Aristotle used in the *Poetics* to describe the 'purification of the emotion' through tragedy. When Breuer employed the term, it had already acquired a medical meaning through Jakob Bernays (1857–80).[6] It is the most spectacular phase also in that the development of the cure is simultaneously the story of the 'discovery' of psychoanalysis. Case Histories and early writings on hysteria tell us the 'story of suffering' of Freud's patients but also that of the reasoning that led to the postulates about the unconscious. The other two phases of development, which have no name-tag, involved the discovery of the therapeutic role of resistances and interpretation. We will consider these three phases in the order in which Freud presented them in 1914.

Breuer elaborated the 'cathartic method' when treating Anna O. (Bertha Pappenheim, 1859–1936), between 1880 and 1882, a method which Freud also practised on a number of female hysterical patients. *Studies on Hysteria*, co-authored by Freud and Breuer, presented the case histories of these treatments.[7] Breuer and Freud's work was a continuation of Charcot's study of hysteria, which the French neuropathologist carried out during the early 1880s (for them hysterics were typical of all psychoneurotics [SE 7: 164]). Charcot's work modified accepted views on hysteria, notably the idea that it was an imaginary disease or that it was due to an irritation of the womb or uterus. He noted that the formation of symptoms did not obey anatomy, but ordinary conceptions of the body. For example, a hysteric may have a paralysis of the arm that corresponds to the cut of her sleeveless garment rather than to physiology (Wollheim 1971: 22–3). In Freud's aphorism of sort: '*in its paralyses and other manifestations hysteria behaves as though anatomy did not exist or as though it had no knowledge of it*' (Freud's emphasis, SE 1: 169). Charcot had observed that traumatic paralyses, which appear in hysteria, could be produced artificially, by a traumatic suggestion. For example, a workman was suffering from paralysis of the arm some time after receiving a blow on the shoulder. Charcot put the patient under hypnosis and reproduced the paralysis by giving a light blow on the patient's arm, which became paralysed. More importantly, the blow could be replaced by a verbal suggestion: 'your arm is paralysed' (SE 3: 28). The example showed that if verbal suggestion, an idea, could play the role of a trauma and artificially produce a paralysis, it could be that ideas always play a part in the appearance of symptoms in traumatic paralyses. Charcot's research indicated that bodily symptoms could be related to ideas formed at the time of the traumatic experience, even if for him the causes of hysteria were nevertheless related to deterioration of the brain and were hereditary (Wollheim 1971: 23).

Let us consider briefly the steps leading to Breuer's elaboration of the cathartic method when he treated Anna O., who became one of the emblematic women of the early moments of psychoanalysis.[8] In his detailed description of the treatment, Breuer noted the patient's own contributions to its terminology (it is Anna O. who called the treatment a 'talking cure' or, jokingly, 'chimney-sweeping' [SE 2: 30]). Breuer said of her that 'she possessed a powerful intellect' and had 'great poetic and imaginative gifts' (SE 2: 21). He compared her 'mental creations' to Hans Christian Andersen's *Picture-book without Pictures* (1839) (SE 2: 29) and recorded the poetical degree of her narratives (SE 2: 29). The daughter of a puritanically-minded family, in which she experienced a lack of intellectual occupation, Anna O. had developed the ability to daydream intensively while engaged in her domestic duties. She described her daydreaming, her 'living through fairy tales in her imagination', as her 'private theatre' (SE 2: 22).

Anna O. fell ill when she was twenty-one, while she was nursing her father (who died a few months after the onset of her illness). During that time she suffered from a number of symptoms: the rigid paralysis and the loss of sensation of both extremities of her body; problems of vision, nervous cough, inability to speak German following the gradual loss of grammar and syntax, and so on. The most significant one among these was the state of confusion and the alteration of her personality, which she experienced during her states of *absence* or *condition seconde* (SE 2: 31). While in these states, she was hallucinating 'terrifying figures, death's heads and skeletons' (SE 2: 27), to which she gave a clue by muttering words. After these *absences*, she would fall into a state of hypnosis, which she called 'clouds' (SE 2: 27), during which she narrated her hallucinations. It was as though she was haunted: 'her mind was relieved when, shaking with fear and horror, she had reproduced these frightful images and given verbal utterances to them' (SE 2: 29–30). Breuer spoke of these moments of relief as 'hypnotic relief' (SE 2: 30). In a state of somnambulism, Anna O. uttered indistinctly 'mental creations': 'They were profoundly melancholy phantasies – "day-dreams" we should call them – sometimes characterized by poetic beauty, and their starting-point was as a rule the position of a girl at her father's sick-bed' (SE 11: 12). What was so striking was the effect that her speech had on her. She 'was as if set free' by the voicing of her *phantasies* (SE 11: 12) (her 'poetical compositions' [SE 2: 29]). The discovery came accidentally: some words could evoke the hallucinations she had had during her *absences*, and triggered the telling of stories (Anna O. went on to write children's stories). Breuer could produce a 'cathartic effect' from the stories by making Anna O. narrate them.

A year after she had fallen ill, and shortly after the death of her father, Breuer observed that in some of her *absences*, 'she was carried back to the previous year', and relived events of that time 'day by day' (a diary kept by her mother enabled Breuer to confirm his observations) (SE 2: 33). Most particularly, the stories she narrated referred back to the 'psychical events' which occurred during the period of incubation of her illness from the moment when her father fell ill in July 1880, until she herself fell ill in December of that year. Strikingly, when she narrated the events dating from that period, her symptoms disappeared. Breuer first observed this astonishing fact when the narration of an episode of that period relieved her of her inability to drink water. Telling Breuer 'forgotten memories', moreover, removed more serious symptoms, such as the paralysis of her right side. Symptoms disappeared when Anna O. remembered the circumstances in which they first appeared. For example, she once recalled that in the early days of attending to her father, she had had a waking dream in which she saw 'a black snake coming towards the sick man from the wall to bite him' (SE 2: 38). Her paralysis of the arm was related to that episode in that when trying to use her arm to keep the snake off, she had been unable to move her right arm that had gone to sleep over the back of the chair where she was sitting. She also remembered that when the snake had vanished, she had tried to pray: 'but language failed her: she could find no tongue in which to speak, till at last she thought of some children's verses in English and then found herself able to think and pray in that language' (SE 2: 39). In telling the story of that 'waking dream', Anna O. recovered her ability to speak German.

Yet it was impractical to wait for the patient to attain 'naturally' the hypnotic state in which the narration took place. Hypnosis had been useful in demonstrating that physical ailments had a psychical rather than physiological cause. Breuer surmised that by reproducing the auto-hypnotic *absences* (SE 2: 36), by inducing 'a kind of hypnosis', one would be able to make her remember certain events. Freud later said that Breuer had discovered that symptoms had 'a sense' (SE 15: 83). This was significant in the context of the dominantly physiological understanding of hysteria and mental diseases more generally. To claim that a symptom had a sense meant that it had to be 'interpreted'. The causes of Anna O.'s disease, according to Breuer, could be attributed to the ideas which she formed during her *absences*, or her 'secondary state', and which were 'acting as a stimulus "in the unconscious"' (SE 2: 45). In persisting, the memory formed a *condition seconde*. Hypnosis had shown how 'in one and the same individual there can be several mental groupings, which can remain more or less independent of one another, which can "know nothing" of one another and which can alternate with one another in their hold upon consciousness' (SE 11: 19). Hypnosis demonstrated that there could be a kind of mental functioning that was unconscious, but that the latter nevertheless effectively entertained relations with consciousness.

Breuer used hypnosis with Anna O. in order to induce a 'hypnoid state' in her, so that she could have access to significant but otherwise inaccessible memories. The 'second state' was not yet specified but the idea of the unconscious emerged out of the observation that patients could speak about memories, of which they otherwise knew nothing (Freud and Breuer believed that 'a neurosis would seem to be the result of a kind of ignorance – a not knowing about mental events that one ought to know of' [SE 16: 280]). It is a 'state of mind in which one knows and does not know a thing at the same time' (SE 2: 117 n. 1), which Freud poetically describes as 'the blindness of the seeing eye' (SE 2: 117 n. 1).[9] The cure consisted in a particular kind of talk or of narration. Communicating the memory of an event was meant to make the patient experience the 'affect' or the emotion that s/he had not experienced at the time of the trauma, and which was suppressed or repressed. It was the very telling of the memory that had a therapeutic effect (among other places, SE 2: 6; SE 7: 251). For making the symptom disappear in that way, however, the narration had to arouse the accompanying affect. It had to bring about the 'affective colouring' (SE 2: 9) that had been suppressed at the time of the trauma (SE 2: 6). The treatment consisted in 'unravelling' pathological symptoms in order to 'remove' them (SE 4: 100), for 'symptoms vanish[ed] when their sense [was] known' (SE 16: 281), when one had established their 'psychical genealogy' (SE 2: 281).[10] This was one of the first steps in the development of psychoanalysis, which established a link between symptom and amnesia, or what Freud also called 'a gap in the memory' (SE 11: 20). The treatment involved 'filling up this gap' by going back to what 'led to the production of the symptom' (SE 11: 20). Significantly, part of the efficacy of the treatment came from the fact that pathogenic ideas (which could be images) were translated into words, as though 'putting into words' had the power to cure.

Freud, following Breuer, used hypnosis between 1887 and 1896 (SE 2: 110–11). However, not all patients could be hypnotized. Fräulein Elisabeth von R. and Miss Lucy R., two of Freud's patients whom he treated in 1892, would not be hypnotized (see too Frau Emmy von N. [SE 2: 48]). The treatment by hypnosis, he believed, could be replaced by obliging the patient to communicate their memories (Freud often came back to the 'question of insistence' (SE 2: 270), to how intensively one should exert what he also called 'psychical compulsion' [SE 2: 270]). In order to trigger memories without altering the normal state of the patient, Freud used the 'pressure technique', which he had learned from Hyppolite Bernheim, a physician who practised suggestion, and whose work *De la suggestion et de ses applications* (1886) Freud had translated in 1887. Through 'suggestion' Bernheim aimed to show that the hypnotic subject did not act magically. The obedience of the hypnotized subject was caused by the 'normal' dynamism of ideas, which can remain active in an unconscious state, as 'post-hypnotic suggestions' showed. The term post-hypnotic suggestion refers to one of Bernheim's experiments, whereby he would hypnotize a patient, and order him/her to accomplish an action after waking up, say to eat a raw onion. When the patient came out of the hypnotic state, and was fully conscious, s/he would then carry out the ordered action without knowing why. Freud later said that the idea 'grew *active*': 'it was translated into action as soon as consciousness became aware of its presence' (SE 12: 261). The significant aspect of that action is that only the ordered action became 'active'. Everything else – Bernheim's suggestion – remained 'unconscious'.

The pressure technique consisted in exerting a pressure of the hand on the forehead of patients so as to help them to remember 'forgotten' experiences: 'I press for a few seconds on the forehead of the patient as he lies in front of me; I then leave go and ask quietly . . . "What did you see?" or "What occurred to you?" ' (SE 2: 270). In Freud's account of the treatment of a girl suffering from a nervous cough, the emergence of memories seemed directly to be due to the pressure exerted on her forehead:

> Under the pressure of my hand she first of all remembered a big dog. She then recognized the picture in her memory: it was a dog of her aunt's which became attached to her . . . it now occurred to her . . . that her cough started on her way back from the funeral [of the dog]. I asked why, but had once more to call in the help of a pressure. The thought came to her. (SE 2: 273)

The treatment unfolded as an alternation of the 'prompting question' ('Why was that?'), the baffled response of the patient ('I don't know'), and the renewed pressure – 'I pressed again' – until the pathogenic idea, which had to do with 'love', emerged (SE 2: 273). Freud eventually abandoned the pressure technique and anything having directly to do with hypnosis, as he enquired further into the circumstances in which certain ideas were forgotten, and most importantly, reappeared. However, the use of the pressure technique illustrates in a physical (and burlesque) manner the early aim and technique of the cure, whereby 'the physician's activity consisted of urging [the patient] on incessantly' (SE 11: 141). There are other instances when gestures would seem to illustrate the power of the cure, for example, when Freud stroked one of his patients, Emmy von N., 'several times over the eyes' in order to reinforce his suggestion that the patient should 'wipe away' the disturbing pictures which made up her hallucinations (SE 2: 55). The gestures give expression to how the treatment involved the exertion of a certain force against another.

The cathartic method rested on the observed fact that bodily symptoms were related to certain ideas, rather than being determined organically ('the development of hysterical symptoms are to be looked for in the sphere of psychical life' [SE 3: 27]). Neurotic symptoms could 'be traced back to something in the past' (SE 14:

17), which continued to act long after it had been experienced. Symptoms were 'precipitates' of emotional experiences (SE 11: 14) that were associated with forgotten ideas, as the well-known formula goes: '*Hysterics suffer mainly from reminiscences*' (SE 2: 7). The patients had memories of certain events, without knowing it, and without having any access to them. It was only when they were questioned under hypnosis that memories emerged 'with the undiminished vividness of a recent event' (SE 2: 9). Sometimes, the connection between the precipitating event and the symptom was clear. For example, a man had witnessed an operation performed on his brother's ankylosed hip-joint. 'At the instant at which the joint [during the operation] gave way with a crack, he felt a violent pain in his own hip-joint, which persisted for nearly a year' (SE 2: 5). At other times, the link was more obscure (such as the bond between Lucy R.'s olfactory hallucinations and her repressed love for her employer [SE 2: 106–24]). It is the variety of 'associative paths' between the symptoms and the causes that Freud explored.

For example, the relation between the cause and the pathological phenomena could be 'symbolic', that is, the genesis of the symptom could occur by means of verbal symbolization. An illustration of this is the case of Frau Cäcilie – Freud's 'most severe and instructive' one (SE 2: 178) – who had suffered from facial neuralgia, which recurred regularly for many years. Under hypnosis, Freud was able to discover that her pains were related to scenes from the past when her husband had regularly insulted her. When recounting the scene she had exclaimed: 'It was like a slap in the face' (SE 2: 178). Remembering with these words how insults from her husband had affected her had caused her symptoms to disappear. At fifteen, she had also experienced the 'piercing' look of her grandmother as 'a penetrating pain in her forehead between her eyes' (SE 2: 180).[11] We said above that hysterical symptoms were not a matter of physiology. Frau Cäcilie's symptoms showed how physical ailments could be combined with words and situations that gave rise to narratives (for example, to scenes from her early married life). The realization that mental illness could implicate words was fundamental to the development of the cure. For example, the memories of patients could return as pictures and the patient get rid of them by 'turning [them] into words' (SE 2: 280).

In their investigation of precipitating events, Freud and Breuer noted that it was generally not a matter of a single impression, but of 'a *series* of affective impressions' (SE 3: 31). The impressions had 'a traumatic effect by summation'; they formed part of a 'single story of suffering' (SE 2: 6). Freud represented vividly the accumulation of memories that the cure unravelled. In the patient's mind, hundreds of similar memories were grouped under headings in chronological series 'as though [Breuer and he] were examining a dossier that had been kept in good order' (SE 2: 288). The groupings formed 'a file of documents, a packet' (SE 2: 289). In his account of Anna O., Breuer even counted and classified the instances in which she variously failed to hear (108 instances of 'not hearing when someone came in', 50 instances of 'not hearing when she was alone', 37 instances of 'deafness brought on by fright', and so on [SE 2: 36]). The frequency of certain 'themes' became an index of their force. This counting is significant if we relate it to the way in which symptoms were 'unravelled' by following chains of associations, which 'do not form a simple row, like a string of pearls, but ramify and are interconnected like genealogical trees, so that in any new experience two or more earlier ones come into operation as memories' (SE 3: 196–7). Freud later explained how the quantity of accumulated memories constituted a material limitation to the efficiency of the treatment for people beyond the age of 50 because 'the mass of psychical material is no longer manageable' (SE 7: 254).

How can the memory of certain events not be worn away, not be forgotten, as most of our memories are, and have, instead, a 'pathogenic effect', or, as Freud also said, 'an after-effect' (SE 7: 275)? How can they retain the impression or the 'affect' that was experienced in relation to them? For in hysterical patients, Freud wrote, 'there are nothing but impressions which have not lost their affect and whose memory has remained vivid' (SE 3: 37).

Sexuality and Phantasy

The discovery of psychoanalysis forms a narrative, which is here only partially recounted, and which is characterized by turning points. One of them is the interruption of Anna O.'s treatment, when Breuer refused to deal with his patient's sexual phantasies – Anna O. claimed to be expecting Breuer's child.[12] Historians have speculated on exactly what happened, following Freud's discussion of Breuer's problem with his patient's transference in 'On the History of the Psycho-Analytic Movement' (SE 14: 12). Whatever the case, the end of the emblematic treatment illustrated Freud and Breuer's contrasting attitude towards sexuality. Both of them noted and recorded as a significant fact that most of the traumatic events reported by hysterics had to do with sexuality. However, it was Freud who pursued the idea that sexuality was not a contingent factor in hysteria, but that it 'provid[ed] the motive power for every single symptom, and for every single manifestation of a symptom' (SE 7: 115).

> If the psychical trauma from which the hysterical symptoms were derived were pursued further and further by means of the 'cathartic' procedure . . . experiences were eventually reached which belonged to the patient's childhood and related to his sexual life. (SE 7: 273)

An early scene of seduction of the child by the adult, at a time when the child was not prepared to react adequately to such a kind of event, triggered the advent of hysteria in the adult. In 'The Aetiology of Hysteria' (1896) Freud stated that 'at the bottom of every case of hysteria there are *one or more occurrences of premature sexual experience*, occurrences which belong to the earliest years of childhood but which can be reproduced through the work of psycho-analysis in spite of the intervening decades' (SE 3: 203). That finding was obtained by going along the associative thread of memories, which eventually led to memories of early childhood.

However, for a number of reasons spelled out in a letter to Wilhelm Fliess dated 21 September 1897 (SE 1: 259 – Draft K SE 1: 220), Freud came to believe that the so-called memories of early sexual traumas were created 'in *phantasy*' or in 'imaginary memories' (SE 7: 274). The change of views was prompted by the observation that '*no hysterical symptom can arise from a real experience alone*', for that experience is associated with memories of earlier experiences which 'play a part in causing the symptom' (SE 3: 197). Among other reasons, the numerous scenes of seduction of a child by an adult seemed to imply an improbable frequency of perversity towards children among adults (SE 1: 259). In 1924, Freud said that in 1896 he had overvalued reality and had had a too 'low valuation' of phantasy (SE 3: 204 n. 1; SE 3: 169 n. 1). The repeated phantasies of seduction narrated by his female patients, he proposed, were in fact a cover up of the 'auto-erotic activity' (infantile masturbation) which is characteristic of infantile sexuality (SE 14: 17–18). They were 'embellishments' of the first years of early childhood. Although Freud no longer believed that an actual scene of seduction took place each time, he retained the idea that neuroses were caused by problems that occur around the development of sexuality in early childhood (up to the age of six). This modified his views on the traumatic origin of neuroses. Hysterical symptoms were not directly caused by the memory of a traumatic experience from early childhood, or even from an actual experience. It was the advent of sexuality itself that was traumatic, and the disposition of the individual to welcome it or to fend it off (sexuality breaks in and the breaking in is assimilated to the individual's history through phantasy and through the formation of neurotic symptoms). The advent of sexuality could be linked with a certain number of phantasies organized around the following themes: 'observation of parental intercourse, seduction by an adult and threat of being castrated' (SE 16: 369). Freud developed these early findings on infantile sexuality, which led to the theory of 'normal sexuality' in the *Three Essays on the Theory of Sexuality* (1905), as we will see in Chapter 2.[13] Commentators have accused Freud of denying the reality of sexual abuse. However, it is not a matter of an alternative between 'reality' and 'falsehood' but rather of a compromise, a combination of the two, which is 'remarkably perplexing':

> If the infantile experiences brought to light by analysis were invariably real, we should feel that we were standing on firm ground; if they were regularly falsified and revealed as inventions, as phantasies of the patient . . . we should . . . look for salvation elsewhere. But neither of these things is the case . . . the childhood experiences constructed or remembered in analysis are sometimes indisputably false and sometimes equally certainly correct, and in most cases compounded of truth and falsehood. (SE 16: 367)

It is from these early findings that Freud developed the distinction between 'psychical reality' or 'historical reality' and 'material reality'. He later elaborated on that distinction in 'Constructions in Analysis' (1937), one of his last technical writings.

Transference

Let us recall the question that we raised at the beginning of the chapter: is it possible to separate the phenomena or 'things themselves' – the manifestations of psychical processes – from the explanations of their mode of functioning? As the cure developed, it became more imperative to elaborate explanations (hypotheses and postulates) for understanding the processes whose existence the cure revealed. For the phenomena observed during the treatments sent us beyond them, towards their psychical causality (Assoun 1997: 118). Nevertheless, before we move at the level of explanations, let us consider one of the ways in which sexuality was manifest during the cure, while pursuing our exploration of the development of the cure.

Freud perceived the importance of sexuality in the origins of neuroses by observing, among other means, that during the treatment, patients were developing an affectionate or hostile relation towards the analyst. He called that phenomenon 'transference', and later said that it was 'one of the foundations of the psycho-analytic theory' (SE 12: 160). In his theoretical contribution to the *Studies on Hysteria*, where the concept of 'transference' [*Übertragung*] appeared for the first time in its psychoanalytic sense, the term referred to a 'false connection' (SE 2: 302). The patient indeed linked the disturbing ideas emerging during the analysis with the doctor in the following manner:

> In one of my patients the origin of a particular hysterical symptom lay in a wish, which she had had many years earlier and had at once relegated to the unconscious, that the man she was talking to at the time might boldly take the initiative and give her a kiss. On one occasion, at the end of a session, a similar wish came up in her about me. She was horrified at it, spent a sleepless night, and at the next session . . . was quite useless for work. (SE 2: 302–3)

There was a *mésalliance* (SE 2: 303): the patient remembered experiences, but instead of recognizing that they made sense in relation to the past, she applied them to the person treating them. Since nothing in the reaction of the patient apparently belonged to the present, the patient's attitude could only be attributed to 'old wishful phantasies . . . which have become unconscious' (SE 11: 51). Failing to remember past emotions, the patient re-experienced them towards the analyst. In the 1890s, Freud perceived that patients were producing 'new editions or facsimiles' of the phantasies which became conscious during the analysis (SE 7: 116). They were elaborating an 'artificial neurosis', through which they relived past conflicts. The 'new impressions or reprints' were more or less well constructed, and more or less ingeniously disguised by being attached to some peculiarity of the physician. The failure to recognize the influence of transference could partly explain the interruption of Anna O.'s and Dora's respective treatments.

Later, Freud specified the kind of reproduction that transference entailed, and discovered that not all neuroses could be treated by means of the therapeutic effects of that special kind of 'love' (SE 12: 159).[14] In *Studies on Hysteria*, it was linked to a compulsion to associate or a 'compulsion to repeat' (SE 2: 270; SE 18: 21–3). Freud appropriated as a 'technical means' what had at first occurred without warning, and which 'arises spontaneously in all human relationships' (SE 11: 51). Transference is not specific to psychoanalytic therapy; it is essential to all therapeutic relations. Just when one believed to have controlled everything about the therapeutic situation (as one would have successfully done an arithmetic sum), something 'creeps in' that has not been taken into account, and which takes many forms:

> Transference can appear as a passionate demand for love or in more moderate forms; in place of a wish to be loved, a wish can emerge between a girl and an old man to be received as a favourite daughter; the libidinal desire can be toned down into a proposal for an inseparable, but ideally non-sensual, friendship. Some women succeed in sublimating the transference and in moulding it till it achieves a kind of viability; others must express it in its crude, original, and for the most part, impossible form. (SE 16: 442)

Transference acted as an 'irrefragable proof that the source of the driving forces of neurosis lies in sexual life' (SE 14: 12), and that something that remained unknown to the patient was not occurring in the 'normal state of consciousness', but rather, at an unconscious level. Conducting the cure entailed for the doctor not to attribute to the special quality of his/her person the emergence of love. In the technical terminology, the doctor had to check his/her 'counter-transference', that is, to check his/her own share in the artificial love-relationship constructed within the set-up of the cure.

Beyond the Cathartic Method

For Freud, 'the history of psycho-analysis proper . . . only begins with the new technique that dispenses with hypnosis' (SE 14: 16; SE 16: 292). Hypnosis allowed a 'widening of consciousness', and gave patients access to memories that were inaccessible to them in their normal state of consciousness (SE 7: 249).[15] The hypnotic method of treatment was efficient, but it removed symptoms only temporarily. For applying the cathartic method, one assumed that memories were retained unconsciously and continued to be operative. One assumed that 'unconscious ideas – or better, the unconsciousness of certain mental processes – [were] the direct cause of morbid symptoms' (SE 7: 266).[16] This is why it aimed to reach back to the sources of the symptoms, to ideas that had been 'dropped out' of consciousness.

When treating Emmy von N. in 1889, Freud observed that it was not necessary to employ hypnosis to make her talk. During their conversations, Freud noticed that Emmy von N. was 'unburdening' herself of memories without being hypnotized or even being prompted to speak: 'It is as though', Freud wrote, 'she had adopted my procedure and was making use of our conversation, apparently unconstrained and guided by chance, as a supplement to her hypnosis' (SE 2: 56). In the course of the treatment, whereby Freud was 'wiping away' the pathogenic memories by persistently interrogating her, Emmy von N. had summoned Freud to stop 'asking her where this and that came from' and 'let her tell [him] what she had to say' (SE 2: 63). She had then fully narrated a novel of sorts involving death, accusations of poisoning and so on.

Hypnosis obscured a decisive observation, which became 'one of the corner-stones of [the] theory' (SE 7: 251). If it was apparently impossible to reach certain forgotten 'pathogenic scenes', it was because something in the patient prevented the latter from becoming conscious. When patients were not hypnotized they used all sorts of means to 'frustrate the work of analysis' (SE 14: 16), in so far as unravelling the meaning of their symptoms caused them unpleasure (SE 7: 266). Their opposition took many forms, which Freud called 'resistances', and which hypnosis concealed. When telling their stories patients hesitated, stopped, confused the chronological order of events, broke causal connections or pleaded a failure of memory. If one asked them to 'fill in' the gaps of memory, they struggled to push aside ideas that came to them.

Hence the technique of psychoanalysis became a matter of learning to 'know what it means when the patient's ideas cease to flow' (SE 7: 252). Freud came to define expressions of resistance as 'anything that interferes with the continuation of the treatment' (SE 12: 162), including when the patient *negates* something (SE 19: 235–9). Freud gradually paid more attention to the circumstances in which the latter occurred.[17] Resistances showed that some ideas (the ones causing the symptoms) had been suppressed or 'repressed'. 'The ideas which are normally pushed aside on every sort of excuse . . . are . . . derivatives of the repressed psychical phenomena (thoughts and impulses), distorted owing to the resistance against their reproduction' (SE 7: 251). For 'symptoms, as we know, are a substitute for something that is held back by repression' (SE 16: 298).

Once the analytic technique no longer involved hypnosis, as 'Remembering, Repeating and Working-Through' indicated, it served the purpose of 'discovering from the patient's free associations what he failed to remember' ([SE 12: 147] see the case of Miss Lucy in *Studies on Hysteria* [SE 2: 106–24]). The aim of the cure became, and remained, that of 'lifting internal resistances' against remembering (SE 16: 451), as a way to undo repressions, and ultimately of 'making the unconscious accessible to consciousness' (SE 7: 253). It was a matter of listening to the rhythm of the patient's talks and detecting in it significant variations, in order to witness the patient's transfer of past emotions onto the physician. This involved interpreting the resistances, and communicating to the patient the results of these interpretations (SE 12: 147). With the cathartic method, the cure also aimed to transform the unconscious material into conscious material, to discover what was repressed (SE 11: 32), and in doing so, to free the patient of his/her symptoms. However, the technical means employed for doing so remained external to the patient, and fell to the analyst's lot. The recommendation to attend to one's own mental activity signalled an important technical change. Hypnosis was used for prompting the patients to speak freely about the origin of their symptoms, without the intervention of their 'moral sense'. The patients' means of opposition and interventions were related meaningfully to their symptoms. It was not a coincidence if their story stopped when they were recounting such and such an episode. For once they had overcome their inability to continue talking, they came up with ideas that were 'incompatible' with their moral sense.[18]

Patients were therefore encouraged to suspend their 'critical activity', and to obey the 'fundamental rule' (which has since been profusely caricatured and popularized). The rule enjoined the patient to 'communicate everything that occurs to him without criticism or selection' (SE 12: 112). 'Involuntary ideas' emerged when patients followed that rule, and 'let themselves go' without fear of discontinuity or randomness (SE 7: 251). What mattered for the analyst were the efforts the patient made against his/her critical faculty (SE 12: 147). Inspired by Friedrich Schiller, Freud compared the process to poetic creation (SE 4: 102–3). According to Schiller, letting ideas 'pour out' without reason closely examining them favours poetic creation. On that view, artistic creativity was linked with the ability to suspend one's rational activity, while 'ideas rush in pell-mell' (SE 4: 103). This is what Ludwig Börne advocated in his satirical piece on 'The Art of Becoming an Original Writer in Three Days' (1823), which Freud considered as an element of the prehistory of psychoanalysis. For its author advocated that the aspiring writer should 'take a few sheets of paper and for three days on end write down, without fabrication or hypocrisy, everything that comes into your head' (quoted in SE 18: 265). After three days, the writer would then be confronted with thoughts that s/he did not know s/he entertained. The 'fundamental rule' in psychoanalysis does not have the satirical and political overtones of Börne's piece; it nevertheless still serves the purpose of overcoming one's inhibitions (which can be moral, political and aesthetic, as in the extract from Börne).[19]

There was a counterpart to the 'fundamental rule'. While the patient put 'his self-criticism out of action' and was instructed to speak, the analyst's primary activity was that of listening. However, in doing so, s/he had to 'giv[e] equal notice to everything', to maintain the same 'evenly-suspended attention' towards everything s/he hears, in order not unduly to treat certain elements as being more significant than others (SE 12: 111–12). The analyst had to be attentive to what the patient said without exerting efforts of attention. For it is only later on that the analyst could elucidate the meaning of what s/he heard. Freud summarized in a formula the technical attitude that the analyst must adopt: the analyst 'must turn his own unconscious like a receptive organ towards the transmitting unconscious of the patient. He must adjust himself to the patient as a telephone receiver is adjusted to the transmitting microphone' (SE 12: 115–6).

Interpretation of Resistances

In the early conception of the cure, the treatment entailed the exertion of 'pressure': the therapist 'insisted' – s/he made use of a 'psychical compulsion to direct the patient's attention to the ideational traces of which he [was] in search' (SE 2: 270). The physical pressure of the hand on the forehead even sometimes accompanied the psychical compulsion. Freud abandoned the idea that employing physical force or urging the patient to talk was necessary to bring about a curative transformation. However, he did retain and develop the hypothesis that symptoms were caused by the patient's *defence* against disturbing unconscious ideas, in so far as they resisted the becoming conscious of certain ideas. The cure was a struggle between the physician and the patient, whereby the physician attempted to match the resisting force – the resistance – that the patient deployed: 'it was necessary to overcome something that fought against one in the patient' (SE 20: 29). The amount of effort necessary on the part of the physician varied according to resistances: the physician had to exert force in proportion to the difficulty which the patient had in remembering: 'The expenditure of force on the part of the physician was evidently the measure of a *resistance* on the part of the patient' (SE 20: 29). Resistance is a dynamic idea, which is 'something variable in quantity' according to the impulses to which they attach (SE 15: 116). A resistance 'always increases when we are approaching a new topic, it is at its most intense while we are at the climax of dealing with that topic, and it dies away when the topic has been disposed of' (SE 16: 293). They also take various forms (SE 16: 287; SE 19: 110). One way of resisting, for example, is by stating during the treatment that 'nothing occurs to one'; another one is by taking an intellectual interest in psychoanalytic therapy instead of submitting to it, and still another consists in repeating things instead of remembering them: 'the patient does not *remember* anything of what he has forgotten and repressed, but *acts* it out' or '*repeats it*' (SE 12: 150). For example, instead of remembering that s/he was defiant towards his/her parents, the patient acts critically towards the doctor. S/he suffers, Freud said, from a 'compulsion to repeat', beginning with the transference, a repetition of the past affective relations in the presence of the doctor. One can make the patient remember instead of repeating by using the patient's transference to reawaken memories, by making the patient 'work-through' the resistances. For it does not suffice to identify resistances. The patient also has to 'become more conversant' with his/her resistances (SE 12: 155).

As various forms of resistances took on more importance for the analyst, the cure became a matter of interpretation. In its third phase of development (at least according to Freud's 1914 account that has guided us so far), the analyst no longer sought 'to bring a particular moment or problem into focus', but studied whatever came up, and employed 'the art of interpretation mainly for the purpose of recognizing the resistances which appear there, and making them conscious to the patient' (SE 12: 147). Rather than the concrete struggles taking place in the early case histories, the cure consisted in a situation where 'nothing takes place . . . but an interchange of words' (SE 15: 16). Had a spectator been allowed to witness it, s/he would have found it 'completely obscure'. The cure became, in Jonathan Lear's word, 'a conversation which changes the structure of the soul' (Lear 1990: 18).

Interpretation became one of the key terms of the analytic technique and therapy through Freud's interest in dreams. During the treatment, patients reported dreams, which could provide some clues about the infantile origin of their symptoms, in addition to whatever else patients were communicating to the analyst. But how exactly could dreams do so? Are they not absurd and made of truncated, disordered ideas? Freud surmised that mechanisms similar to those presiding over the formation of symptoms could produce them. For the way in which it opened the paths for further enquiry, dream interpretation became the 'most direct approach to a knowledge of the unconscious, to his unintentional as well as to his purposeless actions (symptomatic acts) and to the blunders he makes in everyday life (slips of the tongue, bungled actions, and so on)' (SE 7: 252). In 1903, Freud had described *The Interpretation of Dreams* as the first manual of initiation into the technique of psychoanalysis, even though he devoted only a few paragraphs to the overall set-up of the cure in the book.[20]

The Interpretation of Dreams involved recommendations as to how to bring in the relevant state of mind in the patient during the cure so that the latter would consent to follow the fundamental rule. A patient must experience 'an increase in the attention he pays to his own psychical perceptions and the elimination of the criticism by which he normally sifts the thoughts that occur to him' (SE 4: 101). Freud emphasized 'self-observation', which was distinguished from reflection by the absence of a critical faculty (as we saw the analyst too was asked to adopt an uncritical attitude towards what s/he heard). Everything hung upon the patient's ability to let 'involuntary ideas' emerge, to produce 'free associations', to be the passive hearer of the thoughts, of which s/he could not exactly say that they were his or hers.

Although *The Interpretation of Dreams* did not focus on the spatial and physical set-up of the cure, it was one of the most important technical writings of Freud. In conformity with our initial attempt to distinguish 'things themselves' from 'explanations', we tried to remain at the level of 'things themselves' (at the level of 'observable symptoms'). However, the formation of symptoms and the verbal and aural essence of the cure suggest that 'things themselves' cannot be the matter of observation in Charcot's sense, who advocated 'looking at' phenomena. The development of the cure shows that psychoanalytic theory and practice do flow together, as commentators have argued in the vein of Freud himself. Symptoms may rest on 'underlying mechanisms', as Binswanger suggested; the latter are nevertheless concrete. There remains to explore the particular kind of concreteness that applies to the psychical processes involved in Freud's theory of the mind.

CHAPTER 2

THE JUXTAPOSITION OF STORIES AND MECHANISMS

In Chapter 1, we examined what it could mean to be concerned with 'things themselves' in the development of the psychoanalytic cure. In order to sharpen that distinction between 'things themselves' and 'explanations', let us continue to explore the layers that make up Freud's research, and which different kinds of expository styles sign-post. After exploring the first two levels, those of the stories and the explanations, the constructions and interpretations, which are an integral part of the cure, we will turn to the explanations concerning the 'underlying mechanisms', which gradually occupy the greatest part of Freud's writings. In the following chapter, we will concen-trate on elements of the theory of defence, repression and sexuality.

There is, as a first layer or level, the description of the symptoms from which a number of male and female, adult and children pro-tagonists suffered, and which form a number of 'small tal[es] of trouble' (SE 2: 116), some of which we touched on in Chapter 1. Let us enumerate some of them. There is that of the girl who 'if a murder had been committed by an unknown person . . . would ask herself anxiously whether it was not she who had done the deed' (SE 3: 55), or of the woman who had to obey a rule 'that [for going to bed] the pillow must not touch the back of the bedstead' (SE 16: 278). There is the tale of the woman who 'was sitting at a small table and was busy arranging silver florins in little piles (SE 6: 200), and of another one who 'frequently interrupted her remarks by producing a curious "clacking" sound from her mouth which defies imitation' (SE 2: 49). A man 'complained of being unable to work, of having forgotten his past life and of having lost all interest' (SE 18: 181); a woman 'had a feeling that she could not close her open mouth and fell to the floor in a faint' (SE 2: 169 n. 1); another 'was tormented by subjective sensations of smell' (SE 2: 106), or still another one at some point 'spoke only English and could not understand what was said to her in German' (SE 2: 26). The story of the child who 'was afraid of horses biting him . . . of horses falling down' (SE 10: 124) is well known, as is that of Dora who 'had had a very large number of attacks of coughing accompanied by loss of voice' (SE 7: 38), and that of the woman who 'more than once . . . saw [her] father get into bed with [her] mother and heard sounds that greatly excited [her]' (SE 2: 127). Less so is the story of the woman who 'pursued a "society lady" who was about ten years older than herself' (SE 18: 147), or that of the friend E. who 'turns red and sweats as soon as he sees one of a particular category of acquaintances, especially at the theatre' (SE 1: 279), or of the man 'who fell in love with a girl who was a flirt' (SE 1: 196). Sometimes the 'trouble' even remains unspecified: 'I saw something which did not fit in at all with my expectation; yet I did not allow what I saw to disturb my fixed plan in the least . . . I was unconscious of any contradiction in this' (SE 2: 117).

These 'little scene[s]' (SE 2: 115) are only fragments of broader, more complex stories, which sometimes include how Freud came to treat the patient, how the latter looked, what was her/his character. For example, Emmy von N., 'a lady of about 40 years of age . . . still looked young and had finely-cut features, full of character . . . Her family came from Central Germany, but had settled for two generations in the Baltic Provinces of Russia' (SE 2: 48). Sometimes the beginning of the case could be mistaken for the beginning of a novel: 'In the summer vacation of the year 189– I made an excursion into the Hohe Tauern . . . I was not so lost in thought that at first I did not connect it with myself when these words reached my ears: "Are you a doctor, sir?"' (SE 2: 125).[1] Freud's writings contain a number of such stories, which are 'set in the midst of life' (SE 1: 278), or fragments of stories, for the cure develops by 'paying as much attention . . . to the purely human and social circumstances of our patients as to the somatic data and the symptoms of the disorder' (SE 7: 18).

Stories in which figure the symptomatic acts – the 'historical' account (SE 17: 13) – are also integrated into the broader narrative of the analysis, which is made of the patient's recollections and the analyst's constructions and interpretations, which he/she communicated to patients (Freud called that aspect the 'thematic' account). That broader narrative, together with elements concerning the recovery of the patient, constitutes a second level of presentation. There is an example of 'constructions' among other places, in 'Fragment of an Analysis of a Case of Hysteria' (1905 [1901]). Freud wrote:

> Certain details of the way in which she expressed herself . . . led me to see that behind this phrase [ein vermögender Mann ('a man of means')] its opposite lay concealed, namely, that her father was *'ein unvermögender Mann'* ('a man without means'). This could only be meant in a sexual sense – that her father, as a man, was without means, was impotent. Dora confirmed this interpretation . . . (SE 7: 47)

However, she did so 'from her conscious knowledge', rather than affectively, as the cure recommended. She moreover contradicted herself, by simultaneously insisting that her father was entertaining a common love-affair with Frau K. and that he was incapable of forming such a relationship. The constructions are a technical means through which the analyst retells the story of the patient. Thanks to that retelling, the latter is meant to recollect elements of his/her past, and to recognize the incoherencies, which unconscious mental processes inserted into their conscious life. For in a 'psycho-analysis the physician always gives his patient . . . the conscious anticipatory ideas by the help of which he is put in a position to recognize and to grasp the unconscious material' (SE 10: 104). Anyone wanting to caricature psychoanalysis could easily cite the interpretation which Freud 'boldly' communicated to Lucy R.: 'I believe that really you are in love with your employer, the Director, though perhaps without being aware of it yourself', to which Lucy answered: 'Yes, I think that's true' (SE 2: 117). Freud specified that the doctor's knowledge (what s/he understands, s/he interprets from the patient's speech) does not produce the same effects as that of the patient: '[the doctor's knowledge] does not have the result of removing the symptoms [as the patient's knowledge would do] but it has another one – of setting the analysis in motion of which the first signs are often expressions of denial' (SE 16: 281).

Given that in written reports, the analyst's constructions and the material presented by the patient were sometimes confusing, Freud advised the reader of the case histories not to expect to understand 'everything at once, but to give a kind of unbiassed attention to every point that arises and to await further developments' (SE 10: 65). That is, to pay attention impartially to 'everything that there is to observe' (SE 10: 23) or to remain with 'things themselves'. The understanding of a case, Freud wrote, can only occur through receiving a sufficient number of 'impressions of it' (SE 10: 23), which are acquired through listening (or, in our case, through reading). The advice referred to the 'impartial' attitude the analyst adopted towards the patients' stories, but also, to some extent, to that which the reader should adopt towards case histories. Regrettably, 'no account of a psychoanalysis can reproduce the impressions received by the analyst as he conducts it' (SE 10: 103), 'no means has been found of in any way introducing into the reproduction of an analysis the sense of conviction which results from the analysis itself' (SE 17: 13). Hence, case histories are only ever fragmentary, not only because they are the summary of a broader interchange of words and of more complex stories than snatches from the treatments recounted in Freud. As we saw, it is also impossible for a third party to experience what happens during the cure (through transference and remembering).

Besides 'constructions', and interpretations, which acted as explanations presented to the patients in order to prompt their recollections, there is another kind of explanation in case histories. The latter form a third level of presentation. In 'Notes upon A Case of Obsessional Neurosis' (1909), for example, Freud initiated the patient into the treatment through instructions about the principles underlying psychoanalysis. Such instructions, however, also served the purpose of enlightening the reader, who becomes an addressee in the pedagogical dialogue Freud held with his patient about the conscious and the unconscious: 'The unconscious, I explained, *was* the infantile' (Freud's emphasis, SE 10: 177); 'according to psycho-analytic theory, I told him, every fear corresponded to a former wish which was now repressed' (SE 10: 180). These explanations were involved in the treatment alongside the constructions, because the analyst communicated them to patients as in the treatment of the 'Rat Man' – the patient's nickname (Freud staged dialogues between an analyst and an opponent in some texts, such as, for example, *The Future of an Illusion* or 'The Question of Lay Analysis', the 'Conversation with an Impartial Person' published in 1926.)

Case histories contain explanations of the 'psychical mechanisms and instinctual processes' (SE 17: 105), which Freud sometimes omitted, or which he isolated from the main stories of the cases in chapters variously entitled 'Discussion', 'Recapitulations and Problems', 'Digression' or 'Postscript'. (We saw earlier that Freud suppressed the discussion of transference from the main case history of Dora, and devoted the Postscript to that problem.) For example, still in 'Notes upon A Case of Obsessional Neurosis', Freud explained to his patient one of the underlying principles of psycho-analytic therapy by telling him the way in which there could be 'a *mésalliance* . . . between an affect and its ideational content' as between 'the intensity of his self-reproach and the occasion for it' (SE 10: 175). Eighteen months after his father's death, the 'Rat Man' had recollected that he had not stayed beside his seriously ill father, who had died in his absence. He had 'come to treat himself as a crim-inal', without having committed any crime (SE 10: 175–6). The excessively intense and conscious self-reproaches from which the 'Rat Man' suffered belonged to an unconscious content towards which the latter had been displaced. Freud presented to him argu-ments he developed in 'The Neuro-Psychoses of Defence' (1894) in the midst of a treatment so as to 'initiate' him into the principles of psychoanalysis. The cure took a pedagogical turn as the patient returned each day having formulated questions about the lesson of the previous day. For example, having learned about the unconscious sense of guilt that motivated his self-reproaches, the 'Rat Man' asked: how could knowing about one's unconscious sense of guilt have a therapeutic effect (SE 10: 176)? Freud reported: 'I then made some short observations upon *the psychological differences between the conscious and the unconscious*, and upon the fact that everything conscious was subject to a process of wearing-away, while what was unconscious was relatively unchangeable' (SE 10: 176). Freud stated that he preferred his patients to 'learn by personal experience' rather than by reading his analytic writings. In this way, 'they will acquire wider and more valuable knowledge than the whole literature of psychoanalysis could teach them' (SE 12: 119–20, quoted in Lear, 1990: 119).

Sometimes, as in the case of Fräulein Elisabeth von R., he 'weav[es] the explanations . . . into [his] description of the course of [the patient's] recovery' (SE 2: 161). These were directed at the reader rather than the patient. For example, towards the end of that case, the troubling simultaneity of two thoughts triggered the clarification of the case. For the reader the clarification occurs in the manner of a narrative *dénouement*, while for the patient it acts as a moment of enlightenment:

> At that moment of dreadful certainty that her beloved sister was dead without bidding them farewell . . . at that very moment another thought had shot through Elisabeth's mind, and now forced itself irresistibly upon her once more, like a flash of lightning in the dark: 'Now he is free again and I can be his wife'. (SE 2: 156)

The recollection was also, for Freud, as a 'flash of lightning in the dark'. It made 'everything' clear, even concrete, and provided an opportunity to verify the mechanisms underlying hysterical symptoms:

> The concepts of the 'fending off' of an incompatible idea, of the genesis of hysterical symptoms through the conversion of psychical excitations into something physical and the formation of a separate psychical group through the act of will which led to the fending-off – all these things were, in that moment, brought before my eyes in concrete forms. (SE 2: 157)

After that clarification, we revert to the 'concreteness' of the situation. Because Fräulein Elisabeth's feelings towards her brother-in-law were incompatible with her 'whole moral being' (SE 2: 157), she had converted them into physical pain. There remains for Freud to tell the patient his analytical understanding of her predicament, and to prompt her to engage in 'abreaction'. Indeed, through the recognition of the ideas and affects that were involved in the formation of her symptoms, she could get rid of the latter. Here 'abreacting' also appeared to be a narrative device, in addition to being one of the springs of the early technique. For it consisted of 'prob[ing] into the first impressions made on her in her relations with her brother-in-law' (SE 2: 158). Through that process, they 'came across all the little premonitory signs and intuitions of which a fully-grown passion can make much in retrospect' (SE 2: 158). They could enumerate everyday life incidents involving the fiancée, the brother-in-law and the patient in a succession of events worthy of a romantic novel. It is only in the following 'Discussion' that the story of Fräulein Elisabeth von R.'s illness became more 'abstract', in the

FREUD: A GUIDE FOR THE PERPLEXED

sense in which the emotions of the patients were treated in terms of 'amounts of affect', which came up against the 'ego-consciousness', and so on: 'She repressed her erotic idea from consciousness and transformed the amount of its affect into physical sensations of pain' (SE 2: 164). The myriad of elements belonging to the woman's story would seem to have disappeared 'behind' these processes. We move from the concrete experiential level to the abstract, theoretical level without warning, in order to learn how to decipher the 'physical' language of hysteria.

In the 'Katharina' case history, the shift from the woman's story to explanations of the mechanisms presiding over the formation of her symptoms is clearly signposted by the idea of translation from the language of storytelling to another terminology (the contrast would probably be even greater, had the English translator rendered Katharina's dialect):

> 'Fräulein Katharina, if you could remember now what was happening in you at that time, when you had your first attack, what you thought about it – it would help you.'
> 'Yes, if I could. But I was so frightened that I've forgotten everything.'
> (Translated into the terminology of our 'Preliminary Communication', this means: 'The affect itself created a hypnoid state, whose products were then cut off from associative connection with the ego-consciousness') (SE 2: 128). [A similar translation occurs in relation to Fräulein Elisabeth von R., which gives rise to an 'algebraical picture'. (SE 2: 166–7)]

The dialogue resumed after the 'translation', but the idea of a double language is carried over to the next page. For Breuer and Freud, the symptoms of hysteria were comparable to a 'pictographic script which ha[d] become intelligible after the discovery of a few bilingual inscriptions. In that alphabet being sick means disgust' (SE 2: 129). There is nothing striking about the fact that one thing can mean another, that one thing can be replaced by another. Does the pictographic script not correspond moreover to the way in which being sick always involves some form of disgust?

What appears to be a general feature of meaning is precisely what interested Freud. The analyst asked: 'What is it like when you get "out of breath"?' (SE 2: 126). S/he then found a way of interpreting the symptom by delving into the life history of the patient (the feeling of suffocation was related to two successive scenes of seduction by Katharina's father when she was fourteen years old). These are the two first levels we identified above, that of the symptomatic acts and the events related to them. Another set of questions follows, whose answering creates another expository level: by what mechanisms or principle of functioning is the experience transformed into a symptom? The translation into the theoretical terminology attends to that latter set of questions. The explanations Freud communicated to his patients (for example, concerning the way in which there can be a false connection between an affect and an idea, or the infantile nature of unconscious motivations) indeed extend well beyond case histories, and in fact they outgrow clinical essays and form the greatest part of Freud's writings (excluding Freud's voluminous correspondence).

UNDERLYING MECHANISMS

If we pass from case histories to the rest of Freud's published work, then, the 'palpable stories', which read like late-nineteenth-century short stories and dramatic works, give way to increasingly lengthy theoretical elaborations, until the ratio between stories and explanations is inverted. Freud's later works contain fewer narrative elements and lengthier theoretical developments; and many of his texts are almost exclusively theoretical. It is as though the 'explanations', which appeared only in the 'roughest way' in case histories (SE 10: 177), obtained the floor, following the idea that, in any case, there can be no adequate account of the 'direct experience' of the cure. We saw that unconscious processes were not directly accessible. The stories might provide a more efficient means of access to them, but they are stories from the past, and there is no direct access to the past either. Memories of an event are always associated with other apparently unrelated memories that interfere and transform their content.

Binswanger called the explanations of psychical mechanisms – what we here identified as a third level of presentation – and the increasingly larger role they play in the whole of Freud's work, the 'gigantic empirico-scientific structure of [Freud]'s *technique of unmasking*' (1970 [1936]: 203). He thus referred to the way in which the technique of interpretation, on which we have begun to expound, rested on elaborate theoretical foundations. Freud made postulates about the 'hypothetical trends' determining our psychical life. According to Binswanger, Freud had neglected the level of experience (which is the least transmissible through writing, since the stories only give an impression of the patient's experience). In the rest of this book, we will explore aspects of the *gigantic empirico-scientific structure*, which may be problematic but which is all one has, when approaching Freud through his writings rather than by undergoing a psychoanalytic treatment. The imposing theoretical structure came to occupy the front of the stage, but Freud nevertheless constantly appealed to everyday life and experiences, as a reservoir of stories and examples, in order to clarify the theory. The two realms were never entirely separated from each other. Freud looked for the most telling occurrences of the effects of the unconscious psychical mechanisms on our lives, as though the latter were not simply 'presupposed' or hypothetical but rather took concrete, tangible forms. Granted that nothing is insignificant, one would have never noticed a whole range of minor daily events – dreams, jokes, errors of all sorts – were it not for the unusual attention psychoanalysis paid to them. The psychoanalytic enquiry modified these minor events into ones worthy of our interest. Turning to them was meant to enlarge the theoretical understanding of psychoanalysis, in particular that of the notion of 'pathological defence' and repression, which Freud compared to the 'normal' processes of repelling. In some of the earliest discussion of repression, in the Letters to Fliess, Freud wrote that the normal process of repression had to do with disgust, in a 'crude' description:

> To put it crudely, the current memory stinks just as an actual object stinks; and just as we turn away our sense organ (the head and nose) in disgust, so do our preconsciousness and our conscious sense turn away from the memory. This is *repression*. (Freud's emphasis. Letter dated 14 November 1897 [SE 1: 269])

In the rest of the letter, Freud continued by saying that 'normal repression' is the affective foundation of a wealth of intellectual processes of development such as morality and modesty (Freud 2006: 355). One might point out that Freud spoke of normal repression only after having observed pathological forms of repression.

However, the process of unconscious pathological repression becomes confused with 'acts of pushing aside' on which our individual and social existences are based, and thanks to which we become adults.

Defence and Repression

In Chapter 1, we saw that Breuer and Freud observed how a certain form of forgetting was the condition for the formation of hysterical symptoms. It was a matter of an incomplete forgetting, of a forgetting 'motivated by repression' (SE 6: 7). The patient's attitude during the treatment indicated that 'something' unknown to them operated and influenced their acts (recall the different kinds of ignorance of which the unconscious is formed [SE 16: 280–1]). One of the underlying hypotheses, which guided Freud and Breuer's early research, was that a 'psychical group' of ideas had become disassociated from normal consciousness, because of its distressing content. The latter eventually formed a nucleus that exerted a pathological pressure on the patient's actions (SE 3: 49). There was, in other words, a 'psychical splitting' or a 'splitting of the mind', which created what Breuer called 'hypnoid states' (SE 2: 220 and throughout *Studies on Hysteria*). That line of enquiry led Freud to the phenomenon of 'repression', whereby 'it was a question of things which the patient wished to forget, and therefore intentionally repressed from his conscious thought and inhibited and suppressed' (SE 2: 10). The problem of repression arose in terms of the ideas that were repressed, but also in terms of its process. The reality of repression occurred on two levels: first, that of the 'troubles' which manifest themselves 'in the midst of life' (SE 1: 278), or in other words, the stories that we have just considered. Second is that of the mechanisms, which are presupposed, and take place . . . where? That is precisely the problem.

The idea of repression first appeared in the 'Preliminary Communication' in 1893, and subsequently throughout the *Studies on Hysteria*. It was the object of a separate essay in 1915, and of sections in Freud's two essays on the Unconscious ('A Note on the Unconscious in Psycho-analysis' [1912] and 'The Unconscious' [1915]). In *The Ego and the Id* (1923), Freud returned to the notion of repression and modified it further in accordance with the second model of the mind, which he therein developed, and to which we will turn in Chapter 5. Freud later noted in the 'History of the Psycho-Analytic Movement' (1914) that when he was working with Breuer, he 'had taken the matter less scientifically' than his collaborator had done, by 'everywhere [. . .] discern[ing] motives and tendencies analogous to those of everyday life' (SE 14: 11). Accordingly, for him 'psychical splitting' was 'an effect of a process of repelling' (SE 14: 11). The unconscious mechanism corresponded to what one does in everyday life when confronted with an unwanted topic of conversation. One says: 'Let's not talk about that', in order to invite interlocutors politely to drop the topic and be relieved of the tension occasioned by it. Likewise, if the method of defence adopted by the ego is successful, it will push away from itself 'the intolerable experience with its affective consequences', which will not remain as a memory (SE 7: 276). The 'normal defence' – 'the ostrich policy' (SE 5: 600) – corresponded to the way in which 'it is quite generally the case that we avoid thinking of what arouses only unpleasure, and we do this by directing our thoughts to something else' (SE 1: 351). Certain ideas would therefore be repressed by being 'ignored', avoided. In many of Freud's examples, what arouses unpleasure is egoistic, jealous or hostile 'impulses' whose existence one would rather ignore (SE 6: 276). One defends oneself against acts or thoughts that would induce remorse or pangs of conscience (SE 6: 147). What provoked that kind of reaction are impulses that have to do with sexuality. Freud's theory did not cease to evolve, even though Freud retained in later works some of his earliest ideas. For our purpose, the early explanations of defence and repression usefully present repression in a more concrete manner than the later formulations, which deal with repression at the level of drives and the ego. Freud also spoke of how repression was replaced by a 'condemning [conscious] judgment', when the cure was successful (SE 11: 53).

Defence, a concept that Freud first used in 'The Neuro-Psychoses of Defence' (1894), and repression became equivalent notions. Freud eventually used repression as the general name of all 'defensive processes', but reverted, in 1926, to using 'defence' as the broader term to designate the process of 'protection of the ego against instinctual demands' (SE 20: 164), of which repression became one example. When the disagreeable thing that one wishes to push aside comes from the external world, one can attempt to escape from it, or condemn it. Repression in that respect is 'something between flight and condemnation' (SE 14: 146). Defensive processes prevent 'the generation of unpleasure from internal sources' (SE 8: 233). It is the instinctual correlative of physical 'flight'. It designates the method of defending oneself against instinctual impulses or demands, from which one cannot take flight. One cannot escape from one's own internal demands, especially when the latter are not conscious ones.

Repression Freud wrote, is 'the oldest word in our psycho-analytic terminology' (SE 21: 153), which 'could not have been formulated before the time of psycho-analytic studies' (SE 14: 146). It consists in *turning something away, and keeping it at a distance, from the conscious* (Freud's emphasis, SE 14: 147). Yet, there is a conception very close to his own in Arthur Schopenhauer's account of insanity in *The World as Will and Representation* (1819). Schopenhauer linked the onset of madness to troubles of memory, and to the propensity of human beings to 'cas[t] out of [their] mind' things that 'powerfully prejudice [their] interests, wound [their] pride, or interfere with [their] wishes' (Schopenhauer 1958: 400–1). For, as Freud believed during the 1890s, 'no experience could have a pathogenic effect unless it appeared intolerable to the subject's ego and gave rise to efforts at defence' (SE 7: 276). In view of the way in which the incompatible idea was only insufficiently 'expulsed', Freud strikingly both said that hysteria resulted from 'an act of moral cowardice' and suggested that the person could have prevented herself from falling ill had s/he displayed 'a greater amount of moral courage' (SE 2: 123; see Lear 1990: 65–8). As the reference to moral courage indicates, Freud did not at first explain the formation of symptoms with reference to the unconscious. Rather, it is by reflecting on the conflict presiding over the formation of symptoms that Freud slowly established the theory of the unconscious (SE 2: 127). The normal process of repression would seem to be modelled on acts of pushing ideas aside (morally or in disgust) only for them to be gradually 'internalized'.

Accordingly, mental illness is closely related to whether or not our acts appear to be morally acceptable ('shame and morality are the repressing forces' [SE 1: 221]). At the least, Freud saw these repressing forces as precipitates of the conflict between the drives and civilization on which the latter rests. A failure to cope with the thought of immorality appears to be a cause of illness (SE 6: 147). (Freud's theory of civilization accounts for the origin of society in remorse.)

Symptoms, then, were the products of acts of defence against incompatible ideas.[2] When asked to remember what caused one of their symptoms, patients remembered their effort at ' "pushing the thing away", of not thinking of it, of suppressing it' (SE 3: 47). That a 'conflict' provoking the 'shutting off' from consciousness of what is unacceptable should be the condition for the formation of symptoms obliged Freud to specify who or what were the adversaries in the conflict. During the cure, there appeared to be a conflict between the patient and the analyst (through transference the latter can embody any number of persons). It was also a matter of incompatibility between 'ethical standards', or the 'moral sense', and forbidden sexual attraction, the 'ego' against ideas, or sexual impulses (or of 'conflicts between the ego and such of the sexual impulses as seem to the ego incompatible with its integrity or with its ethical standards' (SE 18: 246). Freud also spoke of impulses that were incompatible with the subject's 'aesthetic standards' (SE 11: 24).[3] In *Studies on Hysteria*, some of the symptoms of Freud's patients emerged from the irreconcilable duty of nursing a sick parent and from simultaneously experiencing erotic feelings for someone. We saw above how, for example, Fräulein Elisabeth von R.'s symptoms formed as the 'circle of ideas embracing her duties to her sick father came into conflict with the content of the erotic desire she was feeling at the time' (SE 2: 164). It was possible to confirm her resistances when she reacted in a particularly violent way to Freud's interpretation of her pain: 'She cried aloud when I put the situation drily before her with the words: "So for a long time you had been in love with your brother-in-law" ' (SE 2: 157).

Freud found the patient's resistances towards certain ideas relevant, even before he had totally abandoned the use of hypnosis and of any of the procedures related to it: 'It turns out to be a *sine qua non* for the acquisition of hysteria [and other psychoneuroses] that an incompatibility should develop between the ego and some idea presented to it' (SE 2: 122).[4] However, the expulsion is not always successful. It is precisely the inability to 'push the thing away' that poses a problem, when the ego does not succeed in fulfilling the task of defence. In such cases '[b]oth the memory-trace and the affect which is attached to the idea are there once and for all and cannot be eradicated' (SE 3: 48). For the rejected idea 'pursued its activities in what was now an unconscious state, and found its way back into consciousness by means of symptoms and the affects attaching to them, so that the illness corresponded to a failure in defence' (SE 7: 276). There are means for the ego partially to fulfil the task, notably by '*turning this powerful idea into a weak one*, in robbing it of the affect – the sum of excitation – with which it is loaded' [Freud's emphasis] (SE 3: 48). However, the 'sum of excitation' does not disappear, it is merely 'transformed' or 'converted', such as in hysteria (SE 2: 122). It has 'the power to construct a symptom' (SE 16: 294). The patient then retains the 'psychical reminiscence' (the incompatible idea) but 'suffers from the affect which is more or less clearly attached to precisely that reminiscence' (SE 2: 122–3). In transforming ideas into bodily sensations, among other transformations, the ego created a 'sort of parasite': the 'mnemic symbol' of the idea or the memory-trace of the repressed idea 'persists' (on 'parasitic form', see SE 6: 276).

Defence and repression touched on one of the most fundamental aspects of Freud's research into unconscious psychical processes. It was possible to compare defensive processes in hysteria to normal defensive attitudes, to the 'casting out of one's mind' of anything that annoys one in everyday life. Indeed repression had to do with keeping something away from consciousness, something that nevertheless continued to have some ill effects. A question, however, arose as to the state in which that repressed element 'was kept away' and the 'place' where it was kept. We will see in Chapter 5 that these are some of the questions that the metapsychological points of view sought to elucidate. One could not simply answer that 'it is kept in one's mind', since, until the treatment had begun to work, the person ignored the existence of these ideas and emotions that were hidden from consciousness. How could something in 'my' mind, of which I am not even aware, have an influence on 'my' actions?

Today, one would readily say that anything that is 'hidden from consciousness' is 'unconscious', and this without even having read, or even heard, very much about Freud. That some 'ideas' could be unconscious and nevertheless have an influence on our everyday actions and thoughts is the phenomenon that interested Freud from the 1890s up until his death in 1939. At the turn of the century, anything one considered to be mental, anything having to do with the mind, was located within 'consciousness'. 'Consciousness', according to Freud, mistakenly encompassed everything mental (the processes of forgetting, thinking, etc.). There reigned what Paul-Laurent Assoun called a 'conscientalist prejudice' (Assoun 1976: 30). The concept of repression required one to explore a type of 'mental' activity that occurred 'at a distance' from consciousness, in what Freud at first called 'systems', and subsequently 'agencies'. In other words, it required one to explore 'the structure of the succession of psychical agencies and . . . the differentiation between what is conscious and unconscious' (SE 14: 148). (See SE 16: 295–9 on the analogy of rooms in succession, in which 'the mental impulse jostle one another like separate individuals'.)

PRINCIPLES OF MENTAL FUNCTIONING

The 'pushing aside' of unpleasurable ideas occurs because the mind functions according to a principle of discharge. Freud introduced that principle early on and conceived of it in terms of the regulation of pleasure/unpleasure within the mental apparatus, around which the theory of the drive is organized. There is a normal tendency in human beings towards discharge, which make them react 'adequately' when confronted with disagreeable experiences. Freud first described this normal 'tendency' in 1893 in the terminology in which he presented his early hypotheses, that is, by referring to the 'nervous system':

> If a person experiences a psychical impression, something in his nervous system which we will for the moment call the sum of excitation is increased. Now in every individual there exists a tendency to diminish this sum of excitation once more, in order to preserve his health. (SE 3: 36)[5]

For example, when someone has been insulted, the offence can be 'abreacted' when it is received, by means either of a physical action or of words of abuse directed to the insulting party. Alternatively, one can defend oneself by producing 'contrasting ideas', such as reminding oneself of one's own worthiness, or defuse the traumatic idea (in this case, the insult) by associating it with other less disagreeable ideas. If, however, someone does not react at all to the unpleasant experience, by getting rid of the increase of stimulation that it occasions, the experience can later become a psychical trauma and be the condition for the formation of symptoms (SE 3: 37). In hysterical patients, the reaction is 'less adequate', or is altogether lacking, and causes the affect to be blocked or strangulated (SE 3: 36). When the person has not reacted adequately, the memory of the event comes with the affect – or the increase, the excessive charge, or the 'affective tension' – that was felt at the time of the event (SE 2: 174). For, according to that early conception of hysterical phenomena,

> hysterical symptoms are the permanent results of psychical traumas, the sum of affect attaching to which has, for particular reasons, been prevented from being worked over consciously and has therefore found an abnormal path into somatic innervation. The terms 'strangulated affect', 'conversion', and 'abreaction' cover the distinctive features of this hypothesis. (SE 7: 272) (see also SE 3: 38; SE 2: 8–11)

As we saw above, Fräulein Elisabeth von R. suppressed her erotic idea and (unconsciously) transformed 'the amount of its affect into physical sensations of pain' (SE 2: 164), because she was unable to reconcile that idea with her ego by thinking (SE 3: 47). The idea (her attraction towards a forbidden love object) was thus 'repressed from the ego's consciousness'. But the 'strangulated' affect, the distressing affect that was attached to the idea, led to the formation of a symptom: the pain in her legs. The process of conversion 'exaggerates' and intensifies a normal process, known as the 'expression of the emotions' (SE 11: 18).[6] For the latter also involves the transformation of mental excitation into physical sensations. This is so in symptoms that are formed through symbolization (as we saw in Chapter 1). In this instance, the person suffered from a physical pain 'inspired' by an utterance, or a verbal expression. For example, is it not the case, Freud believed, that when we prevent ourselves from responding to an insult, we 'swallow it', as the figure of speech goes, and then suffer from the accumulation of tension in our throat.

The view that psychoneuroses were due to processes of defence, and that memories of traumas could be phantasies, modified Freud's views concerning the 'traumatic' origin of neuroses. 'Traumatic' applied to 'an experience which within a short period of time presents the mind with an increase of stimulus too powerful to be dealt with or worked off in the normal way' (SE 16: 275). Freud and Breuer believed neuroses to be caused by 'the inability to deal with an experience whose affective colouring was excessively powerful' (SE 16: 275). However, the onset of neuroses was caused by more than one determining factor. Neuroses could not be brought back to one traumatic event. Explaining the phenomena of hysteria through defence and repression brought it closer to normal mental processes (SE 7: 276). It led Freud to rethink the classification of neuroses, which was, in the 1890s, primarily based on the French psychiatrist Pierre Janet's notion that there was a splitting of consciousness caused by an 'innate weakness of the capacity for psychical synthesis, on the narrowness of the "field of consciousness" [*champ de la conscience*]', in brief, on ideas of degeneracy (SE 3: 46). For Breuer too, as we saw, there was a splitting of consciousness, but it was linked with 'hypnoid states', whereby ideas occurring in that state 'are cut off from associative communication with the rest of the content of consciousness' (SE 3: 46). Both views of neuroses implied a hereditary predisposition. Freud suggested that some forms of hysteria were 'acquired', which he called the 'defence hysteria'. In the new classification, this type of hysteria was connected with phobias and obsessions. Some patients were perfectly healthy until 'their ego was faced with an experience, an idea or a feeling which aroused such a distressing affect that the subject decided to forget about it', for normal thinking would not be sufficient to deal with it (SE 3: 47).

Explaining the formation of symptoms (and the existence of unconscious mental processes) through the theory of repression rested on the view that, as Wollheim stated, mental states 'can be analysed in two components, an idea which gives the mental state its object or what it is directed upon, and its charge of affect, which gives it its measure of strength or efficacy' (Wollheim 1971: 34–5). Another way of presenting the duality is to say that mental acts comprise a representation [*Vorstellung*] and an affect [*Affekt*] (SE 12: 262–3). That separation allowed Freud to elaborate a dynamic view of unconscious mental processes. Both components can be detached, reconnected, displaced. Repression, the pushing away of an idea or of an affect, is possible in so far as both components can separate.[7]

The mobility of the two components allowed the classification of forms of hysteria, phobias and obsessions. The pathologies were determined by the fate of their movements and by the methods of defence they called for. In hysteria, for example, the excessive amount of excitation, which the affect represented, was attached to an idea. Once detached, it was '*transformed into something somatic*' (Freud's emphasis. SE 3: 49), and produced the fits.[8]

However, the detached affect could also be tied to other ideas, and turn the latter into 'obsessional' ones, as there can be an unconscious 'false connection' between the idea and the affect (SE 3: 53). The latter consisted in a transposition, as Freud put it in his 1894 paper on 'The Neuro-Psychoses of Defence', or in a displacement, as he later stated in *The Interpretation of Dreams*, as we will see in Chapter 3. There are more means of defence than conversion and transposition, and the latter are not limited to the transformation of affect. There is notably the 'accentuation of the idea' (instead of the affect), which gives rise to a 'flight into psychosis' (SE 3: 59). However, these few examples should indicate how methods of defence provided a means of classifying neuroses (later Freud attributed these 'methods of defence' to the ego).

Infantile Sexuality and the Sexual Drives

What exactly gets repressed? Is it events, ideas, affects or impulses? We saw that the explanations successively put into play these elements. Who or what are the repressive instances? Is it the ego? Is it one of the parts of the mind that has 'split off'? At first Freud believed that what was 'repressed' were 'incompatible' ideas, and had noted that 'sexual life . . . brings with it the most copious occasions for the emergence of incompatible ideas' (SE 3: 52).[9] However, he soon understood that it was the memories attaching to the events that arouse unpleasure (possibly more than the actual event). As we saw in Chapter 1, he subsequently realized that it was not so much the memories that were repressed, but the impulses which arise from the 'primal scenes' of seduction (SE 1: 247; Wollheim 1971: 40–1). The whole of Freud's work represents an effort to elaborate on these questions, by developing a complete theory that contains 'gaps' which sometimes remain without resolution. The theory is open-ended because the conceptualization is 'the product of continuous and ever deeper-going experience' (SE 7: 271). For example, in 1905 the theory of neuroses depended on a broader understanding of the mechanisms of repression. In the 1915 paper on repression, in turn, it was necessary to postpone investigating too much the process 'until we have learned more about the structure of the succession of psychical agencies and about the differentiation between what is unconscious and conscious' (SE 14: 148). Freud was pointing to the following paper on 'The Unconscious' (1915), and to the reworking of the division between unconscious and conscious presented in 1923 in *The Ego and the Id*, where the concept of repression is still further modified, as we will see in Chapter 4. One of the topics, which noticeably evolved from the early findings around hysteria until 1920, is the theory of sexuality. It slowly emerged from the treatment of neurotic patients, and from the observation that their pain was not purely anatomical but had some imaginative dimension.

Chapter 1 discussed how the phenomenon of transference alerted Freud, among other observations, to the idea that there could be a link between sexuality and repression (see Chapter 1, pp. 27–9 above). The patient made a 'false connection' between an earlier situation and the present, by carrying over an earlier affective relation to the analyst (SE 2: 303). Hysterical symptoms, obsessions and phobias invariably sent patients back to their pasts. Freud extended that property of mental illnesses to make us 'go backward' to the normal development of the individual. We saw too that Freud was at first dismayed by the frequency with which, according to his patients' memories, adults seduced children. At the same time as Freud was 'over-estimating' the incidence of such events, he was unable to 'distinguish with certainty between falsifications made by hysterics in their memories of childhood and traces of real events' (SE 7: 274). According to that theory, the cause of neurosis could be found in childhood traumatic sexual events (in scenes of seduction by the father, for example). However, it was implausible that so many fathers could be 'perverts', including his own (– Note that it is in relation to the frequency of these phantasies that Freud invoked the story of Oedipus, which represented one of the normal impulses shared by everyone). In addition, the patients recurrently interrupted the treatment precisely in relation to their memories of such purported scenes. Instead of always recalling 'real events', Freud surmised, hysterics could be elaborating 'phantasies of seduction' in order to conceal elements of their 'own sexual activity such as infantile masturbation' (SE 7: 274). This did not mean that, for Freud, fathers or carers never seduced their children, but that what could influence the development of neurosis in later life was not only 'provoked' sexual experiences, but more broadly 'infantile sexual activity' itself. It was a mistake, in this context, to say that neuroses were caused by a traumatic event alone, just as it was a mistake to conceive of symptoms as 'direct derivatives of the repressed memories of childhood experiences' (SE 7: 274). Rather,

> between the symptoms and the childish impressions there were inserted the patient's *phantasies* (or imaginary memories), mostly

produced during the years of puberty, which on the one side were built up out of and over the childhood memories and on the other side were transformed into the symptoms. (Freud's emphasis, SE 7: 274) (see SE 20: 33–5)

Childhood memories produced an effect retrospectively – they had an 'after-effect' – by returning 'disguised'. *The Interpretation of Dreams* explored the dexterity of unconscious mental processes in the art of disguise.

The 'reversals' in the theory of the neuroses, then, obliged Freud to elaborate on repression, and to explore further the link between health, perversion and neurosis (SE 7: 271–9). Theoretical elements relating to defensive mechanisms and to sexuality, which remained diffuse throughout the early writings, came together in the *Three Essays on the Theory of Sexuality*, first published in 1905, but subsequently revised in the six German editions published until 1925 (it is, with *The Interpretation of Dreams*, one of the works to which Freud constantly returned by modifying his views and adding reservations).

THREE ESSAYS ON THE THEORY OF SEXUALITY

Even though what was at stake in the *Three Essays* was 'a theory of sexuality', the topic of the book proves considerably more complex than the ideas and images that 'sexuality' may at first bring about. (What images does sexuality indeed call to mind? That is one of the questions that Freud's theory of sexuality asks) The *Three Essays* do not present snatches of romantic scenes and affective imbroglios such as the ones we saw in the case histories (which were themselves far from simple), but rather theorizations purporting to explain patients' symptoms, by situating them in relation to the genesis of a fundamental aspect of human life. As Freud and Breuer's terminology in *Studies on Hysteria* did for Katharina's breathing malaise, the theorizations 'translated' and explained how sexuality participates in our everyday experiences, and creates neurotic conflicts. In the Preface to the Fourth Edition of *Three Essays*, Freud stated that the book makes an attempt 'at enlarging [*Erweiterung*] the concept of sexuality' (SE 7: 134) in order to show the narrowness of the popular conception of the sexual. Elsewhere, the extension is compared to that of the term 'psychical', which is necessary as soon as one admits of the existence of unconscious mental processes, whereas psychical had up until then, according to Freud's account, only referred to what was conscious (SE 16: 321).[10]

For Freud, there is only a difference of degree between the development of a normal person and that of a neurotic: 'A normal person has to pass through the same repressions and has to struggle with the same substitutive structures; the only difference is that he deals with these events with less trouble and better success' (SE 12: 210). The structure of *Three Essays* strikingly puts that view into play, by providing a detailed account of the proximity between normal and abnormal sexuality. Indeed, against those who want to isolate perversions and the so-called aberrant behaviour from 'normal sexual life', Freud believed that 'some perverse trait or other is seldom absent from the sexual life of normal people' (SE 16: 322). However, for that to be true, it is necessary to specify what 'perversions' entail, and to clarify the new concept of sexuality.

As we saw earlier, Freud had noted how 'impulses' and 'sums of excitation' related to certain scenes and memory in the formation of symptoms. In the first edition of *Three Essays*, he introduced the notion of the 'sexual drive' (which was prefigured by the notion of impulses but which did not replace exactly all similar earlier notions (see SE 14: 118; Draft N SE 1: 154). 'Libido' – the scientific name of the sexual drive – expresses a need in the manner in which 'hunger' does in the domain of nutrition: 'It is the name of the force . . . by which the instinct manifests itself' (SE 16: 313). The 'resemblance' between the sexual instinct and hunger is not born of a mere comparison, and stirs important questions as to whether the theory of sexuality is more biological than psychical. With this comes a fundamental distinction: on the one hand, there is the sexual object, from which sexual attraction stems, and on the other hand the sexual aim, the act towards which the drive tends. The normal sexual object is supposedly an adult of the opposite sex, and the normal sexual aim 'the union of the genitals in the act known as copulation, which leads to a release of the sexual tension and a temporary extinction of the sexual drive' (SE 7: 149).

Separation of the aim and the object

Three Essays provocatively opens up with 'The Sexual Aberrations'. Why begin with what deviates from the 'norm' prior to having expounded on the latter? Because the so-called perversions allow us to understand the mobility of the 'sexual drive', which is a composite psychical element, whose constituents can become undone, as happens in perversions and in certain mental illnesses. It is as though the aberrations performed the analysis of sorts of the sexual drive. One feature of the drive on which the entire theory of sexuality rests is that 'numerous deviations occur in respect of . . . the sexual object and the sexual aim' (SE 7: 136). With regard to the variety of perversions, it is striking how limited the 'normal picture' of human sexuality is with respect to the wealth of possible variations that characterize it (SE 7: 148). Freud exaggerated the limitedness of the prevailing view of sexual life by providing an overtly bare definition. As we saw above, the normal sexual aim consists in 'an endeavour to bring one's own genitals into contact with those of someone of the opposite sex' (SE 23: 152). It is not because most people choose an object of the opposite sex for copulation that the sexual drive is bound to such objects. In fact, 'the sexual [drive] and the sexual object are merely soldered together' (SE 7: 148), and can be disunited and reunited. We must, Freud suggested, 'loosen the bond that exists in our thoughts between instincts and objects', for it might be possible that 'the sexual instinct is in the first instance independent of its object', indeed, it is at first 'auto-erotic' (SE 7: 148).

The biological aim of reproduction indeed does not explain the many forms which sexual activity takes: 'human sexuality in its very nature is open to variation' (Lear 1990: 73), up to the point where the object can be altogether unsuitable for the reproductive aim. It looks as though all variations in the invention of new aims and objects are possible independent of their relation to genitals and copulation. For 'certain regions of the body, such as the mucous membrane of the mouth and anus, . . . seem . . . to be claiming that they should themselves be regarded and treated as genitals' (SE 7: 152–3). They are 'putting themselves forward as the paradigm of what sexuality is' (Lear 1990: 78).

One of the ways in which the concept of 'sexual' is extended is emerging: the sexual drive claims for itself a wide sphere of actions, and the protean nature of perversions is itself an 'extension' of the sexual sphere (SE 7: 160). The sexual and the component drives imaginatively seek and obtain sexual pleasure from a variety of objects and situations. One kind of deviation comes from 'over-valuating' aspects of the sexual object, in disregard of his/her genitals, which can lead to fetishism, in which the sexual drive selects as its 'object' some part of the body, or selects sartorial or ornamental objects relating to it (for example, the hair, the foot, or shoes). The example of fetishism illustrates the creative way in which the sexual drive proceeds. This kind of attitude becomes pathological when the pleasure gained from the foot or from shoes altogether '*takes the place* of the normal aim' [Freud's emphasis] (SE 7: 154). What is perverse in perversions is not their particular form, which turns out to be part and parcel of normal sexual life, as 'preparatory or intensifying contributions' (SE 16: 322), but their complete detachment from the reproductive function of sexuality (or the complete detachment from the act which results in reproduction).

However, it is possible to find points of contact between perversions and 'normal love'. A French novel, *The Princesse of Clèves* (1678), well illustrates the way in which normal love involves the adoration of substitutes. In the extract below, a woman, who is overlooked by her lover without knowing it, is enjoying his 'presence' through substitutes:

> He took up a position behind one of the French windows to see what Mme de Clèves was doing . . . She was reclining on a daybed with a table in front of her on which there were several baskets full of ribbons. She picked out some of these, and M. de Nemours noticed that they were of the very colours he had worn at the tournament. He saw that she was tying them in bows on a very unusual malacca cane which for a while he had carried around with him and which he had then given to his sister . . . She completed this task with such grace and gentleness that all the feelings in her heart seemed reflected in her face. Then she took a candlestick and went over to a large table in front of the painting of the siege of Metz that contained the likeness of M. de Nemours. She sat down and began to gaze at it with a musing fascination that could only have been inspired by true passion.[11]

In the extract, the choice of the yellow ribbons relates to an earlier scene in the novel where the Princesse, according to courtly rules, was wearing the colours of her (hidden) love object when appearing at the tournament in which he took part. The play with the ribbons could be said to be 'an after-effect of some sexual impression' (SE 7: 154). Except that in the novel, the earlier impression dates back to a few weeks rather than to early childhood.

The sexual drive varies its aim by forming 'intermediate relations to the sexual object, such as touching and looking at it' (SE 7: 149), that is by overemphasizing (or 'lingering' over) some preparatory acts and by making of them 'new sexual aims' (SE 7: 156). An example of such lingering is provided by the kiss, which, in Freud's distancing anatomical translation consists in 'a particular contact . . . between the mucous membrane of the lips of the two people concerned' but in which 'the parts of the body involved do not form part of the sexual apparatus but constitute entrance to the digestive tract' (SE 7: 150). Independent of the theory, upon reading that clinical description, one cannot but wish for an extension of the concept of the sexual. Touching and looking prepare for the final sexual aim and are themselves pleasurable (SE 7: 150). It is not a coincidence that it is in *Three Essays* that Freud elaborates on the concept of fore-pleasure, which provides a model for the pleasure involved in aesthetic appreciation and in that produced by jokes, as Freud elaborated on in *Jokes and their Relation to the Unconscious* (1905) and in 'Creative Writers and Day-Dreaming' (1908 [1907]). By sending an apparently sexual process back to the realm of aesthetics, it is not so much aesthetic pleasure that gets sexualized, as an aesthetic dimension that is added to sexual pleasure.

The observations of so-called aberrant behaviours, in addition to dispelling obsolete categories such as 'degenerate', then, helped redefine the normal sexual process. Although human sexuality allows for considerable variations with respect to the sexual reproductive aim, there are some stops, or 'resistances', to the extension of the sexual drive: disgust, shame and morality are 'mental forces' that oppose the infinite extension of the drive. These forces play a role in the development of sexuality and civilization.[12] At the same time as Freud introduced the 'plasticity' of the sexual drive, he brought in what resisted it. The most general name for the opposition to the sexual drive is the civilizing factor (civilization is obtained at the cost of the containment of the component drives).[13] Shame, disgust and morality are at the service of civilization, even though the development of each individual's sexuality involves these forces. Freud used the image of the breaking of a dam for describing what the failure to tame the drive could produce (SE 16: 312). The mental forces, 'like dams', which restrict the flow of the drive are erected during the period of latency (SE 7: 177) against unacceptable choices of objects such as one's parents (Oedipus complex). They are as much a product of education as an organic process (there is a phy-logenetic dimension to that process, that is, it sends us back to the evolution of the species). Nevertheless, the sexual drive ('the most unruly of all the instincts' [SE 7: 161]) sometimes 'goes to astonish-ing lengths in successfully overriding the resistances of shame, disgust, horror or pain' (SE 7: 161). The analysis of perversions confirms that the sexual drive is always a composite thing, whose ele-ments are concealed by the 'uniform behaviour of normal people' (SE 7: 162). With the introduction of the concept of the sexual drive, the definition of neuroses gets more precise: 'the human ailments known as "neuroses" are derived from the many different ways in which these processes of transformation in the sexual component instinct may miscarry' (SE 7: 215).

However, perversions are not the only means of getting to know human sexuality. Neurotic symptoms are equally fitted for that purpose because they 'are based on the one hand on the demands of the libidinal instincts and on the other hand on those made by the ego by way of reaction to them' (SE 7: 163). They are, in Freud's provocative formula, *'the patient's sexual activity'* (SE 7: 115); *'the negative of perversions'* (Freud's emphasis, SE 7: 165). Neurotic symptoms are 'transcriptions' or 'imprints' of the repression of impulses, which were derived from the sexual drive.[14] These impulses 'have been prevented from obtaining discharge in psychical activity' (SE 7: 164), and consequently, they 'strive' to find expression by forming symptoms. Symptoms inform us about earlier mental processes relating to the sexual drive. In neurotics one finds the following 'enigmatic contradiction': they experience 'exaggerated sexual craving' but display 'excessive aversion to sexuality' (SE 7: 165). The contradiction gives rise to the conflict out of which symp-toms emerge. Neurotic symptoms confirm the variability of human sexuality, in so far as they proceed from the same kind of extensions, which the perversions display, and model themselves on earlier stages of development.

There is another equally decisive *rapprochement* between infantile sexuality and perversions in the theory of sexualtiy (SE 16: 320). Freud was searching for the best 'port of entry' into human sexual-ity. Perversions served the purpose of demonstrating the composite character of the sexual drive, as 'something tangible and unambigu-ous', while the manifestations of infantile sexuality 'melt into indefiniteness towards their beginnings' (SE 16: 320). By putting together the associations and memories of early childhood obtained during the analysis of neurotics and by observing children (as in the case history of 'Little Hans' in 'Analysis of a Phobia in a Five-Year-Old Boy' (1909), it was possible to link perversions and sexual activity in childhood. The proximity between the two meant for Freud that 'perverse sexuality is nothing else than a magnified infantile sexuality split up into its separate impulses' (SE 16: 311). The idea of 'magnification' is recurrent in Freud whenever he wishes to indicate how mental illnesses (here perversions) differ only in degree from normal mental processes. It may also be one of the ways in which to understand almost in a physical sense the *enlargement* of the concept of sexuality.

What Freud discovered, then, is that we are ignorant of the beginnings of our sexual life, and that we believe that it coincides with the moment when the 'normal picture' of sexual life, which requires physical maturity, is activated. However, the fact that we are unaware of infantile sexual life does not mean that it does not exist (the theory of the unconscious is partly a theory of what it means to be 'unaware'). That one cannot remember one's infantile sexual activity does not entail that it did not take place. On the contrary, not only do humans have an early sexual life, but Freud also suggested that not knowing about infantile sexuality and forgetting about it are intrinsic to their development. Sexuality does not begin at puberty. Indeed, the activity that apparently makes up the whole of sexual life is only the last stage of a long development, during which the genitals play a marginal role, if at all. This is why 'sexual' cannot be equated with 'genitals'. Hysterical women did not repress only elements of their own personal history. Rather, they showed how human beings are characterized by the way in which they ignore the development and nature of sexuality.

DEVELOPMENT

It was one of the highlights of *Three Essays*, so to speak, to propose to lay out the 'ordered course of development' of sexuality from early childhood to adult life (SE 23: 153). If it was possible to show that sexuality is the result of an assemblage, it became possible to show how the latter can become undone. Sexual life passes through an eclectic series of stages of organization (from the less unified stages in early childhood sexuality to the most unified one from puberty and thereafter. In the 1920s, Freud makes of the sexual drive (of Eros) a unifying power, which binds all living substances together, and thus contributes to upholding civilization as developed in *Civilization and its Discontents* (1930 [1929]; SE 21: 108–9). It culminates in the 'subordination of the component sexual instincts under the primacy of the genitals' (SE 16: 328). Before unification occurs, it displays an anarchic structure of sort: 'Infantile sexuality lacks . . . any . . . centring and organization; its separate component instincts have equal rights, each of them goes its own way to obtaining pleasure' (SE 16: 323). How do these separate impulses become unified, or, as Freud put it, 'organized'? The answer to that question is a key to the understanding of the pathological disorganization of sexuality in neurotics.

Even though the gradual organization of sexuality is not an entirely fixed pattern (since the 'phases' of development can overlap, indeed co-exist), Freud's account is chronological. Sexual activity starts 'soon after birth' and undergoes a 'regular process of increase, reaching a climax towards the end of the fifth year' that marks the beginning of the period of latency (SE 23: 152–3). During that period of lull, a number of 'stops' are put in place which we saw above: shame, disgust and morality act to contain the sexual drive, until the second start of sexual life at puberty. The onset of human sexuality is 'diphasic', that is, it occurs in two stages (SE 23: 153). Through that double beginning, it is significant that the events of early childhood are forgotten, are subjected to what Freud called 'infantile amnesia'. Some forces impose the forgetting of that earliest period of development (SE 16: 326). 'Infantile amnesia' concerning our early years is specific to human sexuality, and is explained by the fact that that early period contains the beginnings of sexual life. As we said above, it is constitutive of the beginnings of sexuality that they be forgotten and repressed.

It is within that overall chronology that it is possible to distinguish phases of development in early childhood. Everyone is familiar with them, as with the 'Oedipus complex', as the popular reception of Freud's theory of sexuality has reduced it to these isolated elements. One of its controversial aspects is that Freud developed the theory from the biological need of self-preservation, and is therefore too biological. Freud uses the notion of *Anlehnung* (anaclisis) to point to how sexuality originates in close relation to vital functions; in particular, to the act of nourishment. The child's sexual activity begins from the moment that s/he engages in sucking without seeking nour-ishment ('thumb-sucking' or 'sensual sucking' serves as a sample of children's sexual activity [SE 7: 176]): 'sucking at the mother's breast is the starting point of the whole of sexual life, the unmatched pro-totype of every later sexual satisfaction, to which phantasy often enough recurs in times of need' (SE 16: 314). The child is not seeking to be satiated by food but to obtain pleasure for pleasure's sake in the first 'oral' phase. The breast is the first sexual object. However, when the child next begins to hallucinate satisfaction rather than seeking to obtain it by sucking, he/she thus takes a part of his/her his own body as an object (he/she turns towards an 'auto-erotic' object). The excitation of the 'zones' destined for the accomplish-ment of the vital functions, for example, the mouth in the oral phase, establishes future sources of sexual satisfaction (these zones are called the 'erotogenic zones', the zones of the body from which sexual excitation will emerge). The diverse 'component drives' at first seek to obtain pleasure from these zones, including eventually from the genitals. Nothing prevents the whole body from becoming an erotogenic zone (SE 23: 151). Some drives are not related to a bodily zone, such as the drive for mastery and the drive for knowledge.

The oral phase is only one of the four forms taken by the sexual drive, which evolves as it seeks new sources of satisfaction. In the second phase, the anal-sadistic phase, the drive no longer 'leans' on nourishment, but seeks sources of satisfaction in aggression and in the excretory function, while in the third, the phallic one, satisfac-tion is sought in the genitals, and in this way it comes near the final 'genital' phase. In that account, the transition from one phase to the other is not clear-cut. However, the arrival of the period of latency marks an important shift, in so far as Freud no longer spoke of 'the sexual development' in general, but of the differentiated paths which male and female sexuality thereafter follow.

We began the chapter by distinguishing narrative and explana-tory levels in Freud's writings. Having moved into the realm of explanations (concerning repression and sexuality, two of the three factors, with 'infantilism', that constitute psychoanalytic theory [SE 12: 210]), we seem to have moved to another level altogether where stories are no longer juxtaposed with explanations. Let us recall that it was in relation to dreams that Freud spoke of 'things themselves' with which he preferred to begin. Indeed, by turning to dreams, we zoom in on the composition of the 'interchange of words'. Moving closer to the paths, the threads, the chains of association that produce dreams, provides an access to the unconscious processes of neurotic and 'normal' life, which we have begun to explore through Freud's early findings. Having explored the explanations of the mechanisms *underlying* the formation of neurotic symptoms, in particular, the nature of defence and repression, and sexuality, we will consider, in the next chapter, dream-interpretation and the dream-work. Dreams as a 'normal' unconscious formation give a tangible form to primary processes, which are only temporarily inaccessible to consciousness.

CHAPTER 3

DREAMS

Freud's general hypothesis, whereby unconscious processes determine our conscious life, confronts us with a contradictory state of affairs, that is with a 'state of mind in which one knows and does not know a thing at the same time' (SE 2: 117), as we saw in Chapter 1. A series of everyday-life phenomena – the forgetting of proper names, of lines of poetry, of objects, the committing of errors of all sorts, accidental actions, joking – as well as neurotic illnesses – make us experience that contradiction. For example, when booking a train ticket from the Reichenhall railway station, Freud could not remember the name of the place where he was next going. Yet he was very familiar with that name. When looking for it in the timetable – *Rosenheim* ('Rose-home') – he realized that it was connected to that of his sister Rosa and to the idea of home (SE 6: 23). Freud did not analyse further that instance of forgetting, but it shows that he momentarily did not know what he knew very well. The feeling of knowing and not-knowing at once is particularly acute in relation to dreams. Freud believed that the dreamer '*does* know what his dream means: *only he does not know that he knows it and for that reason thinks he does not know it*' (Freud's emphasis, SE 15: 101).[1] Freud's theory of dreams and, more generally, his theory of the unconscious draws attention to that puzzling kind of knowledge.[2] It seeks to explain the fact that I am not aware of everything 'that goes on in my mind', but that this does not mean that it does not go on: 'Unless the content of the dream (rightly under-stood) is inspired by alien spirits, it is a part of my own being' (SE 19: 133). The remark applies beyond the content of the dream to every-thing I say or do. Freud said of the 'repressed' that it 'proliferates in the dark . . . and takes on extreme forms of expression' which invari-ably 'seem alien' to the person concerned (SE 14: 149).

The aim of this chapter is to explore the main elements of Freud's theory of dream-interpretation, in the vein of the 'technical innovations' that we considered in Chapter 1. *The Interpretation of Dreams* is the central piece of the theory of dreams, and of the theory of the unconscious. Dreams allow us to zoom in on 'underlying mechanisms'. The distinction between 'things themselves' and 'explanations' is at its most tenuous with dreams, since dreams present themselves as 'mechanisms'. Dreams tell stories and also the story of their composition. Freud revised the initial theory, as he modified some of the fundamental tenets of the theory of the drives. We saw how, upon coming up against the riddle of his patients' dreams, it became necessary to find a way of making sense of them. However, one could not turn to existing 'dream-books', as one would do to a book on how to read tarot cards and proceed to tell someone their future. The notion of interpretation emerged from the theoretical insights obtained when elaborating the hitherto unknown therapeutic set-up. Not only did Freud develop his dream-book while treating neurotics, dream-interpretation was also instrumental in the elaboration of the technique of the cure and of the theory of the unconscious.

According to Freud's 1914 history of the psychoanalytic movement, recognizing the importance of dreams for understanding the mind was one of the factors that transformed the cathartic method into psychoanalysis. The other two, which we have already explored in Chapter 2, were the theory of repression and the discovery of the role of infantile sexuality in the onset of neurosis. Dreams are not simply the irrational productions of neurotic patients, or of gifted individuals who could create 'unrestrained and unregulated structures' (SE 9: 9). Everyone concocts and experiences such absurd fictions. For, assuming that most of us dream at night, the difference between the normal and the pathological 'holds only during the day' (SE 16: 256). Even so, we cross the conventional and fluctuating frontier between normal and pathological 'many times in the course of a day' (SE 9: 44). Neurotic symptoms permitted the analyst to form hypotheses about repression and the unconscious; nevertheless, it is dreams that are the 'most convenient means of access to a knowledge of the repressed unconscious' (SE 16: 456). In the oft-quoted formula, the interpretation of dreams is *the royal road to a knowledge of the unconscious activities of the mind*' (Freud's emphasis, SE 5: 608). Freud went so far as to say that 'psycho-analysis is founded upon the analysis of dreams' (SE 12: 265). Dreams give a concrete form to the conflictual nature of unconscious processes. They inform us about the entire field of unconscious formations. Dreams, in the same way that the language of the obsessional is, appear to be 'protected from being understood' (SE 9: 226). However, unlike neurotic symptoms (which can be photographed, as Charcot did with hysterical women), and unlike 'tumours as big as apples compressing the organ of the mind, haemorrhages, chronic inflammation, in all of which the changes in the tissues can be demonstrated under the microscope' (SE 15: 84), dreams form an unpractical object of research. Although everyone regularly dreams, it is impossible to have any certainty about one's dreams, for 'we know a dream from what seems as a rule a fragmentary memory of it which we have after waking' (SE 8: 159–60). Worse, 'what we exercise our interpretative arts upon has been mutilated by the untrustworthiness of our memory . . . which may well have lost precisely the most important part of its content' (SE 5: 512). We saw in Chapter 1 how Freud slowly discovered that his patients had a falsifying memory, in that they both remembered and embellished scenes from their past. The concept of phantasy encompassed that activity. Freud believed that every memory was composed of various elements based partly on past events and partly on the imaginative enlargement of them (see 'The Aetiology of Hysteria' [1896] SE 3: 197). Our active memories are the only means of access to our dreams.

Most problematic for the constitution of the theory, 'as a rule no account at all can be given of [dreams]' (SE 15: 84) just as there could be no adequate account of the cure. We saw that when one consciously tries to remember something, a host of substitute thoughts come up. Writing one's dream helps remembering more of them (Freud did not simply 'write down' his dreams, he rather rendered them in the form of narratives, using literary techniques, such as descriptions, dialogues, interjections or free indirect speech). Every dreamer experiences dissatisfaction towards the rendering of their dreams. Our dream-narratives are always inadequate, too short for how much we dreamt (there is always more to tell). Dream-narratives are usually incoherent; they string together unrelated ideas; they do not respect spatio-temporal limitations; they present technological feats worthy of science fiction. The *suspicion* towards dreams, that is, the surmise that they have a double meaning, however, did not arise solely from their incoherence, but also from their *apparent* rationality. For the clarity and coherence of dreams is no less intriguing than their obscurity. However, that no dream-narrative can ever be entirely reliable as the faithful record of an oneiric experience, is not an obstacle for the theory of dream. Quite the reverse: all features of the dream, beginning with the appearance of irrationality or rationality, have a role to play in them.

THE INTERPRETATION OF DREAMS (1900)

Before we explore the main elements of dream-interpretation on which Freud worked from around 1896, let us describe in broad outline the content of *The Interpretation*. It was first published in 1900 (it actually appeared in 1899, but the editor altered the date so that the book could be regarded as a twentieth-century book). It was reprinted and revised eight times.[3] Freud reworked his theory of dreams in *The Interpretation* itself and in later papers, notably after the publication of *Beyond the Pleasure Principle* (1920). One of his forays into literature deals with a class of dreams that 'have never been dreamt at all' (SE 9: 7), which creative writers invent or which are attributed to fictional characters such as in Wilhelm Jensen's *Gradiva*, which Freud studied in 'Delusions and Dreams in Jensen's *Gradiva*' (1907 [1906]). He even became interested in the controversial problem of dreams, telepathy and occultism in 'Dreams and Occultism' (1933 [1932]). Together with *Three Essays on the Theory of Sexuality* (1905), *The Interpretation* is one of the works to which Freud most regularly returned. For that reason, it constitutes an archive of sorts of Freud's thinking and of the psychoanalytic movement. For example, the addition of sections on symbolism in Chapter VI records the development of the application of psychoanalysis during the 1910s, in relation to the development of the human sciences during the first decades of the twentieth century.[4]

The opening chapter of the book reviews ancient and late-nineteenth-century theories of dreams, and provides a point of reference for evaluating the novelty of Freud's views. The survey begins with classical antiquity, notably with the fourth-century BC Greek philosopher Aristotle, for whom dreams became an object of psychological research, and had the property of magnifying 'small stimuli arising during sleep' (SE 4: 3). It moves on to the physiological theories of his predecessors and contemporaries, such as, Alfred Maury, Joseph Delboeuf, F. W. Hildebrandt and Johannes Volket.[5] For the ancients, dreams were 'deceitful and worthless' or they were 'truthful and valuable', in that they could warn the dreamer about an imminent danger. They could foretell the future (SE 4: 3). Whereas for contemporary medical science dreams were unworthy of scientific interest beyond their so-called somatic function, for Freud their absurdity would seem to lure anyone experiencing or listening to them into 'interpreting' them. One cannot help but be fascinated by them and ask how such composite figures, or juxtaposition of images, could be possible. The unintelligibility of dreams constitute a 'bait'.

To take dreams seriously, then, is to 'embrace the prejudice of the ancients and of the people' (SE 15: 87) according to whom dreams were significant. There is no need, then, to discard every idea from the medical authorities and previous authors on dreams. On the contrary, Freud presented some of the main tenets of his theory of dreams in the first chapter, where he introduced his first dreams. To take only two examples, Freud underlined the idea of 'psychical localities', which he borrowed from Gustav Theodor Fechner, for whom *'the scene of action of dreams is different from that of waking ideational life'* (Freud's emphasis, SE 4: 48; SE 5: 536). That dreams occur in a 'change of location' was not the expression of an anatomical localization. Rather, the idea of localization could prove fruitful by applying it, as Freud did in Chapter VII of *The Interpretation*, 'to a *mental* apparatus built up of a number of agencies arranged in a series one behind the other' (SE 4: 49).[6] To call attention to the 'scene of action' of dreams was also to underscore, as previous authors had done, that dreams 'dramatize' and make us experience situations in visual modes (SE 4: 50). We will see below the importance of that property of dreams. Freud also retained from existing sources – this is our second example – the idea that, as the English psychologist James Sully and others had stated, 'dreams have a disguised meaning' (SE 4: 60).

Among many topics in Chapter 1, 'Memory in Dreams' stands out, for it introduces the idea that dreams, as neurotic symptoms, have to do with the past, rather than being turned towards the future.[7] They have to do with memory in the banal sense that we indicated above, as we need to remember them in order to analyse them. They can 'bring back to our minds, with a wonderful power of reproduction, very remote and even forgotten events from our earliest years' (SE 4: 15). Dreams confront the dreamer with what s/he 'knows without knowing', as their use of forgotten quotations and obscene words indicates, or the persistence of certain images and scenes in them (SE 4: 14). For several years, Freud was 'pursued by the picture of a church tower of very simple design, which [he] could not remember ever having seen. Then [he] suddenly recognized it, with absolute certainty, at a small station on the line between Salzburg and Reichenhall' (SE 4: 14). He had seen it for the first time in 1886 and only recognized it in the mid-1890s, after having dreamt about it. The book closes with the idea that dreams derive from the past. They nevertheless maintain some link to the future, because they slightly modify the past: 'By picturing our wishes as fulfilled, dreams are after all leading us into the future. But this future, which the dreamer pictures as the present, has been moulded by his indestructible wish into a perfect likeness of the past' (SE 5: 621).[8]

That dreams have to do with wishing is the leading idea of Freud's theory of dreams. They indeed 'picture our wishes as fulfilled', or replace ' "Oh! if only . . ." by "It is" ' but the wish is not readily accessible (SE 8: 162). Freud introduces the psychoanalytic method of interpretation with reference to the 'Dream of Irma's Injection', which is the first dream Freud almost 'fully analyzed'. It is possible to give some of the significant elements of that famous dream: Freud dreamt that he had told Irma, one of his patients, that it was her own fault if she still had pains. Yet he might have missed an organic illness. She was recalcitrant. He had called on his friends to examine her, and to confirm the infection that Freud detected. He could then trace the infection back to an injection of '*a preparation of propyl, propyls . . . proprionic acid . . . trimethylamin*' which his friend Otto had given Irma (SE 4: 107). The analysis of that dream allowed Freud, in the following chapter, to formulate in what indeed the meaning of dreams consists: '*a dream is a (disguised) fulfilment of a (suppressed or repressed) wish*' (SE 4: 160), or as he put it in the lecture on Dreams in *The Introductory Lectures on Psycho-Analysis*, 'the dream as a whole is a distorted substitute for something else, something unconscious' (SE 15: 114). The object of study itself calls for being replaced by something else, by what it distorts. Through an accumulation of examples and a long theoretical chapter concluding the book, Freud demonstrated how dreams exerted that function. He expounded on the processes thanks to which a repressed wish could be fulfilled disguisedly, assisted in that task by the lifting of repression. In the Dream of Irma's Injection, the dream-thought was 'If only Otto were responsible for Irma's illness!', but it was replaced by 'Yes, Otto is responsible for Irma's illness' (SE 5: 534).

After brief chapters on distortion, on the distinction between the manifest and latent content, and on the material and sources of dreams, there follow the central chapters of the book, respectively entitled 'The Dream-Work' and 'The Psychology of the Dream-Processes'. The former contains the essential elements of Freud's theory of dreams, with reference to which we can grasp the transformation of unconscious impulses into something that can reach consciousness, via interpretation. The chapter provides the 'poetical' rules for the elaboration of dreams, and by extension for other 'unconscious formations', such as the *Witz*, the obsessional style, or neurotic symptoms. Excluding the first chapter, then, *The Interpretation* begins with 'things themselves', that is, with a dream and a practical exercise in its analysis by means of the 'correct' method for unravelling its meaning. Up until Chapter VII, we are in the domain of dreams and 'dream-interpretation', and can witness what Wollheim called Freud's 'feat of prestidigitation' (Wollheim 1971: 76). The move into the theory of the 'mental apparatus' in Chapter VII marks a break from the demonstration of the meaningful character of dreams, through interpretation. We go into the domain of 'underlying mechanisms', of unconscious mental functioning, or of the 'theoretical fiction' of an apparatus responsible for the formation of dreams. Chapter VII is a significant text, for it is there that Freud elaborates the *first topography*, that is, the first model of the 'psychical apparatus' that divides into three systems or agencies: the unconscious, the preconscious and the conscious ones. It is also the precursor to the metapsychology. Freud replaced that first model by the *second topography*, a structural (anthropomorphic) model of the mind, composed of the Ego, the Id and the Super-Ego. We will consider both the metapsychology and the second model of the mind below.

'I BEGAN BY ATTEMPTING THIS UPON MYSELF'[9]

We have so far only partially described the book on dreams. Specimen dreams – and not solely the 'Dream of Irma's Injection' referred to as a 'specimen' – tell of Freud's experiences of the loss of his father, of disappointments in his academic career in the political climate of exclusion characteristic of Vienna at the end of the nineteenth century, of his family, of his affective attachments during his early childhood. In elaborating the technique and theory of psychoanalysis, among other things, through the analysis of his own dreams, Freud produced a 'work of confession' (Wollheim 1971: 66), which he began around the end of 1897. The 'confession' – the self-analysis [*Selbstanalyse*] – was carried out in the psychoanalytic fashion, that is, by attempting to discover the mechanisms through which certain memories returned in his dreams. Unlike analysts after him, who had to undergo a psychoanalytic treatment as part of their training from 1922 onwards, Freud had to divide himself into the subject and object of analysis. In embarking on his self-analysis, Freud assumed that it was possible to pursue the research into unconscious mental processes, not with neurotics, but in 'someone who is not at all or only very slightly neurotic' (SE 3: 309). However, there are limits to that endeavour, as he stated in a letter to Fliess, dated 14 November 1897. That analysis, Freud wrote to Fliess, was the most difficult of all the analyses he had carried out so far (that is, before the analytic set-up was established thanks precisely to his self-analysis). One of the problems was the fact that he only disposed of a body of 'knowledge acquired objectively (as a foreigner)'. We saw in Chapter 1 that taking an objective, intellectual interest in psychoanalysis during the cure could constitute a form of resistance. Freud went so far as to state that 'self-analysis is impossible, otherwise there would be no illness' (Freud 2006: 357). Fliess, with whom Freud was linked for thirteen years, played a crucial role in the elaboration of psychoanalytic theory. Among other things, he shared Freud's interest in sexuality and in theoretical speculation about the relation between mental and organic processes. Fliess was developing a theory of periodicity and of bisexuality, which he discussed with Freud, and which appeared in some of Freud's dreams or dream-thoughts (see, for example, SE 4: 331 for a dream involving Fliess's theory of bisexuality). There was eventually a rupture of their friendly relations over the priority and ownership of that idea – the episode is referred to as the 'Plagiarism Affair' – which Freud took seriously when developing the material on homosexuality in *Three Essays on the Theory of Sexuality*.[10]

EARLIER AND PSYCHOANALYTIC METHODS

Freud provided a very broad definition of 'interpretation' in his Lecture on Dreams from *The Introductory Lectures*, whereby 'interpreting means finding a hidden sense in something' (SE 15: 87). It is because dreams have particular ways and motives for 'hiding sense' that they require a specific method of interpretation. Prior to presenting his own method, Freud reviewed two existing popular methods of interpretation: the first 'symbolic' one 'considers the content of the dream as a whole and seeks to replace it by another content which is intelligible and in certain respects analogous to the original one' (SE 4: 96–7). The prophetic dream by the Pharaoh that Joseph explains illustrates what the method entails. The dream about 'the seven fat kine followed by seven lean kine that ate up the fat kine' served the purpose of announcing that there would be 'seven years of famine in the land of Egypt' (SE 4: 97). The second, 'decoding' method, however, 'treats dreams as a kind of cryptography in which each sign can be translated into another sign having a known meaning, in accordance with a fixed key' (SE 4: 97). A dreamer adopting that procedure would look mechanically for the translation of the elements of his/her dream in a dream-book. For example, dreaming about a funeral might mean, following a certain key, a betrothal; receiving a letter might refer to 'trouble' (there is not a great degree of decipherment necessarily to be done).

The main difference between these earlier methods and Freud's is that the latter grants a crucial role to the dreamer's associations in relation to his/her dream, up to the point where the interpretation of dreams has to take place within the dialogic situation of the psychoanalytic cure. It rests on the idea that understanding a symptom removes it. For 'if a pathological idea [causing the symptom] [. . .] can be traced back to the elements in the patient's mental life from which it originated, it simultaneously crumbles away and the patient is freed from it' (SE 4: 100). The method relies on the distinction between the manifest and the latent contents of the dream, to which we will come back, and which is well illustrated by the following account of the manifest dream:

> [The dream] appears as a meshwork of sense-impressions, mostly visual but also of other kinds, which have simulated an experience, with which thought-processes ('knowledge' in the dream)

and expressions of affect may be mingled. What we thus remember of the dream I call *'the dream's manifest content'*. It is often entirely absurd and confused . . . But even if it is quite coherent, as it is in the case of some anxiety-dreams, it confronts our mental life as something alien, for whose origin one cannot in any way account. (Freud's emphasis, SE 8: 160)

One can relate the strange, manifest dream to some 'rational psychical structures' which Freud calls the *'latent dream-thoughts'* (Freud's emphasis, SE 8: 160). The latter apparently act the 'solutions' to the dream's riddle, once the dream has been analysed. For example, one of Freud's patients had the following dream:

> I wanted to give a supper-party, but I had nothing in the house but a little smoked salmon. I thought I would go out and buy something, but remembered then that it was Sunday afternoon and all the shops would be shut. Next I tried to ring up some caterers, but the telephone was out of order. So I had to abandon my wish to give a supper-party. (SE 4: 147)

For interpreting the dream, one proceeds by setting aside the overall narrative content, its apparent meaning, which is here the fact that a woman had to abandon her wish to give a supper-party because she had next to nothing to offer and shops were shut. However, the recounted narrative is not necessarily the meaning of the dream, for the latter points beyond its immediate 'façade'. The coherence may even be added at the moment of telling the dream (SE 5: 512). One then 'divid[es] the dream's manifest content into its component parts' (SE 8: 160), and encourages the dreamer freely to associate in relation to these elements, once in the appropriate uncritical frame of mind. These latter trigger in the dreamer ideas that are connected with the manifest dream. In the supper-party dream, after much resistance and reluctance to suspend her critical faculty, the woman finally brought up her jealousy towards one of her woman friends, of whom her husband was fond. Everything hung on her willingness to let herself be led by involuntary thoughts that cropped up in relation to isolated elements of the dream, wherever they could lead her (SE 5: 527). The analyst then 'follow[s] the associative threads', which 'interweave with one another' and form a 'tissue of thoughts which are not only perfectly rational but can also be easily fitted into the known context of our mental processes' (SE 8: 160). Here, there is a connection between the wish to give a supper-party, food, and the dreamer's woman friend, who was not entirely suited to her husband, as he preferred 'a plumper figure' and her friend was 'very skinny and thin' (SE 4: 148). Drifting along the path of involuntary ideas allowed one to discover the 'secret' meaning of the dream, which the dreamer could most often recognize. Whereas the dreamer of the supper-party dream believed that her dream was refuting Freud's theory of wish-fulfilment, the dream contained a telling negative wish. Given her jealousy towards her friend, there was no way that she would have thrown a supper-party, because to do so would have made her friend 'grow plumper' and become more attractive to her husband. Involuntary thoughts are only apparently 'involuntary'. In fact, they are 'purposive' thoughts, which are *unknown* to the dreamer or, in other words, are 'unconscious' (Freud wrote later: 'what we call arbitrariness in the mind rests upon laws' [SE 9: 9]).

In Chapter 1, we saw how patients recounted dreams during the cure, as a result of being urged to tell 'everything that comes into their mind', and of having to set their critical faculty aside. The cure changed considerably when Freud understood how memories were related to a network of associations, that one could listen to, and that could inform us about the formation of symptoms. Prompting 'free association' in relation to the remembered dream merely pursued the act of remembering one's dream. Moreover, Freud's method was meant to be the 'mirror-image' of the dream itself: interpretation reproduced the composition of the dream in reverse (let us recall Breuer's analysis of Anna O. by thematic groupings).[11] This began with the telling of the dream: 'whatever the dreamer tells us must count as his dream, without regard to what he may have forgotten or have altered in recalling it' (SE 15: 85; see too SE 4: 281 and Section A Chapter VII). Where, then, did the dream end and where did interpretation begin? In principle, the dreamer could be interpreting his dream when recounting it during the analytic session, in conjunction with the analyst. The conscious remembering, the forgetting of some parts of it, and its interpreting participated in its distortion. Freud based *The Interpretation* on the analysis of his own dreams, in the manner of a patient during the cure. By attributing to themselves the status of analysts, commentators have taken Freud's analytic solutions to his dreams as further material to be analysed, in the diagnostic manner that we pointed out at the beginning.[12] Freud's method of dream-interpretation maintained elements from earlier ones. This is most notable in relation to the problem of symbolism, when it is a matter of interpreting 'diving into the water' as 'being born' (SE 5: 400), or of the 'genitals represented by buildings, stairs, and shaft' – a section added in 1911. Freud would then seem to have adopted a 'dream-book', an approach which he still found problematic in previous authors.

DREAMS HAVE A MEANING: WISH-FULFILMENT

The assertions that 'dreams really have a meaning' (SE 4: 100), that they are 'psychical phenomena of complete validity', which 'are constructed by a highly complicated activity of the mind' (SE 4: 122), no longer appear as shocking as they must have done in 1899. They were then formulated in response to the current idea that dreams were unworthy of scientific scrutiny and that interpreting them would be to engage in 'a fanciful task' (SE 4: 100; see Lear 1990: 71). However, the 'correct method' of dream-interpretation generated ambiguities. Was discovering the 'meaning' of dreams to take cognizance of their processes of formation, which were supposedly universal and unchanging? Or else, did the 'sense' of dreams derive from the particular 'stories' the dream told us about the dreamer, and in which one found the sources and material of the dream? Revealing the meaning of dreams entailed, on the one hand, exploring the rules of their formation (their syntax, their grammar), thanks to which they served the function as wish-fulfilment. From that perspective, 'the' meaning of dreams would seem to be the same for every dreamer, whatever wish may have motivated their dreams. On the other hand, once correctly analysed, dreams told us short stories about professional rivalry, sexual attraction, marriage, homosexuality, jealousy, anxiety, regrets, and so on. Through the act of dreaming, there seemed to be an infinite number of situations in which to 'dramatize' these topics.

There is a tension in Freud's theory of dreams, which is not solely a textual or argumentative concern, between the myriad of stories and situations to which dreams give rise, and the general meaning of dreams – their motives and function. In the case of most dream narratives in *The Interpretation*, a preamble introduces the surrounding events of the dream. The analysis then sends us back to the preamble and beyond, into the dreamer's life history. The tension can be partly reduced when we discover that the stories lead us to the functioning of the 'mental apparatus'. The assertions about dreams would seem to pertain to the domain of motives and processes. The effort to make sense of their absurdity, our efforts to tackle these disjointed, and sometimes also poetical stories, are so to speak redeemed by the fact that dreams in fact tell us about the functioning of the mind. Dream-interpretation was not put at the service of the 'secret meaning' of dreams – did not Freud end up by saying controversially that he did not care about the dream itself, apparently contradicting what he said about his interest in 'things themselves' (SE 5: 517)? Rather, it above all served the understanding of the functioning of the mind.

This is particularly apparent with the notion of wish-fulfilment, which is also the 'psychical apparatus's primary mode of working' (SE 5: 567). For *dreaming is a piece of infantile mental life that has been superseded*, to which the dreamer regresses during the night (SE 5: 567). The 'fulfilment' of a wish has a temporal dimension: it consists in re-establishing a previous state or situation. We noted above that memory was a significant concern in the theory of dreams. Each particular dream indeed 'remembers' elements of our past. But the psychical apparatus itself also works by going back to the past through the wish. There are thus two levels at which to situate the theory of wish-fulfilment. At one level, the aim of interpretation is to discover the wish (the disguised repressed wish). The analyst does not necessarily obtain that result, but it gives an orientation to his/her interpretative act, since wishes are 'the sole psychical motive force for the construction of dreams' (SE 5: 568). The interpretation of dreams has a role to play during the cure. At another level, the wish is a piece in the functioning of the mental apparatus for 'nothing but a wish can set out our mental apparatus at work' (SE 5: 567). Let us explore how dreams have to do with wish-fulfilment.

Dreams of Convenience

Even though for Freud dreams were psychical rather than physiological processes, he maintained that they acted as 'guardians of sleep' by responding to 'internal somatic stimuli'. Dreams somehow 'arbitrate' between two conflicting purposes: they protect the desire to sleep, while they permit hallucinatory experiences to satisfy the striving of psychical impulses towards consciousness (SE 16: 131). The compromise is best illustrated by 'dreams of convenience', which turn out to be the most general category of dreams. The following example recalls the experimental, provoked dreams familiar to previous authors on sleep and dreams:

> If I eat anchovies . . . in the evening, I develop thirst during the night which wakes me up. But my waking is preceded by a dream; and this always has the same content, namely, that I am drinking. I dream I am swallowing down water in great gulps, and it has the delicious taste that nothing can equal but a cool drink when one is parched with thirst . . . The thirst gives rise to a wish to drink, and the dream shows me that wish fulfilled . . . If I can succeed in appeasing my thirst by *dreaming* that I am drinking, then I need not wake up in order to quench it. (Freud's emphasis, SE 4: 123)

Thanks to dreaming that s/he is drinking, the dreamer can continue sleeping, as s/he does not need to get up and fetch a 'cool drink', which made Freud say that 'a dream may be described as a piece of phantasy working on behalf of the maintenance of sleep' (SE 19: 127; see SE 5: 568).[13] It is 'an *attempt* to get rid of a disturbance of sleep by means of a wish-fulfilment' (Freud's emphasis, SE 23: 171).

Children's Dreams: Undisguised Wishes

In order to explain the function of dreams as the 'disguised fulfilment of a repressed wish', Freud also strikingly provided examples of dreams in which the wish was not disguised and was closely related to the prototype of a physical need. According to the idea that earlier states of development were necessarily simpler, Freud believed that children's dreams indeed illustrated the theory of wish-fulfilment better than adult 'dreams of convenience'. They were 'pure wish-fulfilment', not yet rendered more complex by disguise. In children's dreams, the elements of the dream have not yet formed a unified picture such as they do in adult dreams.[14] (children dreams are comparable to the component drives in the theory of sexuality, which show us the composition of sexuality prior to its fixation into the 'normal' picture of sexuality.) Children's dreams showed the wish prior to the distortion: in a child's dream, there is a '*saving in dream-work*' (SE 5: 643; our emphasis). There is oddly a saving of what precisely makes interpretation necessary. For example, Freud's daughter Anna was ill, and had been kept without food for an entire day. The following night, her parents heard her scream in her dream: 'Anna Fweud, stwawbewwies, wild stwawbewwies, omblet, pudden!' which composed a menu of all the things she liked eating (SE 4: 130). When adults are put under the strain of unusual external circumstances', they too tend to dream 'infantile' dreams. Members of an expedition in the Antarctic, for example, dreamt of having 'got through a three-course dinner', 'dreamt of tobacco, of whole mountains of tobacco'. In brief, they had dreamt of the goods and sensual pleasures they missed. It is significant that, according to the diarist, the crew's childlike dreams should show a 'lack of imaginativeness' (SE 4: 131–2 n. 1). It is precisely that unimaginativeness that allows us to see the 'wish' prior to its transformation.[15] Not only, then, did Freud think that dreams bring us back to early childhood memories; infantile dreaming also brings us closer to the function of adult dreams.

The Experience of Satisfaction

It is not a coincidence if the examples of children's dreams involve a wish to eat, which recalls the child's early demands for nourishment. They bring us to the earliest mode of functioning of the mental apparatus. Dreams (both adult and children's) allow us to witness that mode of operation *in statu nascendi*, which 'the experience of satisfaction' encompasses. The latter is the first step *in* the development of the psychical apparatus (from which the development of thinking, of language, of the relation to the other, to objects all spring). The primitive apparatus first functions by 'keeping itself so far as possible free from stimuli' (SE 5: 565), according to the 'principle of constancy'. It tends towards the discharge of excitations towards the external world. What matters here is that, in Freud's explanation, that early mode of operation is conceivable mostly when a second mode of operation comes to disturb it.[16] A baby seeking nourishment, who 'screams or kicks helplessly' until outside help can bring about in him or her an experience of satisfaction, which will get rid of the internal tension, illustrates that mode of functioning. That early experience is attached to a particular perception. When the tension provoked by hunger ceases once the mother has given the breast to the child, the child's satisfaction or the disappearance of the tension gets connected to the image of the breast. From then on, the 'mnemic' image, as Freud called that original image, becomes 'associated with the memory trace of the excitation produced by the need' (SE 5: 565). Every time the need next arises, the child can 'hallucinate' the breast, in order to 're-establish the situation of the original satisfaction' (SE 5: 566). The 'wish' is the *impulse*, which endeavours to *repeat* the experience of satisfaction by making the 'mnemic image' present again. When the latter reappears, there is the fulfilment of a wish. (The 'fulfilment' entails a repetition. The notion of repetition became prominent in Freud's theory of the drives after the introduction of the 'death drive' and the 'compulsion to repeat' in 1920. The idea of repetition, which comes close to reproduction, is, however, present in the earliest writings.) At first then, 'the aim of this first psychical activity was to produce a "perceptual identity" – a repetition of the perception which was linked with the satisfaction of the need' (SE 5: 566). However, the 'primitive thought-activity' did not bring the desired satisfaction. Such a striving for the reproduction of the experience of satisfaction consists in a regression to the 'mnemic image' associated with the perception. Because it was inefficient to hallucinate the means of satisfaction – it did not appease the need – it became necessary to stop, to inhibit the striving for repetition (SE 5: 566). A second system inhibited and diverted the search for satisfaction towards the external world (towards motor activity).

One of the factors of development of the psychical apparatus, then, is the inefficiency of the hallucination for appeasing the need (SE 5: 567–8). When the apparatus is prevented from hallucinating, it can reach a 'real' perception of the object: 'Instead of [hallucinating], the psychical apparatus [has] to decide to form a conception of the real circumstances in the external world and to endeavour to make a real alteration in them' (SE 12: 219). The story Freud told about the development of the psychical apparatus prepares for the extension of his theory to the understanding of the institution of civilization. In both cases, the 'advance' rests on the renunciation of an immediate pleasure (here satisfaction through hallucinating) in exchange for a greater good. The apparatus renounces the hallucinating mode of satisfaction, by establishing the 'principle of reality'. The motor discharge, which was used to divert the accumulation of stimuli, by turning towards the inside of the body, is 'converted' into *action*. Children's dreams, then, bring us closer to the original experience of satisfaction in which it is possible to situate the 'wish', because they are closer to the 'primitive' functioning of the apparatus.[17]

DISTRESSING DREAMS: THE MANIFEST AND LATENT CONTENT

Having briefly explored the earliest mode of functioning of the psychical apparatus, let us return to the idea that dreams are wish-fulfilment of a disguised, repressed wish. From the example of the child's dream (but not necessarily from its explanation), the theory appears to be quite as simple as the proverb Freud quoted in support of it: ' "What", asks the proverb, "do geese dream of?" And it replies: "Of maize" ' (SE 4: 132; on children's dreams, see SE 15: 126–35). One obvious objection against the theory of wish-fulfilment was that some dreams were highly disagreeable, and caused anxiety. That objection anticipated the revision of the theory of dreams after 1920. How could distressing dreams serve the function of 'wish-fulfilment'? In some dreams, the 'most dreadful of all unpleasurable feelings holds us in its grasp till we awaken' (SE 4: 135). It is in relation to distressing dreams (or 'anxiety-dreams') that Freud introduced a very important pair of concepts, on which we touched above. Some dreams may be distressing in their *manifest* content. However, if one interprets their *latent* thoughts correctly, the distressing content leads us to quite another type of content – the latent one, which is a 'new class of psychical material'. In Anna Freud's dream, it is easy to refer the manifest content (the little girl eating the 'stwawbewwies') to the latent content (the wish to eat strawberries). There is a difference between the two (the manifest content shows the wish realized), but the fulfilment is not here concealed – Freud says that the 'manifest and the latent content coincide' (SE 5: 643). Hence, even in infantile dreams, which appear transparent, one finds a 'species of transformation': '*a thought expressed in the optative has been replaced by a representation in the present tense*' (SE 5: 647). In adults' dreams the manifest content most often differs considerably from the latent content. Yet they are not independent from each other, for the dream consists in the transformation of the one into the other.

It is as much a mistake to focus exclusively on one level as on the other. Some objections to Freud's theory of dreams come from the undue separation of the manifest and latent contents.

Commentators exaggerate Freud's interest in the latent content. We saw in Chapter 1 how Binswanger reproached Freud for concentrating too exclusively on 'underlying mechanisms'. In the essay we quoted he formulated his criticisms in relation to the theory of the drives. The distinction between the manifest and latent content brings us back to Binswanger's reproach.[18] For the literary and art critic Susan Sontag, for example, Freud's doctrine (together with Karl Marx's) 'amount[s] to elaborate systems of hermeneutics, aggressive and impious theories of interpretation'. Freud's hermeneutics is 'aggressive and impious', because it is, in Sontag's gloss, 'bracketing' phenomena as 'manifest content'. What matters is what lies 'beneath' that manifest level. Freudian hermeneutics does violence to 'all observable phenomena', which have 'no meaning without interpretation. To understand is to interpret. And to interpret is to restate the phenomenon, in effect to find an equivalent for it'.[19] Instead of dwelling on the dream itself (on the italicized narratives throughout *The Interpretation*), Freud goes 'behind' them, replaces them with a theory of dreams. The idea of the manifest dream presupposes that dreams 'point beyond themselves', that they 'mean more than they seem to be saying', which is not one of Freud's innovations (Lear 2006: 90). For the philosopher Paul Ricoeur, they are a 'symbol' in the sense in which they 'aim to say something else than what they are saying' (Ricoeur 1965: 22). Sontag almost provides a caricature of Binswanger's argument concerning Freud's interest in 'underlying mechanisms'. Whereas the latter formulated his theory of the drives in apparent disregard for Freud's ambiguous definition of the drives, Sontag's and similar kinds of assessments apparently ignore the note Freud added in 1925, which is one of the most important assertions of the book: 'At bottom, dreams are nothing other than a particular *form* of thinking, made possible by the conditions of the state of sleep' (Freud's emphasis, SE 5: 506). In children's dreams the two levels coincide (Freud's nephew wanted to eat the cherries in the basket of cherries, which he was supposed to present to his uncle on his birthday. The next day he was declaring 'Hermann eaten all the chewwies' [SE 4: 131]). There is apparently no transformation of the desire to eat the cherries (however one could ask: how do we know that the 'simple dream' is not a disguise?).

If the dream is not solely or always caused by somatic stimuli, where does it come from? Freud argued that dreams, on the one hand, drew their material from the memory of the immediate past (from the previous days, from the 'day residues', the remains of our multifarious daily activities). For example, Freud and one of his friends took a cab with a taximeter the night before he dreamt about sitting at a *table d'hôte*. In the two situations he was reminded of what he owed (SE 5: 636). But the dream of sitting at a *table d'hôte* in the company of Frau E. L. also referred back to an episode that had occurred in the past when Freud was courting his wife (SE 5: 638).

On the other hand, dreams go as far back as infancy and early childhood (the same dream brings Freud back to his infantile distaste for spinach, which one of his children also shared [SE 5: 639]). Indeed dreams even connect us to the prehistory of humanity, according to the idea that 'dreams and neuroses seem to have preserved more mental antiquities than we could have imagined possible' (SE 5: 549).[20] The 'mental antiquities' refer both to the development of the individual, which, following Haeckel's law, is 'an abbreviated recapitulation influenced by the chance circumstances of life' (SE 5: 548), and in turn, to Freud's theory of the unconscious which is 'by a bold extension' applied to the 'human race as a whole' (SE 22: 239). As with the theory of wish-fulfilment, there is a temporal dimension to the distinction between the manifest and the latent content: 'every dream [is] linked in its manifest content with recent experiences and in its latent content with the most ancient experiences' (SE 4: 218).

DISTORTION, CENSORSHIP

The content of dreams springs from repressed material and the only way that the latter can reach consciousness is through distortion. The dream's incongruities are due to its work of concealment of repressed ideas ('there is a causal connection between the obscurity of the dream-content and the state of repression' [SE 5: 672]). If children's dreams appear to be transparent, it is because in early childhood, wishes are not yet repressed (SE 5: 552). The institution of repression in the individual through shame, disgust and morality is at the service of the civilizing process. For civilization requires repression; it demands a sacrifice from the individual in exchange for which the latter is protected. Until puberty, children are not submitted to that constraint.

Dreams are difficult to interpret, then, because they represent the striving of repressed ideas to become conscious in spite of what opposes their return (they are one of the forms which the return of the repressed takes; see 'Delusions and Dreams in Jensen's *Gradiva*' [SE 9: 3-95]). Censorship is 'the watchman of our mental health'; it prevents unconscious wishful impulses from taking 'control of the power of movement' (SE 5: 567). Freud compared the process of censorship in dreams and the political phenomenon of censorship (he had already presented resistance and repression in hysterics as a form of censoring [SE 2: 269; 282; SE 3: 182]). If we replace 'writer' by 'repressed ideas and affects', Freud would appear to be speaking about the dream:

> A writer must beware of the censorship, and on its account he must soften and distort the expression of his opinion. According to the strength and sensitiveness of the censorship he finds himself compelled either merely to refrain from certain forms of attack, or to speak in allusions in place of direct references, or he must conceal his objectionable pronouncement beneath some apparently innocent disguise: for instance, he may describe a dispute between two Mandarins in the Middle Kingdom, when the people he really has in mind are officials of his own country. The stricter the censorship, the more far-reaching will be the disguise and the more ingenious too may be the means employed for putting the reader on the scent of the true meaning. (SE 4: 142)

The last sentence is especially relevant to Freud's theory of dream-distortion. For the stronger the opposition against the incompatible idea, the greater will be the degree of absurdity, or the 'dexterity' of the dream (Freud speaks of 'unconscious dexterity' [SE 6: 142]). It was through 'resistances' that Freud was able to reach certain unconscious ideas. Censorship and resistances act as signals: the greater the resistance, the more there will be symptomatic manifestations. Why do the phenomena of censorship and of dream-distortion correspond down to their smallest detail, as Freud said? Just as in censorship there are two powers – or one power in the form of the government, and a will in that of the political writer – there are two psychical forces (or 'systems') in individual beings. One of the systems constructs the dream (so as to make the repressed reach consciousness) in response to the strength exerted by censorship against the return of that material to consciousness. The censorship is exercised by the other system. The amount or the degree of distortion is a function of the power of that censorship. What is the nature of that power which exercises censorship? The second agency or system 'allows nothing to pass without exercising its rights and making such modifications as it thinks fit in the thought which is seeking admission to consciousness' (SE 4: 144). When discussing censorship and the dream-work, Freud merely spoke of 'two systems', even if he called one of them consciousness. It is only in Chapter VII that he developed more fully the functioning of the mental apparatus.[21]

THE DREAM-WORK

'The Dream-Work' spells out the ways in which the *form* of the dream: 'the essence of dreaming' (SE 5: 506–7 n. 1). It provides the rules of dream-composition: it is the sum of *unconscious* operations, psychical processes, that 'transform the latent content of the dream into the manifest one' (SE 5: 641). The dream-work comprises four main operations, which act in varying proportion in each dream: '[the dream-work] has no functions whatever other than condensation and displacement of the material and its modification into pictorial form, to which must be added as a variable factor the final bit of interpretation, or what Freud called 'secondary elaboration' (SE 6: 667). Let us consider each of them by means of Freud's examples, and in the order in which he first presented them.

Condensation

Condensation, one of the most important processes of formation of dreams, consists in the 'compression of material'. That reduction is deduced from a comparison between apparently incomparable data, that is, from the content of the manifest dream and from ones obtained only through analysis (which is potentially interminable):

> If . . . we compare the number of ideational elements or the space taken up in writing them down in the case of the dream and of the dream-thoughts to which the analysis leads us . . . we shall be left in no doubt that the dream-work has carried out a work of compression or *condensation* on a large scale. (Freud's emphasis, SE 5: 648)

Although the 'degree of condensation' cannot be evaluated – 'it is impossible to determine the amount of condensation' (SE 4: 279) – the further we analyse a dream, the greater it appears. For dreams are 'laconic' while the analysis of the dream-thoughts that compose them can occupy 'six, eight, or a dozen times as much space' (SE 4: 279). This is at least the case in *The Interpretation*, where the 'text' of the dream can be measured in lines, and that of the analyses of the many portions of the dream in pages (Irma's dream has 28 lines, and its analysis spreads over approximately 12 pages). Dreams are divided into 'elements' which can be as short as the 'the letter "e" ' (SE 4: 303), can be words such as *'Dysentery'* (SE 4: 114), or phrases such as *'In spite of her dress'* (SE 4: 113), and still necessitate one or more pages for their meaning to be unravelled in relation to the other elements of the dream. Or else the elements of the dream concern the set-up (*'The hall – numerous guests, whom we were receiving'* [SE 4: 108]), are expressions of intelligible worries (*'I was alarmed at the idea that I had missed an organic illness'* [SE 4: 109]), or could form part of a larger narrative (*'And probably the syringe had not been clean'* [SE 4: 118]), but still give rise to considerable developments. No matter how fragmentary the elements under scrutiny are, the dream can be 'unpacked', in conformity with the impression that 'we dreamt far more' than we can remember (SE 5: 512). The method rested on the idea that precisely 'the most trivial elements of a dream are indispensable to its interpretation' (SE 5: 513), since before letting associations flow it is impossible to tell where the dream leads us. Let us recall how, as we said above, it often appears to us that 'our memory . . . may well have lost precisely the most important part of the [dream's] content' (SE 5: 512).

The disproportion between the manifest and the latent content comes from the way in which each element of the manifest content triggers a host of associations in the dreamer, just as whole portions of life attach to neurotic symptoms. In their work with hysterics, Freud and Breuer had encountered that kind of disproportion whereby the symptoms acted as a 'summary' of whole networks of associations (let us recall Breuer's counting of the occurrences of certain themes, and arranging them in files, according to Freud). That disproportion is expressed in Jonathan Lear's description of the symptom as 'an eye-catching aspect of *an entire way of life* that is going wrong' (Lear 2006: 66; our emphasis). In Freud's terminology, 'each element in the content of a dream is "overdetermined" by material in the dream-thoughts; it is not derived from a *single* element in the dream-thoughts, but may be traced back to a whole number' (Freud's emphasis, SE 5: 652). Moreover, 'not only are the elements of a dream determined by the dream-thoughts many times over, but the individual dream-thoughts are represented in the dream by several elements' (SE 4: 284). Because of processes such as condensation, 'it is . . . not easy to form any conception of the abundance of the unconscious trains of thought, all striving to find expression, which are active in our minds' (SE 5: 521).

The way in which single elements of the manifest dream act as 'representatives' of larger ensembles gives an almost physical sense to the *compression* [*Kompression*] of material taking place in condensation, to the way in which the material of the dream is 'packed together for the purpose of constructing a dream-situation' (SE 5: 649). Dream-thoughts are 'brought under the pressure of the dream-work, and its elements are turned about, broken into fragments and jammed together – almost like packed ice' (SE 4: 312). In that operation, connecting words, 'logical relations' are excluded – Freud spoke of dreams as 'the Realm of the Illogical' (SE 23: 168). There is no space (or time?) for logical relations. Nevertheless, the dream-work connects, and it is possible to unravel all the various incongruous matches it produces. Interpretation consists in 'restoring' the connections between dream-thoughts that would obtain in 'waking thinking' (SE 5: 660).

One of Freud's dreams illustrates the process, by making a 'connection' [*Beziehung*], and thus creating a 'collective figure', one of the species of condensation: 'I had a dream of someone who I knew in my dream was the doctor in my native town. His face was indistinct, but was confused with a picture of one of my masters at my secondary school' whom Freud still sometimes met (SE 4: 17). After enquiring to his mother, Freud discovered that both the doctor and the schoolmaster were one-eyed. The dream illustrates the hypermnesia of dreams (Freud had not seen the doctor for 38 years), but it is also an instance of the building up of a figure 'by giving it the features of two people' so as to indicate 'an "and" or "just as", or to compare the original persons with each other in some particular respect, which may even be specified in the dream itself' (SE 5: 651). Freud compared what the dream-work does when it suggests that 'all these things have an element x in common' (SE 5: 651) to Francis Galton's *Mischbildung*, or 'composite pictures'. The latter were invented, among other purposes, for the identification of hereditary defects through the superimposition of the members of the same family. This was meant to show their common defective features and it was done on the assumption it would that be possible to delimit the distinctive features of criminality.[22]

The dream of an indistinct face condensing two one-eyed figures is related to a later dream, which showed the process of condensation even more strikingly, and involved a more complex set of links:

> I. . . . My friend R. was my uncle. – I had a great feeling of affection for him.
> II. I saw before me his face, somewhat changed. It was as though it had been drawn out lengthways. A yellow beard that surrounded it stood out especially clearly. (SE 4: 137)

Freud wished to be appointed to a higher academic post, but he and his friend were prevented from that because they were Jewish. The friend and the uncle were linked through simple-mindedness but also by virtue of their physical features. By making R. and N. (Freud's other colleague included in the dream) a simpleton and a criminal, Freud found reasons other than their common Jewishness for their failures to be appointed to higher posts. His Uncle Josef (who had committed criminal acts in his youth) represented Freud's two colleagues who had not been appointed to professorships. Freud could thus continue hoping to be promoted since he was not a simpleton or a criminal.

Another example of the formation by the dream of a 'composite structure' is that of the two objects featured in one of Freud's dreams: 'I dreamt . . . that I was sitting on a bench with one of my former University teachers, and that the bench, which was surrounded by other benches, was moving forward at a rapid pace' (SE 5: 651). The moving object is 'a combination of a lecture theatre and a *trottoir roulant* [a moving roadway]' (SE 5: 652), but Freud did not pursue the analysis further than pointing out the unification of a moving to a non-moving object, and left us with a poetic image. More generally, condensation produced all sorts of 'composite structures', which called for being 'dissected' into the common elements of which they were made (see Freud's dream of dissection, SE 5: 452–5). Dreams moreover combine, abbreviate or compress features of things and persons together not only in order

to highlight common elements, but also sometimes so as to underline relations of dissemblances or contraries (see 'the "flowery"
dream' [SE 5: 347–8]).

Dreams also produce verbal condensations, which appear by
themselves or in conjunction with other types of composite structure. Verbal condensation most clearly showed the process of compression the dream-work performs (let us recall that therapy and
theory have developed through the analysis of words and associations of words, and how Freud found significant Cäcilie's linguistic
symptomatic invention). The analysis of the neologisms and nonsensical verbal forms in dreams makes us pass from syllables, indeed
letters, to broader, all-encompassing situations. Some dreams well
illustrate the emergence of a wealth of associations out of sparse
material, such as the following preamble, dream and analysis, involving nonsensical words:

> On one occasion a medical colleague had sent me a paper he had
> written, in which the importance of a recent physiological dis-
> covery was, in my opinion, overestimated, and in which, above all,
> the subject was treated in too emotional a manner. The next night
> I dreamt a sentence which clearly referred to this paper: *'It's
> written in a positively norekdal style'*. The analysis of the word
> caused me some difficulty at first. There could be no doubt that it
> was a parody of the [German] superlatives *'kolossal'* and *'pyra-
> midal'*; but its origin was not so easy to guess. At last I saw that
> the monstrosity was composed of the two names 'Nora' and
> 'Ekdal' – characters in two well-known plays of Henrik Ibsen's [*A
> Doll's House* and *The Wild Duck*]. Some time before, I had read a
> newspaper article on Ibsen by the same author whose latest work
> I was criticizing in the dream. (Freud's emphasis, SE 4: 296)

The analysis stops short of stating the wish fulfilled by the dream,
and is quite laconic (we are not much informed about the thought
processes taking place between 'There could be no doubt that . . .'
and the final 'At last I saw that. . .'). However, it fits in with Freud's
other dreams of ambition and professional jealousy. It confuses
literary and medical concerns, even though Freud did not elaborate
on the relation between the characters of Ibsen's play and the
topic of the article or the relation to his colleague. Nevertheless, the
extract gives us a good indication of the processes and the kind of

'material' the dream used. Not only did the manifest dream appeal to literature, but its process also resembled that of poetry. For the process of connecting dream-thoughts by altering the phrasing of one of them recalls a similar one, that of making a rhyme 'where a similar sound has to be sought for in the same way as a common element is in our present case' (SE 5: 651).

As in other dreams, the 'monstrous' word draws its elements from dramatic and literary works, which either Freud or his entourage read (elsewhere, it is a matter of a character in Émile Zola's *L'Oeuvre*, of the contradiction between two women in George Eliot's *Adam Bede*, or of verses from a poem by the German poet Uhland). References to works of literature do not necessarily consist in references to the story of the novel, or of the play. In Marcel Proust's *In Search of Lost Time*, the narrator presents the singular way in which every reader remembers a book: remembering a book could be not so much to retain its plot and its characters, but rather the colouring of its cover in a particular light when one has first read it. Similarly, the dream-work seizes on any element it chooses, to create new 'objects' of interests, names and words (see SE 3: 182, where Freud explains how the formation of hysterical symptoms is linked with the associations that come to join in the passages of a book. Both memories and reading never come without triggering associations, which threaten to blur them). The dream 'takes' freely what it needs from everyday life, and unreservedly cuts existing wholes into how many elements it requires for its 'work'.

The transformation of words and names, the invention of new verbal forms, is more disquieting than the creation of composite objects, for it touches more intimately on the possibility of meaning. Analyses of nonsensical verbal forms may be few in *The Interpretation*; however, Freud developed further these analyses in two subsequent works, *The Psychopathology of Everyday Life* (1901) and *Jokes and their Relation to the Unconscious* (1905), for there are analogies between the formation of the dream and that of jokes, to which we will turn in Chapter 5.

Displacement

Among the four factors of transformation of latent thoughts into the manifest content, condensation and displacement are the 'governing' ones 'to whose activity we may in essence ascribe the form assumed by dreams' (SE 4: 308). Freud called the second mode of transformation 'displacement' or 'dream-displacement'. It is 'by far the most striking' (SE 5: 671). It makes ideas of central importance in the dream-thoughts (the latent content) appear as unimportant in the manifest dream. For example, the 'Dream of the Botanical Monograph' pertained to a monograph Freud had written. However, '*[t]he book lay before me and I was at the moment turning over a folded coloured plate. Bound up in each copy there was a dried specimen of the plant, as though it had been taken from a herbarium*' (SE 4: 169). Through the associative thread prompted by the elements of the dream, 'botanical' turns out to have a minor role:

> All the trains of thought starting from the dream – the thoughts about my wife's and my own favourite flowers, about coca-ine, about the awkwardness of medical treatment among colleagues, about my preference for studying monographs and about my neglect of certain branches of sciences such as botany – all of these trains of thought . . . led ultimately to one or other of the many ramifications of my conversation with Dr Königstein. (SE 4: 173)

The word 'botanical', which had a central place in the manifest dream, has a secondary position in the latent dream-thoughts. Botany figures as the object of Freud's neglect (SE 4: 302). Displacement relates closely to the idea of transference (SE 5: 562 n. 2). It involves a change of intensity (something, which is remembered very vividly, turns out to conceal a peripheral element or vice versa). It is a matter of varying 'psychical value', or the 'significance or affective potentiality of the thoughts' (SE 5: 654): essential elements, which have a high 'psychical intensity', appear in the dream as having only small value. Moreover, 'it is often an *indistinct* element which turns out to be the most direct derivative of the essential dream-thought' (Freud's emphasis, SE 5: 654).

We noted above the physical overtones of condensation. As for displacement, it directly refers us to a 'psychical force', that imposes the *transference and displacement of psychical intensities* (SE 4: 307). Freud borrowed the idea of 'transvaluation' from Friedrich Nietzsche, and spoke of a 'transvaluation of psychical values' (SE 5: 655). Something, the attempt to avoid censorship, imposes a change in the distribution of psychical intensity. Freud spoke of endopsychic defence (SE 4: 308). One can witness the 'transvaluation' only retrospectively, after having 'undone' the displacement (SE 5: 655). In constructing their content, dreams moreover have a preference for what are indifferent and trivial elements from the previous day or days – the day-residues. However, the triviality of dreams is almost a proof that 'dream-displacement' is taking place, because through analysis 'insignificant and uninteresting' ideas lead to 'things that are of the highest psychical importance' (SE 5: 656).

Means of Representation

Condensation may be the most easily detectable transformation performed by the dream-work, but all means of transformation raise the objection as to how to identify the undistorted elements in the first place. With the 'pictorial arrangement of psychical material' – the third transformation of which the dream-work is capable – we enter into an even more difficult area of Freud's theory of dreams. For it touches on the special 'mode of expression' of dream-thoughts, which is not ordinary verbal language, but which nevertheless has a syntax, a grammar, and obeys a certain logic.

From the outset, we have been concerned with the translation of stories into mechanisms. With the dream it is also in some way still a matter of translation: 'a dream is recognized as a *form of expression* of impulses which are under the pressure of resistance during the day but which have been able to find reinforcement during the night from deep-lying sources of excitation' (SE 4: 614). In what way can impulses be 'expressed'? Given the origin of the dream in early childhood, and as a return to the primitive mode of functioning of the apparatus, the 'means of representation' stands out among the other elements of the dream-work. For it raise the question as to how impulses can give rise to representations. How indeed can certain impulses influence the fate of someone's life; how can excitations 'create stories'?

We said earlier that 'The Dream-Work' provided the rules of composition of the dream. Having considered the creation of nonsensical verbal forms, we saw that this is not a mere figure of speech, for the dream does create linguistic entities according to certain operations, or rules which resemble the 'hammering of a rhyme'. When dealing with the 'considerations of representability in the content of the dream' – the transformation that dream-thoughts undergo for 'entering' into the composition of the manifest dream – we move into the realm of linguistic similes and metaphors, but also into that of pictorial representation. We saw above how the process of condensation had to be understood also in a physical sense. With the 'pictorial arrangement of psychical material' (SE 5: 666), the formation of dreams moves even closer to sensory experience itself. For the manifest dream 'consists for the most part in *pictorial situations*' [our emphasis] (SE 5: 659), and dream-thoughts gain a right of entry into the dream by being 'transposed' into sensory perception. 'Dream-images . . . are clothed in the psychical appearance of perceptions' (SE 5: 678).

Let us recall how the experience of satisfaction forms a point of reference to which the mental apparatus regresses in dreams. Early childhood impressions instigating the dream (as well as the day-residues) have a 'visual subject-matter' (SE 5: 659). It is that visual nucleus that has a strong influence on the formation of the dream, and that determines its pictorial nature. Interrogating the 'conditions of representability' leads us to the 'sources and material of the dream', and to the way in which dreams tend to 'go backwards'. For the 'visual' instigator of the dream fits in with other material: 'The content of dreams . . . does not consist entirely of [pictorial] situations, but also includes disconnected fragments of visual images, speeches, and even bits of unmodified thoughts' (SE 5: 660). Examples of such pictorial situations are ready-made lines of reasonings, calculations and, as we saw, remembered literary residues (literature, especially poetry and theatre, is omnipresent in the theory of dream-interpretation). The emphasis on pictorial situations reveals that dreams incorporate 'ready-made' material through regression. The conditions of representability, therefore, do not solely impose a pictorial transformation, but encompass various other modes of representation.

Many of the elements of the dream have not been constructed by the dream, but 'turn out to be repetitions or modified versions of scenes from infancy' (SE 5: 667) or the repetition of elements from the dream-thoughts unmodified. For example, there may be a calculation in the dream-thoughts, but when the dream-work 'processes' it, so to speak, one might be faced with 'the wildest results'. Whereas one might be tempted to think of the dream-work as a productive force, Freud insists on the way in which the manifest dream sometimes just reproduces elements of the dream-thoughts, that have been 'heard or read . . . whose wording is exactly reproduced . . . while . . . their meaning is violently changed' (SE 5: 668). It is precisely the power of the dream to reproduce that caused problems to the theory in 1920, when Freud isolated the 'compulsion to repeat', as we will see below.

With respect to the 'conditions of representability', condensation and displacement would appear to be preliminary 'destructive' steps, for in order to be transformed into a dream,

> the psychical material will be submitted to a pressure which will condense it greatly, to an internal fragmentation and displacement which will, as it were, create new surfaces, and to a selective operation in favour of those portions of it which are the most appropriate for the construction of situations. (SE 5: 660)

Having 'destroyed' connections (SE 6: 660), the dream-work combines the material according to 'formal means employed . . . for the expression of logical relations in the dream-thought' (SE 5: 662). It imposes its own means of representing logical relations, which Freud spelled out in a manual of logic of sorts, the dream's unique one. However, these logical connections are also those presiding over the process of condensation, in so far as the dream favours the relation of *'similarity, consonance, the possession of common attribute'* (Freud's emphasis, SE 5: 661). Among other logical connections, the dream-work groups elements by *approximation in time and place*; it represents causal relations between two thoughts by 'a *sequence* of two pieces of dream of different lengths'. Or else, it represents the relation of cause and effect by showing 'an immediate *transformation* of one thing into another'. Most interesting is the way in which the dream-work represents contradiction through the 'sensation of *inhibition of movement*', which points to a *conflict of will*. The dream-work does not admit of the alternative 'either-or' (Freud's emphasis, SE 5: 661). It treats it as 'and' just as 'No' seems not to exist as far as dreams are concerned (see 'Negation' [1925]). It is thanks to these means of representation that some dreams appear more 'absurd' than others. Absurdity and nonsense become a 'method' employed to express *'contradiction, ridicule and derision'* (Freud's emphasis, SE 5: 662).

Secondary Revision

The last of the dream processes – secondary revision or elaboration – brings us back to where we started and to the problem of access to the dream. Secondary elaboration appears to enter into action once the manifest dream has been constructed: 'Its function would then consist in arranging the constituents of the dream in such a way that they form an approximately connected whole, *a dream-composition*' (SE 5: 666; our emphasis). It aims at making the dream apparently intelligible, but in fact it consists in a 'glaring misunderstanding of the dream-thoughts' (SE 5: 666). What sort of misunderstanding? The activity of revision is at the service of distortion and arranges the dream as though its elements were intelligible; in other words, it inserts intelligibility where the dream has 'distorted' ordinary logical relations. Freud indeed comes back to the 'non-disguised' dreams, such as a child's dream, through the idea of 'secondary revision', whereby dreams pretend to be rational and to be acceptable to conscious thought. Jonathan Lear pointedly stated how 'psychoanalysis tends to move simultaneously in two directions . . . it tries to discover a hidden irrationality in the thought, speech and action which presents itself as rational [and] it tries to find rationality hidden within the irrational' (Lear 1990: 71). This is true for dreams, even if the majority of dreams 'seem *disconnected*, *confused*, and *meaningless*' (Freud's emphasis, SE 5: 642), and if there exist misleading 'rational dreams'. In the latter case, what must be shown is the rationality of dreams (which points to the ingenuity of the dream-work). The distinction between the manifest and latent content of the dream, and the transformation that takes place between the two, takes on its full importance the more incoherent the dream appears.

Secondary revision also consists in a misunderstanding when one is faced with a succession of unknown words, namely, when it falsifies what is given by perceiving sense where the latter is in fact absent, so as to neutralize the unfamiliarity of the sequence. Under secondary revision the dream appears to be 'beautifully polished and provided with a surface', as opposed to being 'hopelessly confused' (SE 5: 667). However, it is necessary to demolish the 'surface', the 'dream-façade', for it is one more layer of distortion. Unlike the other processes forming the dream-work that Freud called the primary, unconscious processes, however, the dream-façade is 'nothing other than mistaken and somewhat arbitrary revisions of the dream-content by the conscious agency of our mental life' (SE 5: 667). This is why it does not participate in the formation of every dream.

SYMBOLISM

Freud does not devote a separate section to symbolism. It enters the work through numerous additions elaborated at the same time as other works of applied psychoanalysis during the 1910s. It is important because it touches on the 'discovery' of the Oedipus complex. Let us note how the juxtaposition of 'stories' and of 'explanations' recalls the important and intriguing role literature plays in psychoanalysis. For Freud recurrently refers to literary works. Verses from Goethe's *Faust*, among others, are inserted everywhere as though they could also 'translate' the experience into words, besides the evolving scientific terminology.

The most well-known example of a literary work that has been, by now, assimilated to Freud's writings is Sophocles' *Oedipus Rex*, the first published reference to which appears in *The Interpretation*. The appeal to Oedipus is twofold. On the one hand, the tragedy is useful for illustrating one of our childhood sexual impulses ('It is the fate of all of us, perhaps, to direct our first sexual impulse towards our mother and our first hatred and our first murderous wish against our father' [SE 4: 262]). However, the illustration also serves the purpose of 'validating' the psychoanalytic findings. It acts as a testimony that such impulses exist independently from psychoanalytic theory (Bowlby 2006: 115–18). Besides *Oedipus Rex*, there are hundreds of references to canonical and less canonical literary works (including works by Shakespeare and Goethe, to name only the most recurrent ones). According to many commentators, Freud's conception of the psyche would seem to have something essentially literary about it, in so far as the 'analysis begins . . . with nonsense that calls for interpretation', and that it is above all a matter of interpreting the 'meaning' of symptoms (Ricoeur 1969: 185–6).

To have offered here a comprehensive account of Freud's theory of dream would require us to submit it to 'an extensive process of condensation' (SE 4: 279). Instead, we aimed to show that the problem of 'underlying mechanisms', which Binswanger raised in relation to the theory of the drives, presents itself acutely in the case of dream-interpretation. Binswanger evaluated Freud's neglect of phenomena by overemphasizing the extent to which Freud's theory of the drives gave a biological account of human beings. For many commentators, the distinction between the manifest and the latent content, and Freud's so-called excessive interest in the latent content, meant that he did not much care about dreams themselves (and by extension, that he neglected everything he interpreted, whether it be works of art, of literature, or indeed neuroses). It is possible to avert that criticism by insisting, as this chapter aimed to do, on the dream as a *form* of thinking. Hence, the dream poses the problem of interpretation in analysis, by drawing our attention to the form of what there is to interpret (let us recall that the elucidation of neurotic symptoms came from the association that Freud made between certain verbal expressions and Cäcilie's bodily 'translation' of that verbal expression. Freud would appear to have focused on the various ways in which ideas and meanings can send us back to something else: a memory sends us to another memory, an idea to another idea). It is not clear that in Freud's theory, the 'double' meaning is underlying, or hidden. It might be precisely because it is not necessarily hidden that it poses a problem (when I try to remember something, the most troublesome aspect is that I remember something other than what I need to recall).

Not only are dreams as much about their composition as about their contents (drawing us into the particular patient's history), they also display the functioning of the mental apparatus. Whatever dreams may tell us about each particular dreamer, they tell us about the psyche in general. This is why, when concluding our study of psychoanalytic interpretation, we are oscillating between a theory of dream-interpretation that can be easily caricatured as doing violence to its very object, and a theory of the mental apparatus, which Freud presented in Chapter VII of *The Interpretation*, and developed thereafter.

The multi-levelled theory of dreams may allow us to show that to be 'underlying' does not mean necessarily to be 'hidden'. In what sense could one say that the primary processes responsible for the dream are hidden when they confront us with as complex an object as dreams? Dream-interpretation would appear to demonstrate that unconscious processes take form 'in the world'. It might be that, just as he did for the idea of sexuality, of what is psychical, Freud extended our conception of what it is for something to be 'underlying', concealed. When one recalls some of Freud's declarations

about the unconscious, as not being the 'mysterious' unconscious of
the Romantic or about the necessity of having a concept for describing what is active in the mind without being conscious, it might be
that the theory of the unconscious proposes to make us precisely
reflect on what appears and what does not appear (to make us reflect
on the contradictory kind of knowledge with which we began).

CHAPTER 4

AFFECT AND REPRESENTATION

In Chapter 2, we saw that for Freud mental acts were made of two components: an idea or a representation and a quota of affect. Psychoanalysis is concerned with how the ones are 'converted' into the others, how they combine and form neurotic symptoms. Freud presented that duality, among other places, in the paper on 'The Neuro-Psychoses of Defence' (1894), where he advanced the hypothesis that a dynamic 'quota of affect', a 'sum of excitation' or, indeed, a quantity accompanies repressed ideas and memories (SE 3: 60). It is through the dynamic character of that 'quantity' that Freud explained the process of repression. Repression was the keeping at a distance, the separation of, that 'quota of affect' from the idea to which it was once attached. The psychoanalytic cure worked on the principle that it was possible to free that 'quota' through speech, up until it was possible to bring the affect back to another idea, or to the idea or situation with which it arose (SE 5: 460). In Freud's words:

> the release of affect and the ideational content do not constitute the indissoluble organic unity as which we are in the habit of treating them . . . these two separate entities may be merely *soldered* together and can thus be detached from each other by analysis. (SE 5: 461–2)[1]

It was in relation to dreams that Freud presented the first model of the psychical apparatus, with its stratification into agencies: *'the architectonic principle of the mental apparatus lies in a stratification – a building up of superimposed agencies*; and it is quite possible that [defence] belongs to a lower psychical agency (Freud's emphasis, SE

6: 147). According to that model, dream-stories forced their way into consciousness from the 'lower psychical agency'. The staging of ideas, the compression of the features of many persons into one, the rendering conscious of a repressed idea occurred through the displacement of an unconscious 'psychical energy', which 'activated' ideas presented in the dream. Dreams allowed Freud to 'observe' the making of associations and disassociations between ideas, images and their energetic substratum (the impulses or excitations to which the latter are linked). They were the means by which it was possible to perceive 'psychical activity during sleep' (SE 23: 165). They gave us access, more generally, to the 'laws that govern the passage of events in the unconscious' (SE 23: 167). Sleep showed that the psychical apparatus 'consists in a particular distribution of mental energy' (SE 23: 146). Dreams seize everyday, indifferent situations, childhood memories, forgotten readings, overheard conversations, and 'dramatize' unconscious mental processes (almost in the manner in which Freud 'represented' the process of resistance by analogy with the hypothetical expulsion from a lecture of a rowdy man, who nevertheless seeks to re-enter the lecture hall out of which he has been thrown [SE 11: 25–6]).

The dream, then, showed how mental acts were made of two mobile components, whose movements are determining the course of our actions. It is an error, Freud wrote, to 'picture the link between content and affect as too intimate' (SE 15: 215), just as it was also an error to picture the link between the sexual aim and its object too narrowly. Freud loosened the connections between these domains. One 'gloomy' example from *The Interpretation of Dreams* well illustrates this. A young girl had dreamt that she saw her nephew '*lying before [her] dead . . . in his little coffin . . . with candles all round – in fact just like little Otto*' (Freud's emphasis, SE 4: 152–3), but she felt no pain or grief, in spite of her attachment to him. This is because 'the dream merely disguised her wish to see the man she was in love with once more' (SE 5: 463). On the occasion of the death of her other nephew – Otto – the man she loved had visited her sister (the mother of the dead child), with whom she lived. The absence of emotion was not appropriate to the scene of mourning, but it disguised an inappropriate erotic feeling. Nevertheless, the repressed wish to see the man again was able to emerge thanks to the 'dream-work'.

There is another illustration of the displacement of affect in the case history of the 'Rat Man' ('Notes upon a Case of Obsessional

Neurosis'). This patient was suffering from obsessional self-reproaches, and treated himself as a criminal. However, his sense of guilt, which appeared a few months after his father's death, had only apparently been triggered by the death of one of his aunts. For, as Freud discovered during the analysis, it was caused by the fact that, while nursing his father, the Rat Man had allowed himself to sleep for an hour, during which time his father had died. The reaction to his aunt's death was seemingly 'exaggerated'. But the intensity of the sense of guilt was otherwise justified. There was a 'false connection' between his aunt's death and the supposition that he was a criminal. The affect was displaced from the idea of his father's death to that of his aunt's. The latter served as a substitute for the unconscious idea, which generated the affect in the first place. This was only one of the false-connections against which logical processes had no hold, and which the analysis revealed (SE 10: 175–6). Freud discovered such 'false-connections' in his study of the origin of hysterical symptoms, among other places. One assumed that the hysterical vomiting of a patient could be traced 'back to an experience which *justifiably produced a high amount of disgust* – for instance, the sight of a decomposing dead body' (SE 3: 194). But one might have to enquire further into the formation of symptoms if it turns out that they in fact relate to a fright from a railway accident. Let us recall how the dream made use of 'indifferent material' to allow for the return of the repressed.

It has been possible to circumscribe at least one of the components of a mental act. In the two examples above, it is a matter of a hidden love and a feeling of guilt towards a so-called moral failure. Ideas such as these form familiar themes. Leafing through Freud indeed confronts us with a catalogue of unrequited love, jealousy, excessive attachment to the mother, fear of the father, delusions, desires for revenge, ambition, fear of castration. In addition, it involves us in poetic analyses, for the form of expression matters.[2] According to some commentators, these stories refer us back too exclusively to *fin-de-siècle* Vienna. However, it is not so easy to grasp the nature of the other component, which leads to the very core of the 'psychical', or the unconscious. Freud's theory of the unconscious entails a conflict, but between what or whom does it take place? According to some of the early explanations of repression, it occurred between groups of ideas, or between groups of ideas and the ego, which acted as the 'repressing agency'. One group of ideas could remain in a state of unconsciousness because of 'an active opposition on the part of other groups' (SE 11: 213). It looked as though the conflict was only active between 'groups of ideas'. But mental life is also 'an interplay of forces that favour or inhibit one another' (SE 11: 213). It is not exactly ideas or representations that enter into conflict with each other, but ideas in so far as they represent these forces, or the drives. The affect too comes to be the 'representative' of psychical energy. Unlike ideas that get repressed and that bring us close to the themes of fictional works, it is improbable that we would ever encounter the 'interplay of psychical forces' in such works.

One of the earliest ways in which to describe the 'sums of excitations' that represent the psychical forces is the concept of 'affect' [*Affekt*] (it is sometimes also translated as 'emotion'). Freud's conception of the affect sends us back to the received idea (and to the philosophical tradition) whereby the passions are opposed to reason. Although Freud only indirectly refers to the passions, in *The Ego and the Id* (1923) the ego is said to represent 'what may be called reason and common sense, in contrast to the id which contains the passions' (SE 19: 25). We will turn to the notion of the ego below. Freud appropriated for the most part a popular understanding of that opposition, which is apparent in the idea that civilization is built upon the renunciation of the drives. He also approached the affect *scientifically*, adopting elements from existing psychological conceptions of it developed by German scientific psychology from the end of the eighteenth century onwards. For example, in *Principles of Physiological Psychology* (1874), Wilhelm Wundt defined the affect as a mobile element of the psyche, which had the property of 'setting into motion and which comes from sensibility' (Assoun 1997: 392). Freud's definitions of affect throughout his work, however, are equivocal. Just as it is the case with the notion of the unconscious, one needs to look in more than one text to find an answer to the question 'what did Freud mean by affect?' and even so, the notion remains as André Green stated 'a challenge to thought' (Green 1986: 174). Let us recall one of the earliest quantitative hypotheses from 'The Neuro-Psychoses of Defence', whereby:

> in mental functions something is to be distinguished – a quota of affect or sum of excitation – which possesses all the characteristics of a quantity (though we have no means of measuring it), which is capable of increase, diminution, displacement and

discharge, and which is spread over the memory-traces of ideas somewhat as an electric charge is spread over the surface of a body. (SE 3: 60)

In defence hysteria, Freud had 'discovered' that female patients wanted to *push something away*, for example, a governess unconsciously wanted to suppress the idea of her employer, to detach the disturbing idea of him from the intense emotion she felt towards him. The 'sum of excitation', the quota of affect joined to the idea could be *'transformed into something somatic'* (Freud's emphasis, SE 3: 49). If the symptom was not formed in that manner, the idea could become an unconscious 'sort of parasite', which had an effect either on the body or produced hallucinations (SE 3: 49).

The affect makes itself felt as a quantitative discharge: 'there is "affect" only when *something happens* in psychical life'; for this transformation to occur, there has to be some discharge of the psychical energy (Assoun 1997: 392). It is the process thanks to which the sums of excitation are felt, when the latter have been detached from the idea. However, Freud also defined the affect as itself the 'quota', the 'sum of excitation'. In *Studies on Hysteria* (1893–5), Freud invoked *The Expression of the Emotions in Man and Animals* (1872) by Darwin, who conceived of the emotions as the weakened figurative expression of actions 'which originally had a meaning and served a purpose' (SE 2: 181). On that view, affects sent us back to traces of actions performed in the prehistoric times of the species. Freud surmised that the formation of hysterical symptoms through conversion was due to a similar process.[3]

The uncertainty surrounding the notion of affect in 1894 did not subsequently disappear. The affect has a polemical status in psychoanalytic theory and practice because, amongst the two representatives of the psychical forces, Freud treated the affect more biologically than ideas or representations (Green 1986: 176). This had implications in the whole of the theory. To put it in general terms, the diverging treatments of affects and representations instituted a separation between the so-called *energetic* and the *hermeneutic* dimensions of Freud's theory of the unconscious. That separation roughly corresponds to that between everything that relates to psychical energy (to quantity) and everything that relates to ideas, representations, meaning and language (quality). It does not, however, quite fit in with that of unconscious/conscious. For our immediate purpose, the affect is a significant notion in so far as it poses the problem of quantification, to which we will turn below. For Freud the notion of affect related to the simultaneous dispositions of the psychical apparatus towards seeking pleasure and avoiding tension. From being defined neutrally as a 'quota', a 'charge', it came to be defined as a disturbing quota, as a creator of tension that must be discharged.[4] Affect pointed to the effects of quantitative variations on the functioning of the psychical apparatus. Even though the affect raised such problems, Freud did not specify that by defining one of the components of mental acts as a quota, which yet cannot be measured, he was 'enlarging' the idea of quantification (as he had done explicitly with the concept of sexuality and the psychical). Consequently, the extended meaning of quantification only emerged slowly through Freud's research, as did the extended meaning of sexuality and of the psychical.

To circumscribe the impulses, the 'quantities', the magnitudes and the forces at work, then, is apparently a more difficult task than that of identifying repressed ideas. One of the ways in which Freud approached mental processes was by following out 'the vicissitudes of amounts of excitation and [of] arriving at least at some *relative* estimate of their magnitude' (SE 14: 181). In *Beyond the Pleasure Principle* (1920), Freud nevertheless stated that he knew 'nothing of the nature of the excitatory process that takes place in the elements of the psychical systems' (SE 18: 30–1), an admission which he repeated, among other places, in 'An Outline of Psycho-Analysis' (1940 [1938]): 'we assume . . . that in mental life some kind of energy is at work; but we have nothing to go upon which will enable us to come nearer to a knowledge of it by analogies with other forms of energy' (SE 23: 163–4). At the most, it is possible to describe the dynamic relations of the two types of energy, which the psychical apparatus transforms. Taking up a distinction Breuer established, one type of energy is freely mobile and 'presses towards discharge', while the other one is 'bound' (SE 18: 31). Freud also called the energy the 'cathexes' of psychical material, which referred to the various levels of investment of the psychical energy, given that ideas and affect are more or less intensely 'charged' with psychical energy (SE 23: 164). Moreover, 'the conflict between two trends does not break out till certain intensities of cathexis have been reached' (SE 16: 374).

We have now become immersed in Freud's apparently most abstract explanations, in what Binswanger called the *gigantic empirico-scientific structure* of his work (in our exploration of dreams, we had focused on dream-interpretation, rather than on the theoretical Chapter VII). In the rest of the chapter, we will dwell on what we described in the Introduction as the most 'cumbersome' aspects of Freud's work.[5] We will first explore Freud's theory of the drives. Its development touched on all aspects of Freud's writings, from *Three Essays on the Theory of Sexuality*, where the concept of drive first appeared by name, to the introduction of the notion of the ego-instincts, in 'The Psycho-analytic View of Psychogenic Disturbance of Vision' (1910). Changes in the theory of the drives had repercussions on all the tenets of psychoanalytic theory, including the relation between ideas and affect. It led to the reworking of the model of the psychical apparatus (the id becomes the reservoir of the drives; the model becomes more biological). One significant step towards that reworking is the notion of the ego in the vein of the discovery of the ego-instincts.

THE THEORY OF THE DRIVES

Freud affirmed the indefiniteness of the concept of the drive. There are a number of statements in Freud that could form a set of aphorisms on it. Here is an oft-quoted one: 'The theory of the instincts is so to say our mythology. Instincts are mythical entities, magnificent in their indefiniteness. In our work we cannot for a moment disregard them, yet we are never sure that we are seeing them clearly' (SE 22: 95). The drive is yet a fundamental concept of psychoanalysis (and of the metapsychology, which we will explore in Chapter 5), around which it was possible to systematize the early findings on repression and the existence of the unconscious. It is, Freud wrote, 'an obscure subject' for psychoanalysis as well as for other sciences (SE 20: 263). The sentence 'But it must be admitted that we do not understand . . . [instinctual life] very well' (SE 22: 97) is a recurrent type of admission in the domain of drives. The theory develops from *Three Essays* up until the introduction of the death drive and the compulsion to repeat in *Beyond* and the second topography in *The Ego and the Id* (1923). Among the many definitions of the drive, here is one of the most striking ones:

> an 'instinct' appears to us as a concept on the frontier between the mental and the somatic, as the psychical representative of the

stimuli originating from within the organism and reaching the mind for work in consequence of its connection with the body. (SE 14: 121–2)

The definition presents two related aspects of the drive, and shows Freud's attempt to establish its general nature prior to any differentiation. On the one hand, it posits the drive as a 'frontier' between the psychical and the somatic (the drive is a limit-reality between the psychological and the biological). It is not purely one or the other; but it articulates the two together. Let us recall Binswanger's criticism of the concept: did he take into account the limit nature of the concept to formulate his views on the determinism of Freud's concept of the drive? It is a limit concept by virtue of the way in which it 'represents' bodily excitations to the psyche. It entails that psychical life is always tied to something other than itself. It expresses a form of exteriority within the psyche that is not psychical, but that nevertheless cannot be avoided: it is impossible to flee from a drive (Benoist 2006: 114–18). The double nature of the drive troubles the delimitation between the inside and the outside (just as the opposition between affect and representations does).

That function of representation depends on another characteristic of the drive, which is that of 'a certain quota of energy which presses, in a particular direction'. It derives its name – in German *Trieb* – from that 'pressing' (SE 22: 96). Subsequent definitions of the drive retained a quantitative dimension up until the last writings when Freud re-described the drives as 'alloys' or the result of fusions and defusions ('every instinctual impulse that we can examine consists of similar fusions or alloys of the two classes of instincts. These fusions . . . would be in the most varied ratios' [SE 22: 104–5]). For drives are 'all qualitatively alike and owe the effect they make only to the amount of excitation they carry, or perhaps, in addition, to certain functions of that quantity' (SE 14: 123). The quantitative dimension goes together with the vicissitudes, or the fate of the drives (since the drives, as we will see, can activate reversals of love into hate, among others). Freud stated: 'We have reckoned as though there existed in the mind – a displaceable energy, which, neutral in itself, can be added to a qualitatively differentiated erotic or destructive impulse, and augment its total cathexis' (SE 19: 44); that is, that unspecified quantity would seem to become qualitative by virtue of its alliance with a qualitatively differentiated impulse. However, the erotic or destructive impulse acquire a quantitative dimension.

The theory of the drives tells a story of development. On the one hand, it does so because Freud kept modifying the relation of the drives to the mental functions. On the other hand, dealing with the drives necessarily involves making a history, because they are 'the true motive forces behind the advances that have led the nervous system, with its unlimited capacities, to its present high level of development' (SE 14: 120). In spite of the way in which he focused on the general characteristics of the drives, Freud tried to avoid subsuming instinctual life under a single psychical energy.[6] To do so would have eliminated the essentially dynamic and conflicting nature of the unconscious, from which everything else unfolded.

'The Machinery of the Mental Forces' (SE 16: 415)

Freud introduced the sexual drives in *Three Essays*; however, he had previously alluded to something like the drives under a number of names, such as: ' "excitations", "affective ideas", "wishful impulses", "endogenous stimuli", and so on' (Strachey SE 14: 114).[7] In 'Instincts and their Vicissitudes' (1915), the first attempt to systematize his findings on the instincts or the drives as part of the metapsychology, Freud attributed to it three characteristics: 1) an instinctual stimulus 'does not arise from the external world but from within the organism itself' (SE 14: 118); 2) 'it operates as a constant force'; 3) 'the subject cannot avoid it by flight' (SE 22: 96). In 1905, drive pointed to a force coming from the inside of the body, which reached the psyche as something external. It gradually came also to refer, as we said above, to the 'representative of the stimuli', to the form that endogenous stimuli take in the psyche (SE 14: 122).

Freud did not initially explain the principle of constancy and the pleasure principle in terms of the drives, but rather in terms of 'stimuli'. However, in 'Instincts and their Vicissitudes' he did insert the drive into the functioning picture of the mental apparatus, and in relation to the 'experience of satisfaction' (which was the model of development par excellence). Let us recall that its function is 'to keep as low as possible the total amount of the excitations with which it is loaded', given that 'unpleasure is in some way related to an increase of excitation and pleasure to a decrease' (SE 20: 266). We saw that instead of hallucinating, given the inefficiency of hallucinations to bring about satisfaction, the apparatus had to perform an action in the 'external world'. It is in similar terms that Freud described the role of the drives in the development of the psychical apparatus. They fulfil the economic task of *mastering stimuli*, whereby the apparatus (or the nervous system, in Freud's early writings), 'has the function of getting rid of the stimuli that reach it, or of reducing them to the lowest possible level' (SE 14: 120). The apparatus thus aimed to maintain itself 'in an altogether unstimulated condition' (SE 14: 120). The 'helpless living organism' (SE 14: 119) discovered the distinction between the 'outside' and the 'inside' by means of the 'efficacy of muscular activity': muscular action succeeds in avoiding certain stimuli that have a *momentary* impact, while it is of no avail against 'instinctual needs' that give a *constant* one (SE 14: 118–19). The drives are thus linked with the acquisition of the distinction between the internal and external (they have the paradoxical status of being an 'internal exteriority' ([Benoist 2006: 117]). The stimuli that have a momentary impact and that can be eliminated through muscular movement come from the outside. The apparatus cannot maintain itself free from stimuli when it is confronted with the drives, as the latter 'maintain an incessant and unavoidable afflux of stimulation' (SE 14: 120). It learns to tolerate the constant pressure that they exert from the inside of the body (indeed learning to control the drives is at the basis of Freud's account of the process of civilization. For cultural reasons, Freud moreover writes that 'the most intense repression falls upon the sexual instincts; but it is precisely in connection with them that repression most easily miscarries, so that neurotic symptoms are found to be substitutive satisfactions of repressed sexuality' (SE 20: 267; see too SE 12: 209). However, the drives are also related to the pleasure principle that regulates the apparatus towards the avoidance of unpleasure. As 'quotas of energy', the drives submit to that automatic regulation (SE 14: 121).

We saw how, in Freud's view, the sexual drive undergoes a development, how it is the result of an assemblage that can become undone. The 'normal picture' of sexuality resulted from 'the repression of certain component instincts and constituents of the infantile disposition' (SE 7: 277). Perversions were caused by 'the disturbances of this coalescence', and neuroses by an excessive repression of the sexual drives. In *Three Essays*, Freud had discussed the *object* and the *aims* of the sexual drives. In 'Instinct and their Vicissitudes' he added the *pressure* and the *source* of the drive to the terms from which it is possible to analyse the drives. The latter entailed further possibilities of 'deviation' (the 'vicissitudes'), in addition to those that occur around the aim and the object (SE 7: 168–9).

Let us consider in turn each of these terms, including the object and the aim. As we said above, it is in the very essence of the drives to exercise pressure [*Drang*], since 'every instinct is a piece of activity' (we will see that the notion of the death drive challenges the definition of the drive as pressure, as a movement forward). The pressure is 'the amount of force or the measure of the demand for work which it represents' (SE 14: 122). The aim of every drive is satisfaction, which means that every drive aims at the removal of the state of stimulation it provokes. But drives take different paths to reach their aims (the latter can be combined, partial, inhibited, and so on). The 'paths' are the vicissitudes that sometimes create pathological phenomena. Together with the aim [*Ziel*], the drives have an object [*Objekt*], that is 'the thing in regard to which or through which the instinct is able to achieve its aim' (SE 14: 122). One of the striking features of Freud's theory of sexuality is to have shown how the object is contingent, and can vary infinitely. Contrary to what the 'narrow picture' of sexuality may lead us to believe, normality is defined partly in terms of the mobility of the drive towards its object, even if sexuality implies a certain degree of fixation ('for complete health it is essential that the libido should not lose this full mobility' [SE 17: 139]). For when the latter becomes 'fixated' to an object, it can trigger neurotic behaviour. The phenomenon of mourning can give rise to exaggerated fixations of the pathological kind, as Freud explained in 'Mourning and Melancholia' (1917 [1915]). In normal mourning one manages to replace a lost object by another one, while in melancholia one suffers from the inability to do so.[8] Mourning can involve a moment of 'affective fixation' to the lost object, and Freud compellingly stated that it involves 'the most complete alienation from the present and the future' (SE 16: 276). The detachment from the object is a normal process that people accomplish without falling ill (Freud supports that claim, strikingly, by invoking Faust freeing himself from the world 'by uttering his curses', and that detachment only results in a 'certain general frame of mind', rather than in falling ill [SE 12: 72]). The most uncertain element of the drives is the source [*Quelle*]. As with the pressure, the source would also seem to be the most defining

FREUD: A GUIDE FOR THE PERPLEXED

element of the drive, as every drive comes from the inside of the organism. The source is 'the somatic process which occurs in an organ or part of the body and whose stimulus is represented in mental life by an instinct' (SE 14: 123). The biological, somatic dimension of the drive hovers over the whole of the theory of the drives, as we will see below, and colours the elaboration of the second model of the mind.

Reclassification of the drives

With the concept of the sexual and component drives in *Three Essays*, as we saw in Chapter 2, it became possible to specify further what enters into the psychical conflict. The reclassification of the drives after 1905 entailed a further reframing of the psychical conflict. One of its basic steps, after *Three Essays*, was the separation of the drive into two great classes, the 'ego-instincts' and the sexual drives (SE 14: 124). In 1910, Freud described the psychical conflict between ideas, not only in terms of an opposition between groups of ideas, but also in terms of a conflict between incompatible drives. He asked: 'But what can be the origin of this opposition, which makes for repression, between the ego and various groups of ideas?' (SE 11: 213). The ego is here defined as a 'collective concept', that is, as 'a compound which is made up variously at different times' (SE 11: 213), whereas in *Studies in Hysteria*, it remained unspecified. At the most, it was constituted by a 'dominant mass of ideas' (SE 2: 116), which acted as a repressing force. The answer is that it is possible provisionally to classify ideas into those that are compatible with the ego, and those entering into conflict with it, given that drives attach to ideas. For ego-instincts clash with the 'various groups of ideas' that attach to the sexual drive:

Every instinct tries to make itself effective by activating ideas that are in keeping with its aims. These instincts are not always compatible with one another; their interests often come into conflict. Opposition between ideas is only an expression of struggles between the various instincts . . . [for there is an] undeniable opposition between the instincts which subserve sexuality, the attainment of sexual pleasure, and those other instincts which have as their aim the self-preservation of the individual – the ego-instincts. (SE 11: 213–14)

Hysteria and obsessional neurosis had shown that these mental illnesses rested on a conflict between sexuality and the ego (SE 14:
124). He related the opposition between the drives to Schiller's
classification of all instincts 'as "hunger" or "love" ' (SE 11: 215),
and described it as a 'common, popular distinction' (SE 14: 78).
Freud also spoke of an opposition between the drives for self-preservation (the ego-instincts) and those aimed towards the preservation
of the species (the sexual drives) (SE 22: 95). It was the matter of the
'preservation of the species' because sexuality transcends the individual by serving the purpose of multiplying them (SE 14: 125). That
opposition was one of the first modifications of the 'libido theory'.
It eventually obliged Freud to rethink the relation between repressed
'contents' and repressing agencies; in fact, to rethink the entire
model of the psychical apparatus. It allowed Freud to redefine the
onset of neurosis in terms of a conflict between two antagonist
classes of drives, that of the ego and the sexual ones. That distinguished the 'mental conflict' in which psychoanalysis is interested
from the everyday life situations of 'mental conflict'. The latter are
'exceedingly common'. The ego often attempts to avert painful
memories at a conscious level, without any pathological consequences (SE 11: 26). However, that reframing of the conflict did not
so much clarify the nature of the drives as if provided criteria for
their further differentiation. In spite of the new classification of the
drives, the 'energetic', quantitative component of every mental act
still remained indefinite. The problematic 'exteriority' to which
repressed ideas are attached, and without which the process of
repression (the notion of a dynamic unconscious) would be incon-
ceivable, remained largely unspecified, by Freud's own admission, as
we mentioned above.

Concerning the 'vicissitudes' of the sexual drives, we could here be
dealing with imaginative processes similar to those responsible for
the formation of dreams. For the drive can 'revers[e] into its opposite', it can 'tur[n] round upon the subject's own self', it can be
repressed, or sublimated (SE 14: 126). The sexual drives are 'notice-
able to us for their plasticity, their capacity for altering their aims,
their replaceability . . . and their readiness for being deferred' (SE 22:
97). These processes are manifest in certain disturbances, such as
sadism–masochism and scopophilia–exhibitionism (SE 14: 127).
For example, in these two vicissitudes, 'the active aim (to torture, to
look at) is replaced by the passive aim (to be tortured, to be looked

at)' (SE 14: 127). Sometimes it is possible to observe the opposite aims or content alongside each other, and Freud borrowed the term 'ambivalence' to describe that co-existence. One can have ambivalence towards one's parents. Ambivalence may render intelligible some unexplainable attitude towards them. The 'vicissitudes' of the instincts touch on 'moral feelings' (that of pity, for example: see the case history of the 'Wolf Man' [SE 17: 88; 26]). Let us recall how Freud related the process of repression to 'normal repression', which consisted in moving away in disgust or in 'moral disgust'.

Ego

The clarification of the concept of the ego went together with the changes in the libido theory, for 'it is only when Freud realized that an I can be the object of its own sexual instinct that the concept of an I became the focus of psychoanalytic attention' (Lear 1990: 137). Later Freud wrote that the ego could be split: 'it can take itself as an object, can treat itself like other objects, can observe itself, criticize itself, and do Heaven knows what with itself' (SE 22: 58). The ego had in Freud's early work the meaning of 'self' among others. It gradually acquired a more precise role within the theory of the drives (see 'The Libido Theory and Narcissism' in SE 16: 413). Freud re-ordered the theory of the drive also around the concept of the ego, and more generally, beyond the ego, he re-ordered the model of the mind around the drives. In *Three Essays on the Theory of Sexuality*, Freud had explored the sexual drives, thanks to the findings obtained through the study of neuroses. He had established that it was the 'history of the sexual function that explained its aberrations and atrophies' (SE 22: 98). Freud had written in 1896 that hysterical symptoms made 'themselves heard as witnesses to the history of the origin of the illness' (SE 3: 192, 'The Aetiology of Hysteria'). Some of these alterations were temporal: the sexual drive could be 'fixated' at an earlier stage, through regression.

The collapse of the distinction between ego-instincts and the sexual drives – which was the foundation of the libido theory – occurred, among other factors, when the psychoanalytic treatment proved inefficient against certain types of illnesses. Some patients, who were suffering from schizophrenia and dementia praecox, seemed 'to have withdrawn [their] libido from people and things in the external world, without replacing them by other in phantasy' (SE

14: 74). The sexual drive, the libido, characteristically chose 'objects' (and it is the history of that varied choice of objects that makes up the sexuality of subjects). The libido becomes detached from objects, and finds substitutes. Not to direct libido towards objects appeared to give rise to the magnification of the ego, or to 'narcissism', which is 'an extreme exaggeration of a normal state of affairs' (SE 22: 103). Just as psychoneuroses had been instrumental for understanding normal sexuality, the pathological form of narcissism helped Freud to extend the libido theory. In addition, the observation of 'children and primitive' reinforced Freud's findings, for children overestimate their power, they believe in the omnipotence of thoughts (SE 14: 75). These phenomena of aggrandizement led Freud to believe that there is 'an original libidinal cathexis of the ego, from which some is later given off to objects' (SE 14: 75). That corresponded to the 'auto-erotic' stage of development of the libido 'in which a person's only sexual object is his own ego' (SE 12: 72). For example, megalomania consisted in a 'reflexive turning back' and was equivalent to an overvaluation of the erotic object (such an overvaluation introduces variation in the aim and object of the sexual drive).

The ego, then, comes with a certain quota of libido, which it later distributes. The novelty with respect to *Three Essays* is to have identified the ego's process of 'allocation' of libido, which explains that there should be within the ego 'an antithesis between ego-libido and object-libido' (SE 14: 76). Hence, whereas Freud at first believed that there was an opposition between the sexual drives and the ego-instincts, he now treated the ego as a 'great reservoir' of libido (SE 17: 139), whence the ego-libido and the libido directed at objects both emerged and returned. Freud called to mind a similar situation: let us think of an 'amoeba, whose viscous substance puts out pseudopodia, elongations into which the substance of the body extends but which can be retracted at any time so that the form of the protoplasmic mass is restored' (SE 17: 139). The opposition between ego-instincts and the sexual drives turned out to be internal to the ego. It was no longer possible to maintain an opposition between self-preservation and the preservation of the species. That the ego could be a 'reservoir' is explained by the way in which 'the narcissistic libidinal cathexis of the ego is the original state of things, realized in earliest childhood' (SE 7: 218). In spite of later 'extrusions of libido', that state nevertheless persisted (SE 7: 218).

Once the ego acquired an instinctual basis (or is it the drives that acquire an 'egoistic' – Freud says 'narcissistic' – basis?), it was possible to conceive of it in terms of 'its composition out of various organizations and their constructions and mode of functioning (SE 16: 415). The development of the ego could follow a similar course to that of the sexual drive. Freud showed that just as there existed 'component drives', there could be 'component egos'. In his lecture on creative writing in 'Creative Writers and Day-Dreaming' (1907), Freud underlined the way the special character of 'psychological novels' was due to the way in which the writer 'split up his ego, by self-observation, into many part-egos, and, in consequence . . . personifies the conflicting currents of his own mental life in several heroes' (SE 9: 150). The theory proposed a similar 'dissection', as Freud expounded in Lecture XXXI, entitled 'The Dissection of the Psychical Personality', of the *New Introductory Lectures*, which presents the second topography (SE 22: 57).

Ego, Super-Ego, and the Id

In addition to dividing the apparatus into three 'abstract' agencies on the model of a 'compound instrument' such as the microscope, it was also divided into the anthropomorphic agencies of the *id*, *ego*, and *super-ego* (Freud spoke of the 'psychical personality' [SE 22: 57] in addition to the psychical apparatus). It allowed for a more refined classification of mental illnesses (such as, for example, the pathological delusions of being observed). The names, if not the model of the mind, are probably more familiar to the reader than the first topography (with its system and agencies unconscious, preconscious/conscious). The new division does not replace the first one, but is articulated to it (especially in Chapter VIII of Freud's last work 'An Outline of Psycho-Analysis' (1940 [1938]). The reworking of the model of the mind in *The Ego and the Id* consisted in rethinking the apparatus genetically, and 'dating', so to speak, the formation of the 'provinces' of the mind in relation to the external world. In that model the ego is no longer associated with the preconscious/conscious systems (as it was in the first topography). The repressed is no longer only what is 'unconscious', but also what relates to the drives. It was necessary to redefine the model of the mind, when Freud observed that 'portions of the ego' were also unconscious (the super-ego is an unconscious portion of the ego). Whereas in the first topography, the ego had the function of inhibiting the primary processes, it now included repressed material. Just as the id did not have the sole character of being unconscious, portions of the ego could have the character of being unconscious without being 'primitive and irrational' (SE 22: 75).

The *id*, a term borrowed from Georg Groddeck and Nietzsche, is the instinctual pole of the 'personality' (SE 23: 72). It is the oldest one, and the 'reservoir' of psychical energy; its repressed contents are acquired and hereditary (through the phylogenetic inheritance, which one cannot assimilate with modern genetics).[9] The id has the characteristics of the unconscious mental processes discovered in *The Interpretation of Dreams*. Its processes are dominated by the quantitative factor. Freud describes the id as 'a chaos, a cauldron full of seething excitations . . . It is filled with energy reaching it from the instincts . . . it has no organization, produces no collective will . . . only a striving to bring about the satisfaction of the instinctual needs' (SE 22: 73). As we saw with dreams, the law of contradiction does not apply in the id; there is no negation, and 'contrary impulses exist side by side' (SE 22: 73). Importantly, in the id 'space and time are [not] necessary forms of our mental acts' and 'no alteration in its mental processes is produced by the passage of time' (SE 23: 74). Some wishful impulses are indeed 'virtually immortal' and can reappear. Freud here both addressed a number of philosophical questions in relation to the province of the instinctual and described it in terms of chaos and 'seething excitations'. The id becomes both the instinctual pole of the personality, and for Freud, the source of philosophical questioning about space and time (which goes together with granting an unconscious dimension to moral conscience through the *super-ego*). The id is in conflict with the *ego* and the *super-ego*, which arise out of the id. Defence against the repressed meant defence against the instinctual side of the psychical personality, rather than against what is unconscious.

The *ego* depends on the demands of the *id* and on the 'moral' exertions of the *super-ego*. Freud defined the *ego* by contrast with the two other provinces. The ego is related to the external world genetically and structurally. It is confusing to read Freud's description of it, since it involves a peculiar localization with respect to the system *Pcpt.-Cs* – Freud's abbreviation for the system Perception Consciousness – 'in the outermost superficial portion of the mental apparatus'. The ego is 'that portion of the id which was modified by the proximity and influence of the external world . . . [which] has become the decisive factor for the ego; it has taken on the task of representing the external world to the id' (SE 22: 75). In that account the ego accomplishes the task of 'reality-testing', distinguishing what comes from the inside and the outside. It institutes the activity of thought to which we will return in Chapter 5. The ego 'dethron[es] the pleasure principle . . . and replac[es] it by the reality principle' (SE 22: 76). By contrast with the id, the ego introduces the idea of time, which is linked with periodicity and therefore with quality. The ego is also, however, serving 'three tyrannical masters . . . the external world, the super-ego and the id' (SE 22: 77), and has to submit to their demands.

The *super-ego* is unconscious. It has the three functions of self-observation, moral conscience and is the site of the formation of ideals. There are conflicts between the ego and the super-ego, which result in the feeling of guilt or the feeling of inferiority on the part of the ego.[10] The id and the super-ego are in conflict. In seeking instinctual satisfaction, the ego attempts to push aside the 'voice' of the super-ego. The super-ego, together with the id, is an heir to the influence of the past, in that it is a precipitate of parental influence and of that of other authority figures, whereas the id goes back to an immemorial past. It is with reference to its relation between the ego and the super-ego that the ego can be said to be the 'precipitate' of earlier identifications (Freud elaborated the notion of identification in *Group-Psychology and the Analysis of the Ego* [1921]).

From the introduction of that structural model of the psychical personality onwards, Freud reworked many earlier aspects of the theory of the unconscious. Among other elements, he would seem to have redefined the aim of the treatment in the last sentences of the 'Dissection of the Psychical Personality'. Having provided a genetic account of how the ego arises out of the id, and has dependent relations with the super-ego, Freud wrote that the intention of psychoanalysis is:

> to strengthen the ego, to make it more independent of the super-ego, to widen its field of perception and enlarge its organization, so that it can appropriate fresh portions of the id. Where id was, there ego shall be. It is a work of culture – not unlike the draining of the Zuider Zee. (SE 22: 80)

These prescriptive sentences would appear to reduce considerably the scope of psychoanalysis, by making it a tool of adaptation of the ego to the restricting demands of culture. Or else, that model has been thought to diminish the importance of the hermeneutic, interpretative strengths of psychoanalysis. However, the move towards the second topography is only one of the major turning points. The other concerns the speculative notion of the death drive.

The Death Drive. The Compulsion to Repeat

The phenomena of sadism and of masochism led Freud to reflect on the aggressive instinct. (He had done so in *Three Essays*, under the heading of component drives. Sadism and masochism are associated respectively with activity and passivity, and with 'normal' components of sexuality.) Masochism especially provided a model for the fusion of two classes of drives. For in masochism, there is 'a mixture of the two classes of instinct, of Eros and aggressiveness' (SE 22: 104). The idea of fusion and defusion was connected with the way in which Freud had described human sexuality as the result of an assemblage that can become undone. Each stage could provide an opportunity for 'fixation' and regression (Freud developed the idea of the 'choice' of neurosis, on the basis of the possibilities of fixation and regression).

In his last revisions of the theory of the drives in *Beyond the Pleasure Principle* (1920), Freud still divided the drives into two classes – first into Eros, which is 'by far the most conspicuous and accessible to study' (SE 19: 40). The second class of drive (in the new classification) is the death drive or the destructive instinct. On that view, the 'contrast between the instincts of self-preservation and the preservation of the species, as well as the contrast between ego-love and object-love falls within Eros' (SE 22: 148). The task of the death drive is to 'lead organic life back into inanimate state', to 'undo connections, and so to destroy things' (SE 22: 148), while that of Eros is to 'establish ever greater unities and to preserve them thus . . . to bind together' (SE 22: 148). One of these elements can overdevelop, or the 'alloy' between the two of which the sexual instinct is made can become undone. The death drive was related to the compulsion to repeat, which Freud posited as the most fundamental characteristic of all drives (which 'never ceases to strive for complete satisfaction . . . which consists in the repetition of a primary experience' [SE 18: 42]).

Changes in the conception of the drives, especially the introduction of the compulsion to repeat, had a notable impact on the theory of dreams as wish-fulfilment. Freud observed that dreams 'which occur in traumatic neuroses . . . arise . . . in obedience to the compulsion to repeat'. The function of these dreams would seem to be to 'conjure up what has been forgotten and repressed' (SE 18: 32). Dreams also responded to the instinctual demands of the return to an earlier state, which the compulsion to repeat propelled.

BIOLOGICAL OVERTONES

As we saw above, Freud defined the drive as 'lying on the frontier between the mental and the physical' (SE 7: 168). Even though he wondered 'how far psychological investigation [could] throw light upon the biology of the sexual life of man', and underlined how the 'libido has somatic sources . . . and streams to the ego from various organs and parts of the body' (SE 23: 151), he claimed that the psychoanalytic approach was independent from the 'findings of biology' on the subject (SE 7: 131). Such declarations do not mean that the theory of sexuality – indeed, the theory of the unconscious – is not imbued with biology. In Binswanger's vein, the psychoanalyst Jean Laplanche spoke of Freud's biological 'mistake' in two respects. On the one hand, and as we saw earlier, the sexual drive *imitates* the source, aim and object of the vital functions (the self-preservative drives). On that view, the sexual drive only emerges in the vein of the biological function of feeding (witness the affirmations – the 'slogans' – of *Three Essays*: 'a child sucking at his mother's breast has become the prototype of every relation of love', or, 'the finding of an object is in fact a refinding of it' [SE 7: 222]). Freud called that method for finding an object the 'anaclictic' one (see Chapter 2 above). On the other hand, the drive is defined as the representative of the somatic. The sexual drive takes its source in the somatic, and is itself later the source of the id, the reservoir of drives.

For other philosophers, the biological and somatic anchorage of the drive marks an interesting 'ontological ambiguity'. It signals the unconventional kind of dualism Freud introduced (see Assoun 1981: 48–50 and Bergo 2004: 344–5, among others). He was not endorsing what in psychology is called the hypothesis of the psycho-physiological parallelism (whereby to each physical event there corresponds a psychical one, as two parallel series).[11] The ambiguous nature of the drive raised the question as to whether psychoanalysis is above all concerned with meaning (the formation of symptoms through symbolizations), or whether it presents a machinery of mental forces, determining our lives (the energetic substratum). The drive and the affect the elements of Freud that appear most biological – are points of reference for debating whether one should develop an hermeneutic and/or an economic, determinist understanding of psychoanalysis.[12]

WHERE DO CONCEPTS COME FROM?

Just as the early case histories related to contemporary imaginative writings (the material of the *Studies on Hysteria* resembled 'detailed description of mental processes such as we are accustomed to find in the works of imaginative writers' [SE 2: 160]), Freud's early theoretical work was closely related to existing fields of research. He employed concepts developed in natural sciences and in scientific psychology. Following Freud's own history of the psychoanalytic movement, and at least since Ernest Jones's biography and studies on the epistemology of psychoanalysis, it is possible to identify the provenance of certain psychoanalytic concepts, as Freud himself did.[13] We saw in Chapter 2 how he acknowledged the proximity of Schopenhauer's concept of repression to his own. In *Beyond the Pleasure Principle*, Freud conceded his debt to the biologist A. Weismann, for introducing the morphological theory of 'the division of the living substance into mortal and immortal parts' (SE 18: 45). He also referred in the same work, and in *Civilization and its Discontents* (1930), to the 'Eros of the poets and philosophers which holds all living things together' (SE 18: 50).[14] During the 1890s, Freud and Breuer elaborated *Studies on Hysteria* and the traumatic theory of neuroses in the vein of the psycho-physiology elaborated by the School of Helmholtz, to which their teacher Ernst Brücke belonged.[15] According to its materialist doctrine, it was possible to explain all natural phenomena, and life processes, with reference to physical and chemical forces, which could be regulated (SE 2: xxii). Following Charcot, Freud and Breuer aimed to develop a psychological explanation of hysteria, instead of considering the illness as a result of degeneracy or hereditary weaknesses. That symptoms should involve 'psychological' processes, however, did not prevent them from relating symptoms to the increase and decrease of 'sums of excitations', and to the circulation of 'psychical energy', which would explain why Freud had physicalist prejudices. At first, they did connect symptoms to ideas, but also referred them back to the nervous system, the functioning of which Breuer compared to that of an electrical lighting system (SE 2: 198–9).

We saw how the pleasure principle was elaborated with reference to Fechner's 'tendency towards stability' (SE 18: 9), to which Freud repeatedly returned. It is possible to find for almost every aspect of Freud's theory an existing scientific hypothesis, which Freud considerably modified and distorted. Commentators have described that feature of Freud's writings in terms of the construction of an 'interdisciplinary theory of the mind'.[16] For example, the topographical model is indebted, among other sources, to Wilhelm Wundt's *Principles of Psychological Psychology* (1874), just as the dynamic point of view is closely related to the 'mechanics of representation' [*Vorstellungsmechanik*], which was elaborated by the German psychologist Johann Friedrich Herbart at the beginning of the nineteenth century.

Scientific experimentation requires measure and quantification, and psychology had to find means of measurement of mental phenomena. One way of doing so was to turn to physiology, since the only means of 'measuring' phenomena was through their effects, that is, through movements or sensory impressions. Debates ensued concerning the possibility of measuring in the field of psychology, and the 'relativity' of measurement in psychology, which entailed calling into question the conditions of the experiment. During the 1860s, the possibility of measuring 'the duration of psychical acts' had been raised (following earlier attempts in astronomy). Interests in quantification developed in the vein of Helmholtz, Fechner and others such as Ernst Mach. For Mach it was possible to measure sensations, and in order to do so, he proposed a general law, which bound physical and psychical phenomena, whereby sensation increases as the logarithm of excitation (Assoun 1981: 150–1). Such were the questions, among others, circulating in scientific laboratories, when Freud began his medical education at the University of Vienna in 1873.

Freud, then, appropriated problems presiding over the foundation of experimental psychology at the end of the nineteenth century (Assoun 1981: 144). One way in which Freud reflected on the relation between physiology and psychology was through quantification, in the 'Project for a Scientific Psychology' (1895), where he aimed to unite physiology and psychology. That text, which was published posthumously during the 1950s, aimed to 'furnish a psychology that shall be a natural science: that is, to represent psychical processes as quantitatively determinate states of specifiable material particles, thus making those processes perspicuous and free from contradiction' (SE 1: 295). Just before writing the 'Project', quantitative considerations 'tormented' Freud, as he said in a letter to Fliess dated 25 May 1895: 'I am vexed by two intentions: to discover what form the theory of psychical functioning will take if a quantitative line of approach, a kind of economics of nervous force, is introduced into it, and, secondly, to extract from psychopathology a yield from normal psychology' (SE 1: 283). From the publication of *The Interpretation of Dreams*, *The Psychopathology of Everyday Life* (1901) and *Jokes and their Relation to the Unconscious* (1905) onwards up until the writings on art, culture and religion, Freud sought to fulfil these two aims. However, even though the scientific climate encouraged the adoption of a quantitative outlook, to develop an economics of nervous force was more arduous than establishing the 'normality' of pathological processes (in fact, the two tasks became closely linked).

THE IMPERATIVE OF QUANTIFICATION

It cannot have escaped our notice that both the psychoanalytic cure and the explanations concerning unconscious psychical mechanisms involve quantification (indeed we began with a quantitative account of laughter). We will pursue the exploration of quantity in Chapter 5, under the heading of the *economic* point of view. For the moment, it will suffice to note some occurrences of the most obviously quantitative concepts (see Strachey's Appendix C, 'The Nature of Q', in SE 1: 392). The idea of quantity first appears in Freud's writings in 1891, and in early publications such as 'The Neuro-Psychoses of Defence' (1894), up until the last, such as 'Analysis Terminable and Interminable' (1937). Yet, although the meaning and importance of quantification is undeniable, its meaning fluctuates through Freud's work, especially around the transformation of quantity into quality, which becomes a pressing problem for Freud in 'The Economic Problem of Masochism' (1924).

Early explanations of the power of the 'cathartic method' have quantitative undertones. Let us recall how, during the psychoanalytic cure, the analyst had to deal with varying forces of resistances, which had to be matched by an effort on his/her part ('The amount of effort we have to use, by which we estimate the resistance against the material becoming conscious, varies in magnitude in individual cases' [SE 23: 160]). The concept of resistance calls to mind a physical resistance. 'Quantity' is an obstacle to the treatment in a banal sense: the treatment is efficacious only up to a certain age limit because of the accumulation of psychical material over many years (see Chapter 1 above). Similarly, 'If the dreams become altogether too diffuse and voluminous, all hope of completely unravelling them should tacitly be given up from the start' (SE 12: 92).

The account of 'traumatic moments' is quantitative (SE 22: 93). Situations of danger provide a model for anxiety states that constitute traumatic moments (birth is the model par excellence). Such a situation 'calls up in mental experience a state of highly tense excitation, which is felt as unpleasure and which one is not able to master by discharging it' (SE 22: 93). It is the 'emergence of a traumatic moment, which cannot be dealt with by the normal rules of the pleasure principle' that is feared in all the kinds of anxiety Freud identified (neurotic anxiety, realistic anxiety and the situation of danger). However, the generation of every form of anxiety is defined in terms of a 'question of relative quantities', for what transforms an impression into a traumatic moment is 'the magnitude of the sum of excitation' (SE 22: 94).

THE 'PROJECT FOR A SCIENTIFIC PSYCHOLOGY'

Rather than clarifying the many understandings of quantity in his theory, Freud insisted on their indefiniteness, for unconscious processes take place 'between quotas of energy in some unimaginable substratum' (SE 22: 90). Nevertheless it is worth becoming acquainted with one of its most striking occurrences by turning to the 'Project'. This will make us go into the scientific framework in which Freud elaborated his quantitative thinking, and explore how Freud introduced certain fundamental concepts. We have already referred to the experience of satisfaction, and to the distinction between primary and secondary processes. One also finds the notion of the ego and some elements of the theory of dreams (which Freud began to elaborate as he was writing the 'Project', the year he had the 'Dream of Irma's Injection' – 24 July 1895). From approximately the end of April 1895 until October 1895, Freud was preoccupied with the 'Project', which he wrote 'in one go'. He sent parts of the manuscript in a letter to Fliess (dated 8 October 1895), but continued to work on it 'in bouts' until January 1896. He had then 'reworked' some of the hypotheses in 'Draft K' on the neuroses of defence, which was inserted in a letter to Fliess dated 1 January 1896 (the manuscript was entitled 'A Christmas Fairy Tale'). Both the 'Project' and its reworking aimed at elucidating the mechanisms of defence, following Freud's clinical observations. The 'Project' is a rebarbative text; it contains many distinctions (between systems of neurones and types of action attributed to these neurones, between functions, and so on). Freud uses abbreviations such as Q for quantity and the reader would seem to require neurophysiological knowledge to understand any of it. Let us recall that it is addressed to Fliess, with whom Freud had a 'scientific' correspondence. It divides into three parts, with Part I on psychology, which comprises a mechanical introduction on the circulation of Q in the nervous system. The 'Project' gradually becomes more concrete. From the first part onwards, it leads to the experience of satisfaction, pain, wishing, the ego, cognition, thought and reality, and finally the dream. Part II presents a case of 'Psychopathology', the story of Emma (Eckstein), which pursues the work of the first part, but by following closely the mechanisms of hysteria. Part III presents what Freud called the 'normal processes' (the secondary processes; psychical attention; cognitive processes of thought, judgement, and so on).

Psychopathology

Part II of the 'Project' presents an interesting illustration of the mechanical line of approach it proposes as 'stories', the genre with which we have now become familiar. It presents a drawing of two scenes involving Emma's trajectory in and out of clothes shops and of her being in and out of reach of shop assistants, with the indications of her state of mind (and her actions). The figure is intended to show the associations and repetitions involved in processes of defence, and to underline Emma's inability to go into shops alone. However, for our purpose, it illustrates clearly the juxtaposition of levels of reality (clothes, shopkeeper, sexual release, flight) that we underlined throughout our exploration of Freud. It is a schema illustrating the 'pairing', if it can ever be represented otherwise than through dreams, misreadings, jokes, errors, bungled actions, and so on.

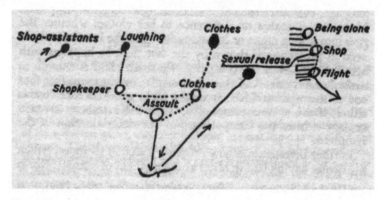

Figure 1

The drawing shows the associative links between two scenes separated by an interval of a few years. On the one hand, there is the scene dating from when Emma was twelve years old, which she most readily remembered: she had been 'into a shop to buy something, saw the two shop-assistants . . . laughing together, and ran away in some *affect of fright* . . . she was led to recall that the two of them were laughing at her clothes and that one of them had pleased her sexually' (Freud's emphasis, SE 1: 353). In connection to that first scene, Emma remembered another one: 'when she was a child of eight she had gone into a small shop to buy some sweets, and the shopkeeper had grabbed her genitals through her clothes' (SE 1: 354). There was a link between the shop assistants and the shopkeeper of the two scenes, the laughing, the clothes and the assault of the first and second scenes, the sexual release in the shop, and the flight (each of these terms being 'points' on the figure).

Quantity in the 'Project'

The 'Project' is one of the earliest and most explicit formulations of the 'quantitative line of approach'. However, it deals with 'an indeterminate entity (the nervous system, the organism, the ego-individual, the psychical apparatus)' (Freud 2006: 597). On the one hand, it brings to the fore the quantitative contents of Freud and Breuer's work until 1895, and, on the other hand, it anticipates the dispersed discussion of the 'quantitative factor' of Freud's later work. It does not clarify fully the quantitative conception, even though this is one of the rare places where one finds an explicit discussion on the concept of quantity. In Part III of the 'Project', Freud attempted to show the relevance of the neurological functioning for 'normal mental processes', and proposed to explain the origin of moral conscience (notably, through the account of the individual original state of help-lessness), and of the emergence of ethical feelings. One of the few places where Freud directly addressed 'ethical' problems is also where he attempted to specify the quantitative conception (see SE 4: 411).

As for the source of that conception, Freud tellingly stated that it was 'derived directly from pathological clinical observation, especially where excessively intense ideas were concerned [*überstarke Vorstellung*]'. He is referring to his work on hysterical and obsessional neurosis, in which 'the quantitative characteristics emerges more plainly than in the normal' (SE 1: 295). In the opening paragraphs of the 'Project', he did not exactly explain why processes of discharge 'directly suggested the conception of neuronal excitation as quantity in a state of flow' (SE 1: 296). However, he did move from the notion of 'intense ideas' to 'quantity of excitations' (SE 1: 295–6).

Before writing the 'Project', Freud had introduced the idea of quantities in his reporting of the case of Frau Emmy von N. in *Studies on Hysteria*, as a necessary theoretical step ('It is impossible any longer at this point to avoid introducing the idea of quantities . . .' [SE 2: 86]). However, the quantities were not here the matter of an external, theoretical point of view on hysterical symptoms. Conversion itself involves the 'surplus', or the 'quantities' for the formation of a symptoms. The process of conversion – which we considered in Chapter 1 – came about when there was a 'surplus of stimulation', when too great a sum of excitations impinged on the nervous system. For the sum was 'transformed' into a symptom, if it had not been discharged through an external action. The process of conversion involved the transformation of a certain amount into a symptom, but the latter occurred only if the amount exceeded a certain threshold. Even though Freud kept underlining that the quantities were not measurable, symptoms were formed in proportion to the amounts of excitations that had not been discharged. Rather than introducing the idea of quantities, it was the clinical phenomenon itself (the hysterical conversion) that involved quantities (as though quantities were '*found* . . . already in existence' [Freud's emphasis, SE 1: 303]). This is probably why Freud stated that processes, such as conversion, directly suggested the 'conception of neuronal excitation as quantity in a state of flow' (SE 1: 296).[17]

The 'Project' begins with basic elements (Q, the principle of inertia, neurones, contact-barriers, differentiation between neurones), and gradually presents their systematic functioning (Wollheim 1971: 45)[18]. On the one hand, there are the 'material particles' or the 'neurones', which form a complex network. On the other hand, there is the 'energy' or 'quantity', which Freud calls Q, as an abbreviation of Quantity. The latter either flows through the network of neurones (it is then described as being in a 'state of flow', or in terms of the 'passage of excitation'), or it 'fills' or 'occupies' neurones more statically. The notion of 'cathexis' describes the 'occupation' by Q of the neurone, a term that, in German, has the military connotation of occupying a territory. Freud adopted Breuer's distinction between 'free' and 'bound' energy. Q cannot be measured, but its movements are regulated by 'the principle of neuronal inertia' (SE 1: 296). In 1893, Freud had described what he then called 'the principle of constancy', as a normal human tendency:

If a person experiences a psychical impression, something in his nervous system which we will for the moment call the sum of excitation is increased. Now in every individual there exists a tendency to diminish this sum of excitation once more, in order to preserve his health. (SE 3: 36)

The most adequate and powerful manner for 'diminishing' the sum of excitation was a deed (responding to an insult, one would give a blow to one's adversary, but failing that, one could resort to language). The principle determines the structure, development and the functioning of the nervous system. According to the principle of inertia (or constancy) 'neurones tend to divest themselves of Q' (see SE 1: 297 and SE 3: 65). However, they do not all equally do so, since they divide into sensory and motor ones: the sensory neurones receive $Q\eta$, and motor ones 'give it off' through a reflex movement.

Freud introduced the distinction between the primary and secondary processes when presenting the structure of the neuronal system as two types of neurones. The distinction involved a recourse to brain anatomy. On the one hand, 'a primary nervous system makes use of this $Q\eta$ which it has thus acquired [through the external surface of the organism], by giving it off through a connecting path to the muscular mechanisms' (SE 1: 296). This is how it keeps itself free from stimulus. The discharge corresponds to the primary function of the nervous system (or later, of the psychical apparatus). The primary process refers to a state of the apparatus in which Q flows freely without encountering any resistance. However, the principle of inertia or the principle of constancy is 'broken from the first' by the secondary function (or the secondary process). It is the very stimulus ($Q\eta$), which the organism received, that provided the organism the 'energy' for the discharge of Q. In other words, the apparatus gets rid of the stimulus by employing the very energy of the stimulus (it uses the energy of what sets it in motion).

The secondary function thwarts the principle of inertia and the primary process. This happens when the nervous system receives stimuli not only from the external world through perception, but also from the very organism itself, that is, when the cells of the body send stimuli to the organism. These stimuli give rise to the 'major needs' (hunger, respiration, sexuality) or what Freud calls the *exigencies of life*. We saw above that the 'endogenous stimuli', or the stimuli coming from the organism itself, stand in the 'Project' as the 'precursors' to the drives (the drives are not the 'biological needs'). The organism cannot employ the $Q\eta$ of the stimuli for flight, as it would normally do (it cannot flee from itself). The organism can discharge the endogenous $Q\eta$ only through 'a specific action' performed in the external world, at first through the mediation of the 'carer' or the mother. The first specific action is screaming (screaming as the origin of language). For being able to scream and in that way, to get rid of the stimuli, the system breaks the principle of inertia by 'gathering its strength'. That is, it accumulates a reserve of $Q\eta$ against its tendency towards discharge. Even though the secondary function contradicts the principle of inertia by 'storing' $Q\eta$, it seeks to maintain its level 'as low as possible'; in any case it seeks to 'keep it constant' (SE 1: 297). In *Beyond the Pleasure Principle* Freud stated that the principle of constancy is opposed to that of inertia, since it denotes the endeavour of the psychical apparatus 'to keep the quantity of excitation present in it as low as possible or at least to keep it constant' (SE 18: 9). Obeying the principle of constancy prevents the total discharge (which must be avoided if the organism is to stay alive).

How can the system stop the discharge of Q if its primitive functioning is discharge? Freud borrowed from histology, which posited that the nervous system is composed of similarly constructed neurones, which are connected to each other 'through the medium of a foreign substance' or the protoplasm (the basic physical substance of cells). The reception of excitations and their discharge creates 'lines of conduction' in these substances (SE 1: 298). Contacts between neurones trigger different degrees of resistances (Freud calls these points of contacts, the 'contact-barriers'), which prevent the free flow of $Q\eta$ from one neurone to the next. They prevent the total discharge towards which the nervous system aims. In the ψ-system, some neurones are permanently cathected or 'invested' (they are never devoid of $Q\eta$). The 'ego' has the control of the inhibitory, secondary function. It is a 'fund of energy' (a reserve of $Q\eta$), which it allocates to the system, in order to regulate the passage of $Q\eta$ (Freud developed the inhibitory function of the ego in 'Negation' [1925]).

The hypothesis of the contact-barriers is central to Freud's account of memory. The nervous system must perform two contradictory functions: that of memory and that of perception. It has to retain stimuli, while remaining able to receive stimuli. The two neuronic systems fulfil that double requirement. There are the *permeable* neurones (the ϕ-neurones retain nothing, are unaffected by the flow of $Q\eta$, and serve for perception), and the *impermeable* ones (the ψ-neurones, which retain traces of the flow of $Q\eta$, which 'are the vehicles of memory and so probably of psychical processes in general' [SE 1: 300]). Another way to put it is to say that the neurones are either *cathected*, that is, they are filled with a certain $Q\eta$ (they are 'occupied'), or they remain empty. The contact-barriers between the ϕ and the ψ neurones react differently to the reception of excitations. Memory lies in their different degree of receptivity.[19] The repeated passages of $Q\eta$ through neurones leave traces in them, and the contact-barriers create pathways in the two systems (Freud SE 1: 300 and Wollheim 1971: 47–8). The latter allow more or less easily the flow of $Q\eta$. Some of them will offer more resistance than others, for the flow of $Q\eta$ through a neurone is not equally 'facilitated'. The degrees of resistance and the frequency of the passage of $Q\eta$ vary. Memory consists in that unevenness; it emerges from the way in which the flow of energy follows some paths more easily than others: '*Memory is represented by the differences in the facilitations between the ψ neurones*' (SE 1: 300).

The difference between the neurones originates from the location of the neurones and from their function. The φ-neurones are turned towards the external world and receive stimuli from it, which is 'the origin of all major quantities of energy' (SE 1: 304). They get their permeability, as Wollheim vividly put it, from the fact that great passages of quantity have 'battered them into total penetrability' (1971: 48). The φ-neurones discharge directly some of the $Q\eta$ through motor discharge (through the performing of actions). Some amount enters the ψ-system and leaves 'permanent traces' that constitute memory. The ψ-system receives 'endogenous stimuli' from the cells (in addition to the share of Q from the external world, which it receives from the φ-neurones). The amounts of stimuli are small and create the 'major needs'. It is only when there has been a certain accumulation of stimuli that need is felt. Pain corresponds to an irruption of a too great quantity through the φ-system into the ψ-system, which leaves permanent traces.

But how does consciousness fit into the 'Project'? Freud introduces a third system, the ω-neurones, which borders on the φ-s. The function of consciousness is to provide 'qualities'. It is 'the subjective side of one part of the psychical processes in the nervous system' (SE 1: 311). Unlike with the other systems, quantity never reaches directly the ω-system. Quantity never reaches consciousness, even if it is not entirely independent from the flow of quantity. The latter does reach consciousness, but only because the ω-neurones 'appropriate the *period* of excitation' (SE 1: 310). $Q\eta$ becomes a matter of consciousness through the duration and frequency of its flow, and produces the contents of consciousness, which are either sensory or perceptual.

The 'Project' also turns to 'normal processes' such as thinking. In the fiction of the first experience of satisfaction, the giving up by the apparatus of the hallucinating mode of satisfaction corresponds to the institution of the 'principle of reality'. It is a step within a larger development (which includes that of attention, of notation, judgement), even though, through the functioning of the apparatus, all the steps become contemporaneous. Among the 'adaptations' of the apparatus, there is the modification of the function of 'motor discharge'. Prior to the introduction of the principle of reality, motor discharge served to unburden the apparatus from accumulation of stimuli, by directing them towards the interior of the body, so that the individual can make expressive movements and manifest affects – like the screaming and kicking baby. With the introduction of the principle of reality, motor discharge is converted into action, that is, into a means of modifying reality (SE 12: 221).

In that development of *thinking* (judgement), it allows the apparatus to 'tolerate an increased tension of stimulus while the process of discharge was postponed' (SE 12: 221). On Freud's model, thinking has a quantitative dimension, since it is defined as 'an experimental kind of acting, accompanied by the displacement of relatively small quantities of cathexis together with less expenditure (discharge) of them' (SE 12: 221). Thinking involves a 'conversion of freely displaceable cathexes into "bound" cathexes' (SE 12: 221): the dynamic opposition which separates the instinctual energy into 'free' and 'bound' energy also takes on a quantitative character – the 'binding' consisting in a reduction of sort. When thinking is subsequently attributed to the ego, it becomes comparable to a technique for exploring reality, which the ego uses, as Freud stated in the *New Introductory Lectures*: 'Thinking is an experimental action carried out with small amounts of energy, in the same way as a general shifts small figures about on a map before setting his large bodies of troops in motion' (SE 22: 89).

Critical Evaluations of the 'Project'

Commentators noted that Freud established psychoanalysis, not solely through the technical innovations we considered in Chapter 1, but also by moving from 'biological explanations to narrative explanations, from diseased bodies to diseased memories'. Freud would have shifted 'the focus of the search for the causes of hysteria from biological sources to narrative sources', that is, by moving from physiology to memory (Thurschwell 2000: 17; 21). This is an accurate account of Freud's own description of the changes in the theory. However, there remains a problem around what role to assign to the somatic in psychoanalysis. The relation between the somatic and the psychical appears as one of the problems of human experience (as we saw with the concept of the drive [SE 11: 38]). Rather than having accomplished such a shift, and having replaced 'physiology' with 'memory', it might be that psychoanalysis conceived of an interesting way of relating them. The idea that Freud never abandoned the model of natural sciences, then, might be a useful observation rather than a criticism. For even though Freud developed a complete 'psychical' theory of the mind, which would seem to have excluded recourse to these sciences (the unconscious is not a matter of biology or physiology: it cannot be located anatomically), biology and thermodynamics never entirely disappeared from Freud's work. As we saw, even while Freud is discovering the role of infantile sexuality, or the relation between affect and idea in the formation of a trauma, and thus apparently moving away from bodily explanations of mental illnesses, we remain in the realm of mechanisms and processes that are unusually paired with 'stories'. It is the pairing of 'stories' and 'mechanisms' that poses problems of understanding and (philosophical) interpretation.

Critical evaluations of the 'Project' illustrate the perplexity surrounding the scientific framework in Freud. Broadly speaking, commentators have interpreted the overtly materialist aim of the 'Project' along two argumentative lines, which are not incompatible with each other, since they can be viewed as successive states in the development of psychoanalytic theory. On the one hand, commentators consider the 'Project' as a neurological account of the brain and its functioning, which Freud formulated with reference to existing neurological knowledge and following the clinical observations he collected in his work with neurotic patients, and the analysis of his own dreams from 1895 onwards. He was interested in systems of differentiated neurones, the properties and connections of which were the sources of mental functions, such as, for example, memory, the perception of reality, process of thought, dreaming, and neurotic process (Wollheim 1971: 44 and Strachey SE 4: xviii). Scholars have checked Freud's account and compared it to contemporary advances in neurology, in relation to the recent field of cognitive sciences.[20]

However, Freud later rejected the neurological contents of his 1895 work, notably the idea that psychical processes related to the nervous system. He suggested that he abandoned anatomy and physiology for psychical notions. This is what he expressed in *Beyond the Pleasure Principle* after having earlier distinguished the psychological understanding from the neuro-physiological ones, as the following statement from *Jokes* concerning the concept of 'cathexis' also shows:

My experiences of the displaceability of psychical energy along certain paths of association, and of the almost indestructible persistence of the traces of psychical processes, have in fact suggested to me an attempt at picturing the unknown in some such way. To avoid misunderstanding, I must add that I am making no attempt to proclaim that the cells and nerve fibres, the systems of neurones which are taking their place to-day, are these psychical paths, even though it would have to be possible in some manner which cannot yet be indicated to represent such paths by organic elements of the nervous system. (SE 8: 148)

In *Introductory Lectures* (1916–17), this time concerning anxiety, Freud had declared: 'I know nothing that could be of less interest to me for the psychological understanding of anxiety than a knowledge of the path of the nerves along which its excitations pass' (quoted in SE 3: 234 n. 2). But his 'lack of interest' with 'the knowledge of the path of the nerves' does not cancel out the hope expressed in *Beyond the Pleasure Principle*, among other places, of moving further in the understanding of the relation between the organic and the psychical. He believed that biological notions could some day relay the psychoanalytical notions, even that they could 'blow away the whole of [Freud's] artificial structure and hypotheses' (SE 18: 60).

The other more positive evaluation of the 'Project' affirms that the posthumous piece of writing contains Freud's most fundamental concepts (it introduces the distinction between primary and secondary processes, the notion of the wish, the diphasic nature of human sexuality, the notion of the ego, etc.), but that these concepts are still implicated in a 'neurological machinery' (SE 4: xvii), from which they will subsequently be distinguished. The idea that Freud abandoned the neurological framework because he developed psychological views goes together with the idea that one should (retrospectively) interpret the original neurological (naturalist) framework, and what remains of it in Freud's later work as being figurative, metaphorical (if Freud continued to resort to scientific concepts, he did so only metaphorically). Freud encouraged such a judgement by commenting profusely on his scientific constructions as he did in *Beyond the Pleasure Principle*. The psychical apparatus was one such 'construction' or model that was not located anatomically.[21] When we turn to Freud's explanations of the comic in the next chapter, we will see that Freud's extension of the concept of quantity leads beyond an objective scientific understanding of quantity towards aesthetics and ethics.

CHAPTER 5

METAPSYCHOLOGY AND ECONOMICS

'I feel uncertain in the face of my own work', Freud wrote in the preface to *Moses and Monotheism: Three Essays* (1939 [1934–8]). The uncertainty did not arise only in view of his forced exile from Vienna to London in 1938, which formed the immediate biographical and historical context of that work (SE 23: 58). He was more generally upfront about the incompletion of psychoanalytic theory and practice. In 'An Autobiographical Study' (1925), he spoke of the 'Metapsychology' as 'no more than a torso' (SE 20: 59). Freud nevertheless attempted to systematize the findings of psychoanalysis into a theory he called 'metapsychology' in 1915. This referred to 'the method of approach according to which every mental process is considered in relation to three co-ordinates, which [Freud] described as *dynamic, topographical*, and *economic* respectively' (Freud's emphasis, SE 20: 58–9). The ultimate image of a 'torso' could be referring to the fact that there would probably always remain gaps in the understanding of the unconscious. In 1911, Freud had said that psychoanalysis was unfinished by virtue of being the 'outcome of experience' (SE 11: 207). As long as there are psychoanalytic treatments, the theory will be 'open to revision' (SE 20: 266, 'On Psycho-Analysis'), as it has continued to be up until today (psychoanalysis is 'open to revision' also with respect to the way in which it keeps putting forward provisional hypotheses).

In Chapter 4, we saw how some of Freud's theoretical speculation and clinical observation culminated in the theory of the drives. From 1915 onwards, he began writing the twelve projected papers that the metapsychology was supposed to include.[1] In this chapter, we will explore briefly the three points of view of the metapsychology. This will allow us to situate the 'imperative of quantification' within the larger picture of the science of unconscious mental processes. We saw how Freud modified his views on the determinants of repression and, more generally, of the psychical conflict in relation to the theory of the drives. The drive was the object of the first metapsychological paper entitled 'Instincts and their Vicissitudes' (1915). Although the metapsychology precisely postulated three interrelated points of view, it is under the economic point of view that Freud pursued the exploration of the quantitative factor, which he introduced in 'The Project for a Scientific Psychology' (1895) among other early texts. After having examined the three metapsychological points of view, we will turn to what we call 'quantitative considerations' (to distinguish them from the more strictly identifiable metapsychological economic considerations).

Jokes and their Relation to the Unconscious (1905) is one of the most 'economical' of Freud's works that predate the metapsychological writings. It presents an analysis of the production of jokes with reference to the first model of the psychical apparatus. Through that marginal topic, it will be possible to see how the quantitative dimension of Freud's work brings us close to aesthetic and ethical concern. The shift from economic to less strictly economic considerations occurs in Freud's treatment of the comic, more particularly of the comic of movement. The section of *Jokes* where Freud deals with it is one of the rare places where he approached unconscious mental processes through the body. That exploration led to the problem of thinking [*Denken*], which involved the linking and transforming of psychical impulses into thought and action, that is, the passage from quantity to quality.

Having first tentatively designated the principles of a 'psychology that leads behind consciousness' as 'metapsychology' in a letter to Fliess, dated 10 March 1898, Freud first used the term in print in *Psychopathology of Everyday Life* (1901), in the context of a discussion of the psychical root of superstition (SE 6: 259). However, it is in the 1915 paper on 'The Unconscious' that metapsychology appeared as a systematic project of theoretical elaboration: 'I propose that when we have succeeded in describing a psychical process in its dynamic, topographical and economic aspects, we should speak of it as a *metapsychological* presentation' (Freud's emphasis; SE 14: 181). Before 1915, Freud had adopted these three points of view separately to describe mental processes, without grouping them under the heading of theoretical requirements. We have already introduced them, if not always by name, in previous chapters.

THE TOPOGRAPHICAL POINT OF VIEW

Chapter VII of *The Interpretation of Dreams* developed the first topographical conception of the psychical apparatus, which divided into two 'systems' or 'agencies', called *Cs.-Pcs.* (for 'Conscious-Preconscious'), *Ucs.* (for 'Unconscious'). However, the model did not yet form the 'topographical point of view', even though Freud spoke of a 'psychical topography', and of the movement backwards within the apparatus as a *'topographical* regression' (Freud's emphasis; SE 5: 548). In 'A Metapsychological Supplement to the Theory of Dreams' (1917 [1915]), Freud took up again what he had initially described by means of a comparison between the psychical apparatus and a 'compound instrument', such as the microscope or the photographic apparatus, in order to facilitate the spatial, temporal and formal presentation of the process of regression. In that revision to the theory of dreams, Freud indeed re-explained, in metapsychological terms, the relations he had earlier identified as *topographical*. In *The Interpretation*, the idea of *topography* gave a loose spatial and temporal dimension to the backward direction of mental processes during the formation of dreams. Here, it raised the question as to 'within what system or between what systems [a mental act] takes place' (SE 14: 173). In the theory of dreams, this meant wondering about how repressed 'wishful impulses' move from the unconscious to consciousness thanks to the dream (SE 14: 227).

Clinical observations had an impact on Freud's understanding of the localization and the fate of psychical quantities and qualities. He accordingly gradually transformed the model of the psychical apparatus extended in space and divided into a number of 'portions' in and between which psychical processes operated. We saw in Chapter 4 how the elaboration of the theory of the drives, and the specification of the 'ego' also contributed to that rethinking, which culminated in *The Ego and the Id* (1923). Freud provided visual representations of the two models of the mind. The first one, printed in Chapter VII of *The Interpretation*, consists of a graph indicating the regressive directions of the apparatus. Even though none of the topographical models refers us to brain anatomy, it is difficult not to see in Freud's figure of the second topographical model some vague

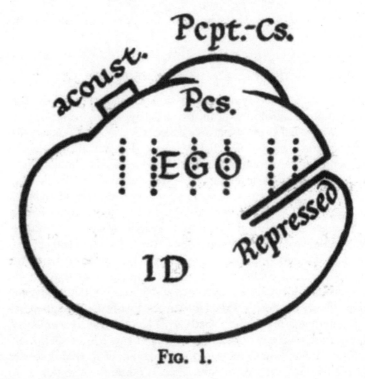

FIG. 1.

From 'The Ego and the Id' (SE 19: 24).

resemblance to a loose drawing of a brain (if it were not for the rectangular 'cap of hearing' [SE 19: 24]).[2]

THE DYNAMIC POINT OF VIEW

The elaboration of the metapsychology also entailed considering the agencies as the stages of an interaction of forces, which moved 'in them and between them', that is, considering the 'systems' from a *dynamic* point of view. According to that approach, mental processes are caused by an 'interplay of forces, which assist or inhibit one another, combine with one another, enter into compromises with one another, etc.' (SE 20: 265). Freud also hinted at the dynamic point of view in *The Interpretation*, where it was a matter of replacing 'a topographical way of representing things by a dynamic one. What we regard as mobile is not the psychical structure itself but the innervation' (SE 5: 610–11). A question arises, however, as to the nature of these 'innervations', which had an organic origin, but which one cannot quite equate with a physiological substratum (see Assoun 1997: 383–6).

THE ECONOMIC POINT OF VIEW

The interplay of forces involves a quantitative dimension, for which a third, *economic* approach to the functioning of mental processes can account. The economic point of view 'endeavours to follow out the vicissitudes of amounts of excitation and to arrive at least at some *relative* estimate of their magnitude' (SE 14: 181). For a 'merely *dynamic* view of . . . mental processes is insufficient' because 'the conflict between two trends does not break out till certain intensities of cathexis have been reached' (SE 16: 374). There needs to be a certain degree of intensity, an invasion of quantities of a certain magnitude for a conflict between ideas to erupt through the drives. Drives represented the somatic to the psyche only thanks to certain levels of cathexis, when they corresponded to important quantities of energy. Freud wrote in *Jokes*: 'The concepts of "psychical energy" and "discharge" and the treatment of psychical energy as a quantity have become habitual in my thoughts since I began to arrange the facts of psychopathology philosophically' (SE 8: 147–8). The pleasure principle is an eminently economic principle of functioning. For on the one hand, pleasure and unpleasure are quantitative, for 'pleasure is *in some way* connected with the diminution, reduction or extinction of the amounts of stimulus prevailing in the mental apparatus, and . . . similarly unpleasure is connected with their increase' (Freud's emphasis, 16: 356). From the economic point of view, the aim of mental activity consists in 'mastering amounts of excitation (mass of stimuli) operating in the mental apparatus and of keeping down their accumulation which creates unpleasure' (SE 16: 375). Freud had therefore introduced that approach to mental processes prior to calling it the economic point of view, or of speaking of 'libidinal economy'. However, Freud also described the pleasure principle as a qualitative relation, when pleasure is envisaged qualitatively, for the aim of mental activity consists 'qualitatively as an endeavour to obtain pleasure and to avoid unpleasure' (SE 16: 375; see also 'The Economic Problem of Masochism' [1924]; SE 19: 160).

The economic point of view stands out among the theoretical aspects of the metapsychology. It is the one to which commentators refer when they seek to show that psychoanalysis is a 'gross psychology', which is 'stuck in facticity and naturalism' (Henry 1985: 348). For many of them, the economic point of view is the aspect with regard to which Freud's theoretical structure is most problematical. In Binswanger's vein, every influential philosophical discussion of Freudian thought called into question in one way or another the *economic* point of view (this does not mean that the other points of view are not subjected to similar forms of criticism). The latter condenses the problematic scientific bias, which Binswanger underlined. The suspicion directed towards the economic point of view does not necessarily entail an overall rejection of Freud. In *Love and its Place in Nature* (1990), for example, Jonathan Lear suggests ways in which to rethink the objectivist position adopted by Freud when he deals with affect. For Lear, there is a discrepancy between Freud's quantitative theorization of affect, and his clinical observation of the role of affect in the psychoanalytic treatment. The concept of emotions which emerges from Freud's clinical practice is that of an orientation towards the world with which the mechanistic picture does not fit (Lear, 1990: 52). We will not elaborate on this rethinking of Freud's theory of affect here. However, Lear provides an example of the ways in which the quantitative framework calls for a transposition of sorts, or a translation. Freud often described his theoretical work as a translation of one language into another, of the hysterical experience into psychoanalytic terminology (for example, the experience of disgust was 'translated' into 'repression'; SE 3: 194). It is interesting that in a discussion of Freud's objectivist stance such as Lear's, it is that initial translation that seems to be retranslated into another, philosophical framework. One might imagine, however, that Freud was raising the question as to whether it is possible to experience quantity as quantity (see SE 8: 149 and Green 1986), as we will see below.

The various ways of conceiving the 'mysterious Q' and the realm of representation (of language, symbols and symptoms) alert us to a problematical aspect of the theory. Freud conceived of psychical processes by means of the category of quantity, even though the latter was mysterious, and remained 'unknown', as the oft-quoted passage from *Beyond the Pleasure Principle* stated:

we know nothing of the nature of the excitatory process that takes place in the elements of the psychical systems, and . . . we do not feel justified in forming any hypothesis on the subject. We are consequently operating all the time with a large unknown factor, which we are obliged to carry over into every new formula. (SE 18: 30–1)

However, the concept of quantity was not contrasted with a more clearly defined concept of quality. What is the order of quality, which Freud sometimes aligned with consciousness, remained as indefinite as the domain of quantity. Just as he did for the 'magnitudes' of psychical energy, Freud insistently underlined the obscurity surrounding the quality of psychical energy: 'the problem of the quality of instinctual impulses . . . is still very obscure and has hardly been attacked up to the present' (SE 19: 44). For example, in 'The Economic Problem of Masochism', Freud suggested that the opposition between pleasure and unpleasure was not simply a ratio between an increase in the quantity of excitation causing unpleasure and a diminution of that causing pleasure. They appear also to depend on qualitative factors such as 'rhythms' and 'the temporal sequence of changes' (SE 19: 160). For 'the factor that determines the feeling is probably the amount of increase or diminution in the quantity of excitation *in a given period of time*' (Freud's emphasis, SE 18: 8). In 'The Project', Freud had linked 'periodicity' with consciousness, but had not elaborated on it.

THE EXTENSION OF THE CONCEPT OF QUANTITY

Now, there are in Freud's thinking quantitative concerns, which cannot easily be assimilated to the naturalist framework in which the theory is couched. Besides the more manifestly economic layers, which dealt with varying magnitudes of cathexes of psychical energy, there are diverse kinds of measurements and evaluations, which confirm that psychoanalytic theory is indeed utterly quantitative. However, by being so extended, 'quantity' loses its strict 'economic' value. Let us recall how in the Preface to the Fourth Edition of *Three Essays* (1920 [1905]), Freud was explicit about the attempt that psychoanalysis made at enlarging [*Erweiterung*], the concept of sexuality. Psychoanalysis was then accused of 'pan-sexualism', which constituted in the eyes of its critics a too radical extension, indeed a 'stretching' [*Ausdehnung*] of the concept. Elsewhere, the extension was compared to that of 'psychical', which one also had to extend in order to be able to point to what is unconscious, whereas it had up until then referred exclusively to what is conscious, as we pointed out in the Introduction. Having so widened the concept of sexuality up to the point where it ceased to refer exclusively to genital sexuality, sexuality had entirely to be redefined. Freud endorsed the 'piece of unification' that language has carried out by creating the word 'love'. The theory of libido made use of the 'wider' concept of love, 'the "Eros" of the philosopher Plato': 'Libido is an expression taken from the theory of emotions . . . [It is] the energy, regarded as a quantitative magnitude (though not at present actually measurable), of those instincts which have to do with all that may be comprised under the word "love"' (SE 18: 90–1). This included, as we saw in Chapter 2, sexual love, self-love, 'love for parents and children, friendship and love for humanity in general, and also devotion to concrete objects and to abstract ideas' (SE 18: 90).[3]

Freud did not speak about a similar extension of the concept of quantity, even though the Freudian theory of the unconscious invite us to rethink that heading. On this view, the rejection by philosophers of the economic point of view might rest on too narrow an understanding of quantification within Freud, one that sees the concept too rigidly within the sciences of nineteenth-century physico-physiological sciences to which Freud was still undeniably indebted. Commentators recognize Freud's ingenuity in extending the concept of sexuality and of 'psychical'. When it comes to the quantitative, economic aspects of the theory, however, it looks as though he had imported the concept of quantity and its derivatives unchanged from the scientific nineteenth-century sources (the chemico-physical laws of the School of Helmholtz). Our presentation of Freud should have allowed us to question that assumption. It is to that extension of the concept of quantity that 'quantitative considerations' point.[4]

QUANTITATIVE CONSIDERATIONS

One finds quantitative considerations at different levels of Freud's thinking. For example, for Freud, as for many other nineteenth-century scientists, the difference between the normal and the pathological is quantitative. The distinction follows on from the quantitative description of psychical activity, which 'The Project' sketches, and whose elaboration the metapsychology pursues. Nevertheless, pathological 'magnifications' do not simply denote a threatening increase of energy (or an upsurge of excitations) (SE 1: 312). When Freud evaluated the 'pathogenic significance of the constitutional factors' in the context of the theory of the drives, it looked as though the quantitative factor was the determinant of illness: 'It may even be supposed that the disposition of all human beings is qualitatively alike and that they differ only owing to . . . quantitative conditions' (SE 16: 374–5). That is, our difference would lie in 'how much *more* of one component instinct than of another is present in [our] inherited disposition' (Freud's emphasis, SE 16: 374). Rather than being synonymous with an objective external view on individual subjects, it is in that quantitative factor that Freud situated differences from one individual to the next. Everyone might have what it takes to develop neurosis – each stage of the sexual development of the human individual is potentially the point of anchorage of an illness. However, it is only when I reach a certain *quota* that I become ill in a particular way. For in neurotic illness, 'it is a matter of *what quota* of unemployed libido a person is able to hold in suspension and of *how large a fraction* of his libido he is able to divert from sexual to sublimated aims' (Freud's emphasis, SE 16: 375). In that context, one could understand the extension of the concept of quantity as a means of modifying existing constitutional and hereditary theories of mental illnesses (see Assoun 1997: 382). In Chapter 4, we considered how the notion of 'trauma' implied that the mental apparatus should be suddenly 'flooded with large amounts of stimulus', which it could not quite control through the pleasure principle, even though the model of the 'autoregulated' mind was aimed at explaining how the apparatus deals with these 'floods' and 'breaches' (SE 18: 29–30).

The distinction between the normal and the pathological introduces ideas of exaggerations and distortions involving quantity in another way. Pathological phenomena have, so to speak, a technical, optical property. 'Pathology', Freud wrote in 1932, 'has always done us the service of making discernible by isolation and exaggeration conditions which would remain concealed in a normal state' (SE 22: 121). For 'neurotics merely exhibit to us in a magnified and coarsened form what the analysis of dreams reveals to us in healthy people as well' (SE 6: 338), and 'perverse sexuality is nothing else than a magnified infantile sexuality split up into its separate impulses' (SE 6: 311). 'The distinction between nervous health and neurosis', Freud stated, 'is of a quantitative not of a qualitative nature' (SE 16: 457). However, quantitative here relates to the way in which pathology connects with normal processes by magnifying them: 'in order to arrive at an understanding of what seems so simple in normal phenomena, we shall have to turn to the field of pathology with its distortions and its exaggerations [*Vergrößerungen*]' (SE 14: 82). Let us recall that the sexual drive and its 'vicissitudes' are our instrument of observation of the drives, and that the problem was precisely that there was not so convenient a means of observation of the ego-instincts. It might be because it was possible to observe the sexual drive through its vicissitudes that it became such a central element of the theory of the unconscious, until Freud found a way to observe the ego-instincts through narcissism. To which quantitative register do the pathological magnifications and exaggerations belong? Quantity would appear both to send us to phenomena of increases (in the sum of excitations) and to the technical – indeed rhetorical – property of amplification.

Freud and others adopted the hypothesis of phylogenesis, whereby the development of the individual presents a reduced version of that of the species. The question arises as to the quantitative dimension of that hypothesis, which underlies, for example, Freud's theory of phantasy. Here, too, it is not a matter of the transformation of 'sums of excitations'; nevertheless there are relevant quantitative variations. Should one assimilate the reduction and the condensation, which the individual represents with respect to the species, with the other estimates of magnitudes?

Freud approached other phenomena through quantitative lenses, even though they were not directly a matter of sums and particles. We mentioned above, for example, the aggrandizement of the ego in 'megalomania', which consists in the extreme form of a normal process, in addition to entailing a magnification of the ego (see Freud's analysis of humour in 'Humour' [1927], which also involves a quantitative transformation of the ego). There is also the process of overestimation, which governs the formation of the super-ego by means of a condensation of experiences accumulated since childhood, as Freud explained in *The Ego and the Id* (1923). We also saw the outcome of the work of interpretation during the cure. In dreams, largeness and smallness relate to the child's desire to become an adult, therefore to the difference between the adult and the child as *The Interpretation* presents ('The appearance in dreams of things of great size and in great quantities and amounts, and of exaggeration generally, may be another childish characteristic' [SE 4: 268 n. 1]). However, Freud sometimes believed that the quantitative factor played no role, as in mass-phenomena, according to his analysis of them in *Group-Psychology and the Analysis of the Ego* (1921). He believed that one could not clarify the mystery of the formation of masses by resorting to the number of people composing them. Rather one must take into account the affective bond or the emotional tie that unites the people fusing in them. How does the quantitative factor, taken in this 'extended' sense, relate to the more restricted sense in which it is normally understood? In other words, do diminutions, increases, impoverishments and enrichments, and the variations of scale that mark psychical life lend themselves to the scrutiny of a unified 'economic point of view'?

We could relate these quantitative considerations to rhetorics (quantity is also a concept of poetics), and consider how Freud's analysis of dreams acquires a quantitative dimension in that sense (the linguistic understanding of the unconscious by Lacan would reinforce the quantitative dimension of Freud's work rather than being opposed to it).[5] Or else, we could say that pathological magnifications are the product of his theoretical work. However, these extensions and exaggerations are not merely figures in Freud's text. They raise an interesting question: what is the relation, if there is one, between the economy of accumulations and discharge, which govern psychical life and which are the object of the metapsychological work, and the more diffuse quantitative variations that organize all aspects of human life, according to the theory of the unconscious?

THINKING AS A QUANTITATIVE REDUCTION

We considered above the experience of satisfaction. One of the factors of development of the psychical apparatus was linked with the inefficiency of hallucinating for appeasing our needs. It had no effect since it was regressive; it did not turn the apparatus towards the external world, but towards an inefficient, superseded means of satisfaction: 'Instead of [hallucinating], the psychical apparatus had to decide to form a conception of the real circumstances in the external world and to endeavour to make a real alteration in them' (SE 12: 219).

The motor discharge, which was used to divert the accumulation of stimuli, by turning towards the inside of the body, was converted into *action*. The introduction of the secondary processes, thanks to which the pleasure principle was replaced by the principle of reality, aimed towards establishing the thinking process, which allowed the apparatus to 'tolerate an increased tension of stimulus while the process of discharge was postponed' (SE 12: 221). In this context, thinking involved a quantitative reduction, which is defined as 'an experimental kind of acting, accompanied by displacement of relatively small quantities of cathexis together with less expenditure (discharge) of them' (SE 12: 221). As thinking also involved a 'conversion of freely displeacable cathexes into "bound" cathexes' (SE 12: 221), the dynamic opposition between 'free' and 'bound' energy also takes on a quantitative character – the 'binding' consisting in a reduction of sort. Subsequently, thinking is a technique used by the ego for exploring reality, involving saving and expenditure: 'Thinking is an experimental action carried out with small amounts of energy, in the same way as a general shifts small figures about on a map before setting his large bodies of troops in motion' (SE 22: 89). Thinking would appear to be a matter of saving and of expenditure.

Giving up of the early mode of satisfaction by hallucinating connects with the doctrine of reward in the afterlife. It is possible to abandon it because there are forms of compensation for that giving up. One can readily renounce an immediate pleasure if it will allow one to gain 'an assured pleasure at a later time' (SE 12: 223). Freud called the first kind of pleasure a fore-pleasure, an *incentive bonus*, a yield of pleasure (or even an aesthetic pleasure). The idea of 'bonus' comes from the fact that the pleasure is 'offered to us so as to make possible the release of still greater pleasure arising from deeper psychical sources' (SE 12: 223). The Christian doctrine of reward would be 'a mythical projection of this revolution in the mind (SE 12: 223)'. Anticipating *The Future of an Illusion*, which proposed a psychoanalytic understanding of religious beliefs, Freud affirmed that science alone fully succeeded in surmounting the pleasure principle by adopting the principle of reality (that constituted a 'normal' step in the development of the ego [SE 16: 357]). We will consider that step further below. For the moment suffice it to note that as we move into cultural domains (such as religion and civilization), the 'quantitative dimension' of phenomena cannot quite be reduced to the economic point of view. Conversely, Freud's psychoanalytic framework attracts our attention to the quantitative dimension of cultural phenomena (the *incentive bonus* of aesthetic pleasure, and the idea of 'projection' in the external world of some surmounted wish). Our perplexity towards the economic, quantitative dimension of the theory of the unconscious, then, might not come from the indefiniteness of the basic concept of quantity (even though it is undeniably so). Rather, it may come from the way in which it makes us pass from the scientific to cultural, aesthetic realms. The economic point of view might show, even more than the extension of the concepts of sexuality and of the psychical, that the unconscious reality with which psychoanalysis is concerned requires the modification of existing concepts.

'IT ALL SEEMS TO BE A QUESTION OF ECONOMY' (SE 8: 42)

In addition to 'The Project', one of the places where Freud most developed the economic approach to psychical processes is in *Jokes*. As a direct outcome of *The Interpretation*, since dreams tended to be witty, Freud investigated jokes, which he deemed to be 'the most social of all mental functions that aim at a yield of pleasure' (SE 8: 179). As in 'The "Uncanny"' (1919), and in 'The Moses of Michelangelo' (1914), among other works, Freud turned to aesthetic theory (Jean Paul Richter, Friedrich Theodor Vischer, Theodor Lipps and Immanuel Kant among others) for collecting existing views on the *Witz*, the better to contrast them with the psychoanalytic one (as he had done in the first chapter of *The Interpretation*). 'A new joke', Freud wrote, 'acts almost like an event of universal interest; it is passed from one person to another like the news of the latest victory' (SE 8: 15).[6] With jokes the juxtaposition of 'stories' and 'mechanisms' is even more striking than elsewhere. Not only do jokes consist in a wealth of stories, and come with an 'urge to tell' them to someone (SE 8: 143), but the pleasure one takes in them would seem to emerge directly from processes themselves; as a case in point, from the process of economy. For, as we will see, economy is the central concern of of Freud's analysis of jokes. But 'economy' in *Jokes* is equivocal. There is 'the economy in the use of as few words as possible or of words as much alike as possible'. However, there is also 'an economy in the far more comprehensive sense of psychical expenditure in general'

(SE 8: 118–19), which Freud eventually discarded for the adoption of a more complex economical account of a process of relief. The latter emerged from the analysis of the social nature of jokes.[7] Let us explore these two senses of economy and indicate how they lead to quantitative considerations.

SAVING AND PLEASURE

Jokes pose problems of translation.[8] However, it is not solely when passing from one language into another that they do so, as when one reads Freud in English. A joke cannot easily be translated into other words altogether. For when doing so, its comical, pleasurable effect disappears. Freud called the process of undoing the joke-work [*Witzarbeit*] a reduction that consists in 'replacing its form of expression by another one, while carefully preserving its sense' (SE 8: 95). The joke depends on its wording, and 'a change in it involves the disappearance of the joke' (SE 8: 52–3). As dreams, jokes consist of a particular form of thinking. It is possible to distinguish between their techniques (the joke-techniques), purposes and mechanisms.

Leaving aside the English examples that Freud provided, the first example of the book is one of the most translatable instances (Freud's choice of them was motivated by whether jokes made us laugh and lent themselves to analysis. Jewish jokes best fulfilled these two requirements [SE 8: 49]).[9] The joke comes from Heinrich Heine, who reported the speech of a man who was boasting about his relations with the Baron Rothschild: ' "And, as true as God shall grant me all good things, Doctor, I sat beside Salomon Rothschild and he treated me quite as his equal – quite famillionairely" ' (SE 8: 16). That joke should illustrate how there is economy in 'joke-techniques', such as in the 'condensation accompanied by the formation of a substitute' (SE 8: 19). That joke says 'in *too* few words' what it has to say (Freud's emphasis, SE 8: 13). Translating it entails adding some sentences, with the hope of being able to produce an 'unjoking expression' of the thought: 'R. treated me quite as his equal, quite familiarly [*familiär*] . . . that is, so far as a millionaire [*Millionär*] can' (SE 8: 18). The 'composite structure' is made up of elements of the two words, which share the letters 'ili' and 'är', thanks to a process that Freud described in physical terms. Earlier we came up against Freud's concrete, almost bodily description of mental processes. Here the description is even more physical. A 'compressing force' exerts pressure on the two sentences – the ones that translate the joke – especially on the second one, which is the 'less resistant one':

> [The second sentence] is thereupon made to disappear, while its most important constituent, the word '*Millionär*', which has succeeded in rebelling against being suppressed, is, as it were, pushed up against the first sentence, and fused with the element of that sentence which is so much like it – '*familiär*'. (SE 8: 19)

However, to note that there is a condensation of two words into one, and that there is the creation of a new word, does not exactly tell us why 'famillionairely' [*famillionär*] should make us laugh, nor whether condensation is a universal feature of jokes.

Other examples and techniques of verbal and conceptual jokes share a 'tendency to compression' or to *saving* (SE 8: 42). Among other techniques there are displacement, faulty reasoning, absurdity, indirect representation, representation by the opposite' (SE 8: 88). Even the multiple use of words entails a saving. This can be illustrated by a play upon words that spread when Napoleon III first gained power and imposed his first acts. People used to say about them: ' "C'est le premier vol de l'aigle" ["It is the eagle's first *vol*"] "*Vol*" means "flight" but also "theft" ' (SE 8: 37). It makes us pass 'economically' from a figure of prominence to criminality.

Condensation, then, best introduced the 'tendency to economy' as the most general characteristic of joke-techniques. However, since 'not every economy of expression, not every abbreviation is . . . a joke' a special kind of economy and abbreviation should be at stake (SE 8: 44). Through the exploration of joke-techniques Freud offered a treatise on the production of puns, absurdities, analogies and comparisons, among others, inspired by and against the views developed in existing aesthetic theory of the *Witz*, in which economy also plays a role. Jokes allow us to observe *saving* at the level of language (they allow us literally to see their processes of composition). For the economy in language is not in itself comical, and this is only one facet of Freud's analysis of jokes. The economy in jokes relates to the functioning of the psychical apparatus, which seeks to save and to maintain levels of excitations as low as possible. The question arises as to why the economy involved in the play with language and conceptual thought should connect with the economical functioning of the mental apparatus.

JOKES EVOKE A FEELING OF PLEASURE

The observation that the character of jokes lies in their form of expression (SE 8: 17) goes together with the common experience that 'the technical methods of joking . . . possess the power of evoking a feeling of pleasure in the hearer' (SE 8: 95). How do they acquire that power? The economical character of Freud's classification of jokes (between verbal and conceptual, 'innocent' and 'tendentious' ones) is of particular interest. Leaving aside the details of that classification, it is tendentious jokes that show most clearly how the pleasure that jokes produce in fact lies in the saving of psychical expenditure (those that aim at proffering an insult by indirect means). They 'liberat[e] pleasure by getting rid of inhibitions' (SE 8: 134). That the jokes '*evade restrictions and open sources of pleasure that have become inaccessible*' is apparent in hostile jokes, among other tendentious jokes (Freud's emphasis, SE 8: 103), since under their cover it is possible to criticize, say, persons in authority or institutions (SE 8: 105). However, the generation of pleasure through the lifting of repression is only one facet of a 'more complex situation of release' (SE 8: 135). For the pleasure from jokes becomes, according to the aesthetic principle of assistance that Freud borrowed from Fechner, a 'fore-pleasure'. That first kind of pleasure has a 'bribing' function: jokes produce laughter, which distracts the hearer's attention by offering a certain amount of pleasure. It is thanks to that bribery that still greater sources of pleasure can be liberated. The 'liberation' of psychical energy constitutes the 'saving', the 'economy' (liberation becomes a quantitative occurrence). That process echoes the struggle between sentences with which Freud opened his study. Tendentious jokes 'put themselves at the service of purposes [aggressiveness, defence] in order that, by means of using the pleasure from jokes as a fore-pleasure, they may produce new pleasure by lifting suppressions and repressions' (SE 8: 137). The mode of operation of (tendentious) jokes involves a struggle between the 'free use of thoughts and words' and 'reason, critical judgement, suppression (SE 8: 137)' (on the distracting of attention, see SE 8: 153).

THE GENESIS OF JOKES

One of Freud's basic assumptions is that civilization rests on the renunciation of the drives (or the renunciation of the pleasure principle; let us recall the way in which the psychical apparatus has to adopt the principle of reality). This occurs through the process of repression and defence against the drives (as we saw with the development of sexuality). A corollary to that process is that 'to the human psyche all renunciation is exceedingly difficult' (SE 8: 101), and the human being is forever seeking means to enjoy a pleasure that it has once known (Freud attributed a similar tendency to the drive itself under the heading of the 'compulsion to repeat' [see SE 18: 36–8]). One keeps aiming to undo the repression on which civilization rests. There are different formulations of that process at different epochs of Freud's research: in terms of the drives, of sexuality, of the ego, of the super-ego (in 'On Humour' [1927]). Jokes have a share in that overall story, but they touch more particularly on the repression that presides over the acquisition of language, and on the relation between language and the world.

Joking makes adults go back (or regress) to a time when they acquired language, and when it was still permitted to play with it. In that way, the various categories of jokes – play upon words, jest and so on – correspond to stages of intellectual development. They make adults regress to 'an embryonic point of view' (SE 8: 171). That pleasure is gradually taken away from the child up until s/he is forced to use language seriously, under the constraints of critical reason. The imposition on the child of logical thinking and of linguistic laws goes together with a rebellion on his/her part against 'the compulsion to logic and reality' (SE 8: 126), to which 'the phenomena of imaginative activity' belong (SE 8: 126).[10] On that view, play and jest are preliminary stages of jokes (SE 8: 129), which are thwarted by reasonableness.[11] For a joke is 'developed play' (SE 8: 179).

A 'PLUNGE INTO THE UNCONSCIOUS' (SE 8: 169)

There is another sense in which Freud provided a genetic account of jokes. The 'mode of operation' of jokes, which could be described as a struggle between reason and the free use of words and thoughts, is repeated each time a joke 'erupts' (jokes are involuntary productions, which require to be told to someone). Where do they take their power of 're-establishing old liberties' (SE 8: 127), of circumventing critical reason? Freud offered a dynamico-topographical account of them. For joke-techniques owe their characteristics to the primitive functioning of the mental apparatus (to primary processes), to which they make adults regress. Their techniques 'arise automatically . . . during thought-processes in the unconscious' (SE 8: 169), which correspond to an infantile way of thinking (Freud speaks of the 'childhood of reason' [SE 8: 170]). Strikingly, uncovering unconscious material is indeed 'comic' (SE 8: 170). However, unlike dreams jokes do not simply 'indulge' in that primitive mode of thinking.

DREAMS AND JOKES

The main difference between dreams and jokes lies in the fact that a dream 'is a completely asocial mental product [which] arises within the subject as a compromise between the mental forces struggling in him . . . it can . . . make use of the mechanisms that dominate unconscious mental processes' (SE 8: 179). By contrast, as we said above, 'a joke is the most social of all social productions that aim at a yield of pleasure' (SE 8: 179). The production of a joke indeed implies the presence of at least three persons, one of whom completes the process that it triggers (SE 8: 179). The social set-up in which joking necessarily occurs imposes a certain degree of intelligibility to the joke (unlike the dream which 'remains unintelligible' to the dreamer and is of no interest to anyone else). Jokes therefore owe something to unconscious processes (their techniques are the same as that of the dream-work), and resemble dreams in that respect. But because they need to be intelligible to someone other than the joke-maker, they cannot entirely be left to the whims of unconscious thought, of the primary processes. In jokes, the thought 'plunges into the unconscious' only momentarily: '*a preconscious thought*', that is, a thought that is capable of becoming conscious, because it is not repressed, '*is given over for a moment to unconscious revision and the outcome of this is at once grasped by conscious perception*' (Freud's emphasis; SE 8: 166). Freud proposes another 'formula': '*the joke* . . . is the contribution made to the comic from the realm of the unconscious' (Freud's emphasis; SE 8: 208).

The social nature of jokes closely relates to the problem of laughter, the analysis of which best shows the economical character of Freud's account of joking. The joke indeed erupts with an urge 'to communicate the joke', for no one can laugh at one's own jokes (SE 8: 143). The mechanism of pleasure obtained through saving is that of the hearer who 'gives evidence of his pleasure with a burst of laughter' (SE 8: 145). Indeed, the 'third person' completes the process that a joke triggers (SE 8: 179). The presence and the absence of laughter tell us whether or not the joke-maker has produced a joke. Laughter tests the success of the joke. Freud provided a quantitative definition of laughter, a modification of Herbert Spencer's view on laughter and discharge: 'laughter arises if a quota of psychical energy which has earlier been used for the cathexis of particular psychical paths has become unusable, so that it can find free discharge' (SE 8: 147).[12] It is in the hearer that the economy of psychical energy directly occurs, for s/he did not have to spend any energy at all to produce a pleasurable effect (the joke-maker can retrieve some of the pleasurable effect *par ricochet* [SE 8: 156]). The hearer is a saver (SE 8: 149), for the 'amount' of pleasure s/he experiences corresponds to the amount of saving produced by the joke (to 'the quota of psychical energy which has become free through the lifting of the inhibitory cathexis' (SE 8: 149); see SE 12: 115–16 and chapter 1 above 'Beyond the Cathartic Method'). Freud goes so far as to state that the hearer of the joke 'laughs this quota off' (SE 8: 149). Laughter gives a concrete character to the social nature of the joke, but also to the economical process of joking, and of the psychical apparatus. Whereas for Binswanger, the mechanisms were underlying, joking, and the comic in particular) displays the mechanisms even more 'visibly' than dreams do. This is the case with respect to the manifestation of laugher, but also because jokes allow one to derive 'pleasure from [one's] processes of thought' (SE 8: 123).[13]

THE COMIC OF MOVEMENT

In order to explore the articulation between stories and mechanisms further, we can turn to a process that Freud calls *ideational mimetics* [*Vorstellungsmimik*], which participates in the production of the comic of movement, according to Freud's account of the comic that follows on from that of jokes. As with the joke, the comic occurs in a social situation and it involves two persons. However, here it shows how Freud's economic account in fact moves us towards non-strictly economical concerns.

The production of the comic differs from that of jokes in many respects (notably with respect to the fact that the knowledge of the dream does not help us to understand its mechanisms, as it does with the joke). However, it rests as much as the joke on the '*economy in expenditure on inhibition or suppression*' (Freud's emphasis; SE 8: 119), a saving of psychical expenditure. The comic comes from contradictory elements: 'sometimes an excess and sometimes an insufficiency seems to be the source of comic pleasure' (SE 8: 196 n. 1). The economy of expenditure is realized when one seeks to understand the other, by putting oneself in someone else's place, by empathy, a notion that Freud borrowed from Jean Paul, one of the sources of *Jokes*.

The source of the comic and of jokes diverges: the production of the comic occurs involuntarily in the social relations between men (and women), notably in movements. The comic of movement lies in the way in which a movement may appear 'extravagant and inexpedient', for we laugh about a too large, unnecessary amount of expenditure manifested by an 'exaggerated, expressive' or 'pointless movement'. How do we perceive or experience that disproportion? By comparing 'on the one hand the psychical expenditure while we are having a certain idea' and 'the content of the thing that we are having the idea of'. The explanation rests on the assumption that the representation of the thing or the 'content of the idea' corresponds to an amount of psychical energy (SE 8: 190–1). For Freud assumed that 'the idea of something large demands more expenditure than the idea of something small' (SE 8: 191). If it is possible to assimilate the 'attribute of the idea' to 'an attribute of what we have an idea of', it is because 'I have acquired the idea of a movement of a particular size by carrying the movement out myself or by imitating it, and through this action, I have learned a standard for this movement in my innervatory sensations' (SE 8: 191). Movements leave memory-traces in the same way as events, words, stages of development do. The gesture is represented by nothing other than the memory-trace of the amount of energy it required (SE 8: 192). The memory-trace constitutes the standard through which I evaluate someone else's gesture (even if in what a memory-trace consists falls within Freud's speculative concepts).

The comparison, then, does not proceed from my imitation of his/her gesture. For 'instead of imitating the movement with my muscles, I have an idea of it through the medium of my memory-traces of expenditures on similar movements' (SE 8: 191–2). Freud refers the substitution of the movement by a memory-trace to the quantitative conception of 'thinking', which we saw above. Accordingly, 'ideation or "thinking" differ from acting . . . above all

154

in the fact that it displaces far smaller cathectic energies and holds back the main expenditure for discharge' (SE 8: 192). Here, however, the reduction explicitly raises the problem of the representation of quantity:

> But how is the *quantitative* factor – the greater or lesser size – of the perceived movement to be given expression in the idea? And if there can be no representation of quantity in the idea, which is made up of qualities, how can I distinguish the ideas of movements of different sizes? – how can I make the comparison on which everything here depends? (Freud's emphasis, SE 8: 192)

Since the comic comes from the perception of excesses, one must be able to distinguish between various magnitudes. Yet how should one evaluate them? The economic component of the metapsychological outlook, which entailed 'following the vicissitudes of amounts of excitation' so as to 'arrive at some *relative* estimate of their magnitude' (Freud's estimate, SE 14: 181) resurfaces. The estimation of magnitudes on which the explanation of symptom-formation and of other mental disturbances rested is now integrated into that of the production and enjoyment of the comic. With the joke, it was possible to perceive the condensation, the 'saving' at the level of the words. Syllables were omitted, joined together, and that economy of material was immediately discernible. Various techniques of condensation presided over the production of jokes. Confronted with play on language by jokes, I can refer myself to the daily use of language. It is possible to compare the amount of expenditure that they make one save with that required for the ordinary use of language. With the comic of movement, during the 'act of representing', innervations go towards the muscles and correspond to a 'very modest amount of expenditure' of energy. It is muscular innervation, rather than truncated syllables, that becomes a means for representing 'the quantitative factor of the idea' (SE 8: 192).

For Freud, it is possible to experience the 'excess' in the following manner: in order to perceive a specific movement I represent it to myself and I thus spend some energy, by putting myself in someone else's place. I compare the perceived movement to mine: 'If the other person's movement is exaggerated and inexpedient, my increased expenditure in order to understand it is inhibited *in statu nascendi*, as it were in the act of being mobilized' (SE 8: 194). I laugh because

I perceive that the other has required of him/herself 'more expenditure' than was necessary. The comical effect rests on a quantitative contrast between two amounts of expenditure. The comparison can take place between the other's expenditure and mine, from empathy, or between two processes that I myself produce. Indeed, the quantitative variations in the function of discharge are comic (and are not solely the matter of neurosis). The 'internal' comparison occurs, for example, around the state of expectation. The latter involves a temporal comparison between a present and a future state. Too great a contrast between various levels of discharge of energy brings about disappointment. (See 'On Humour'. The quantitative factor takes on the quality of a state of mind (SE 21: 165).)

One is dealing with expenditures of psychical investments, but we are not strictly speaking dealing with the economic register of the metapsychology. As with laughter, there seems to be with the comic of movement a concern for the immediate representation of quantity (of the variations between 'small' and 'large'). We pass from exaggerated movements that make us laugh, to the idea that movement in general stands as a quantitative measure. While pathology magnifies normal processes, the comic of movement makes excesses of quantity discernible. (The comic of movement makes discernible the pathological increases of quantity.) For humans indicate 'quantities and intensities' by means of movements. This does not simply consist in paintings with the hands – which would go up and down to indicate greater or smaller sizes and scales – but also includes the raising and lowering of the voice, the opening and the blinking of the eyes, by extension, all modes of expression.[14] One finds the comic among men and women in ordinary human relations. Gestures and facial expressions reveal the quantitative aspect of bodily movements: what they manifest are not 'affects', but rather the 'content of what [one] is having an idea of' (SE 8: 193). That kind of representation does not have a communicative function. It is an element of thinking: it occurs 'as well when the subject is forming an idea of something for his own private benefit and is thinking of something pictorially' (SE 8: 193). The body expresses what is greater and smaller 'by a change in the innervation of his features and sense organs' (SE 8: 193). Let us recall how, in *The Interpretation*, Freud spoke of the bodily features of the attitude of self-observation, which was a precondition to the therapeutic associative work (SE 4: 100). The 'quantitative factor' seems to be limited to the category of the small and large, even though Freud underlined that it was not. For even though the analysis of psychical expenditure is extended to the 'expenditure on the tightening the attention . . . and the expenditure on abstraction' (SE 8: 198), he ends up by considering these other kinds of expenditure in terms of the category of the 'large and small'. For the latter leads to a fundamental evaluation: 'since what is more interesting, more sublime and even more abstract are only special cases, with particular qualities, of what is larger' (SE 8: 198).

Rather than being limited to the domain of the economic description of expenditures and somatic excitations, quantitative considerations lead us to the Freudian theory of culture. The comic of gestures and facial expression in terms of contrasts between smaller and larger expenditures relates to 'the restriction of muscular work and the increase of conceptual work' that underlies the advance towards 'a superior degree of culture' of which we spoke in Chapter 4. Freud presented that idea again among other places in *Moses and Monotheism: Three Essays* (1939 [1937–39]), where the 'advance in intellectuality' depends upon how remote one stands with respect to sensuality. The greatest distance from the sensible world is represented by paternity, that is, by a parental bond that is a hypothesis 'based on an inference and a premiss' rather than on any sensible proof, as is maternity (SE 23: 114).[15] The idea of spiritual progress provided another angle on perceptions of excesses. It is possible to perceive how psychical work represents a spiritual advancement from bodily work through the exploration of the comic. We laugh because of the difference between our perceived superiority and the perceived inferiority of the other (SE 8: 195) (or in a register that is no longer strictly mechanistic, but rather moral, we laugh thanks to the 'greatness' that we are attributing to ourselves). The analysis of the comic occupies a marginal place in Freud's work, and in his studies on *Jokes*. Yet it provides precious indications on how what is described in terms of 'quantitative differences of cathexes' is converted not so much into qualities, but into further 'quantities', as though Freud wanted to give an account of what it would be like to give an account of quantity in the moral and aesthetic registers.

THE FUTURE OF AN ILLUSION (1927)

Freud's critique of religion in *The Future of an Illusion* (1927) is announced in 'Formulation on the Two Principles of Mental

Functioning' (1911), which recounted the gradual adaptation of the psychical apparatus to the 'principle of reality'. This is because for Freud religious beliefs are illusions, beliefs forged by desire (Wollheim 1971: 220), the purpose of which is to ease the renunciation to the pleasure principle on which culture rests. Let us recall that Freud joins religion to myth in that they are both 'projection' of a psychical process in the external world. Religious illusions constitute, with other methods, such as the use of narcotics, or the 'choice' of neurosis, an expedient for supporting the suffering caused by renunciation. Illusions and beliefs should disappear; their disappearance will mark the moment when 'the intellect' will win over and dominate instinctual life. *The Future of an Illusion* repeats what 'Formulations' had already stated: science alone could succeed in eliminating as tenacious illusions as religious ones.

The critique of religion takes up again the problem of desire, of wish-fulfilment and of instinctual demands, of the state of helplessness [*Hilflosigkeit*], but on another scale. Freud sought to understand the discrepancy between the progress made in the domination of nature and in the regulation of human affairs. The pessimistic outlook on the antisocial and anti-cultural character of men is not provoked by all men, but by the masses who do not like instinctual renunciation, and who must be led by exemplary individuals. How can one educate recalcitrant masses, who refuse to submit themselves to the constraint of work and renunciation? Assuredly, a great number of superior leaders will be necessary, given the difficulty of the task, since it is the 'poorer classes' who feel most intensely the dissatisfaction in which culture places individuals (and they are the most dangerous for that reason). It may be possible to find an answer in the genesis of instinctual renunciation, of the establishment of prohibitions and of the means that have been employed to maintain them. Among these (the interiorization of constraint by the superego, the various ideals, art, narcissistic satisfaction, etc.), religious beliefs and illusions are the most significant.

The one who participates in culture is in a state of helplessness (Chapter IV). Culture and nature (in the form of destiny) both protect him/her and inflict upon him/her damages against which s/he must defend him/herself, as the child confronted with his parents, who are both dreadful and protective. One of the ways in which culture protects its offspring against nature is to 'humanize' nature, to give it the forms of gods (who have the characters of the father), and who have a triple function. Religious representations are born of the need to render tolerable human helplessness. It is in this context that religious representations are described as illusions, that is, as 'fulfilments of the oldest, strongest and most urgent wishes of humanity' (SE 21: 30). They hold their strength from that of the wishes. With the concept of illusion, we are not dealing with an error of perception, or with an opposition to reality. We speak of illusions when wish-fulfilment, that is when a regressive form of satisfaction, predominates.

It would be easy to retain from that work only the hackneyed theory of the instinctual renunciation that culture imposes, and Freud's scepticism towards religion to the benefit of science, which is recognized as the sole means of acquiring knowledge about the world. However, Freud here provides another example of the extension of the idea of quantity. Religion gives rise to the problematic application of psychoanalysis, in so far as the properly psychoanalytic concepts are only 'daringly' appropriate to the analysis of culture by means of extrapolations (as Freud states on numerous occasions in *Moses and Monotheism*). In addition to the quantitative variations involved in the mental processes of wish-fulfilment and to the role that helplessness and narcissism play in religion, there is the fact that a great number of individuals contribute to maintain religious illusions. In 'Obsessive Actions and Religious Practices' (1907), Freud had assimilated individual neurosis to religion by conceiving of religion as a collective neurosis. The neurosis in which illusions participate is a mass neurosis, a disproportionate neurosis. Here quantity refers us back to demography. Freud deployed the opposition between religion and the primacy of the intellect against that of a great quantity of people and of a small number, who have access to the highest degree of renunciation, to the pleasure principle which science represents. What Freud reproached religion for, then, is not that it is 'irrational', but that it is 'shared'. In this way, human masses extend the phenomena of the wish-fulfilment, helplessness and narcissism; they exaggerate them. A quantitative contrast is created between intellectual work, thought and religion, which fall into the category of the 'great', before the *restrictive* influence of thought.

NOTES

INTRODUCTION

1 Throughout this book, references to *The Standard Edition of the Complete Psychological Works of Sigmund Freud*, vols 1–24, ed. J. Strachey in collaboration with A. Freud, A. Strachey and A. Tyson, assisted by A. Richards (London: Hogarth Press and the Institute of Psychoanalysis, 1953–74), are given as SE, followed by the volume and page number.

2 For Edmund Husserl, it was possible to criticize natural sciences through scientific psychology, which he did, among other places, in the posthumous *Crisis of the European Sciences and Transcendental Phenomenology* ([1936] 1970).

3 For a recent study of the idea of the unconscious before Freud, see, among others, Rand 2004. Jonathan Lear writes: 'Freud's great discovery is not of the unconscious per se, but of an archaic level of mental functioning that is, at first, so alien as to be unrecognizable' (1990: 6).

4 See 'Heredity and the Neuroses' (SE 3: 151). In *Studies on Hysteria* (1893–5) and in 'The Neuro-Psychoses of Defence' (1894), the new method is called 'psychical analysis' (SE 2: 273 and SE 3: 47).

5 See P.-L. Assoun (1976: 33–6) For a discussion of the contemporary philosophers Freud was referring to, when he reported reactions to the concept of the unconscious. On Freud's transcendental interpretation of hysteria, see Bergo 2004.

6 One finds one of the clearest expositions of the meanings of the unconscious in 'A Note on the Unconscious in Psychoanalysis' ([1912] SE 12: 255–66), and the metapsychological study 'The Unconscious' ([1915] SE 14: 161–215).

7 For a review of some of the critical responses to Freud, see among others Erwin 1997: 671–88, especially 671–96. See too Wollheim 1982 and Mills 2004.

8 For a useful analysis of some attacks against Freud, see Forrester 1997.

9 An early attempt to 'repair' Freud's work is by Roland Dalbiez, in *La Méthode Psychanalytique et la Doctrine freudienne* [The Psychoanalytic Method and Freudian Doctrine] (1936), where the author suggested that

we distinguish between metaphysical constructions and doubtful interpretations and the 'facts' obtained by applying the psychoanalytic
method – the therapeutic cure (Assoun 1981: 35). The typical diagnostic approach to Freud consists in holding Freud to be a 'naive child of
knowledge, revealing worlds of meaning with the epistemological inno-
cence of the non-philosopher' (Assoun 1981: 27 [my translation]). In so
far as it involves the distinction between 'description' and 'explanation',
let us mention Alasdair Macintyre's influential study, *The Unconscious.
A Conceptual Analysis* (1958), where the philosopher argued that 'Freud
treats motives as causes' (1997: 60), whereas 'an essential part of Freud's
achievement lies not in his explanations of abnormal behaviour but in
his redescription of such behaviour' (1997: 61). Macintyre's analysis
converges with Binswanger at least in so far as both commentators
devalue Freud's 'causal story'.
10 See Ricoeur's discussion of phenomenological approaches to psychoanalysis (1970 [1965]: 344–418).
11 See Strachey's comment in SE 1: xxiv–xxv, for the contested translation of
Trieb into instinct. The alternative is 'drive', which most commentators
conventionally use when they wish to distinguish *Trieb* from the biological *Instinkt*, which Strachey also translates into 'instinct'. See Lear 1990:
123–4. For the problems Freud's writings pose to translators, see Ornston
1992. In the following book, we will use 'drive' to refer to *Trieb*, but we will
keep Strachey's translation of *Trieb* as instinct when quoting from *The
Standard Edition of the Complete Psychological Works of Sigmund Freud*.
12 See Hesnard 1960.

1. THE PSYCHOANALYTIC CURE

1 'Report on my Studies in Paris and Berlin' ([1956] (1886) SE 1: 10). Freud
quoted his master's advice again in 'On the History of the Psycho-
Analytic Movement' ([1914] SE 14: 22), and in the 'Letter to *Le Disque
vert*' ([1924] SE 19: 290). He translated into German Charcot's *Leçons
sur les maladies du système nerveux: Tome Troisième* [*New Lectures on
the Diseases of the Nervous System, particularly on Hysteria*] (1886) and
the *Leçons du mardi* (1886). See editor's note to 'Charcot' (SE 3: 10).
2 In a letter to Binswanger, Freud 'affirme que, de même que Kant a
postulé l'existence de la chose en soi derrière l'apparence, il a postulé,
derrière le conscient accessible à notre expérience, l'inconscient, mais qui
ne pourra jamais être l'objet de l'expérience directe'. 'Binswanger's
second visit to Vienna. 15–26 January' (Freud Binswanger 1995: 87). See
Bergo 2004: 342. In a letter to Binswanger, Freud 'affirms that, just as
Kant had postulated the existence of the thing-in-itself behind appearance, he has postulated, behind the conscious realm accessible to experience, the unconscious, which will never be the object of direct
experience' (Freud Binswanger 1995: 87 [my translation]).
3 It was possible to distinguish, for example, between the 'universally familiar hysteria' and the 'obsessional neurosis'. The former is 'obtrusively

noisy' and the latter, 'more like a private affair of the patient's, it dispenses almost entirely with somatic phenomena . . .' (SE 16: 258). Manifestations appear therefore more often to be 'noisy' than 'visible' (see SE 6: 146 n. 1). Freud pointed out that 'in psycho-analysis we cannot do without what is at the same time unconscious and mental, and are accustomed to operate with it as though it were something palpable to the senses' (SE 16: 279).

4 See, for example, the first paragraph of 'Instincts and their Vicissitudes' ([1915] SE 14: 117) on how concepts relate to experience.

5 See Marinelli and Mayer 2003: 12–13.

6 See Bowlby 2006: 164ff.

7 *The Interpretation of Dreams* shows particularly clearly the collective nature of psychoanalysis since Freud's 'disciples' contributed noticeably to the successive revisions of the book, especially in the section on symbolism in Chapter 6.

8 See Appignesi and Forrester 1992 and Freeman 1994. For feminist perspectives on the 'Dora case', see Berheimer and Kahane 1985.

9 See how it is possible to induce blindness artificially through hypnosis in 'The Psychoanalytic View of Psychogenic Disturbance of Vision' ([1910] SE 11: 211).

10 See Derrida 1996: 12, on the two 'directions' in which analysis goes.

11 Freud attributed the profusion of 'symbolizations' by Frau Cäcilie to her special creative gifts and to the sense of form that her poems 'of great perfection' revealed. He was echoing Breuer's praise of Anna O.'s talents (SE 2: 180). Charles Darwin was already interested in the act of taking figures of speech literally in *The Expression of the Emotions* (1872) (SE 2: 181).

12 See Letter to Stefan Zweig, 2 June 1932, quoted in Assoun 1997: 114–15.

13 See Strachey's objection to the view that Freud developed a dynamic view of neuroses only after having replaced infantile traumatic events by infantile traumatic phantasies (SE 2: xx).

14 The case history of 'Dora' has received much critical attention in that respect. See Bernheimer and Kahane 1985 and Borch-Jacobsen 1996, among others.

15 The origin and the date mark of psychoanalysis is an object of controversy. There are many 'histories' of the passage from the cathartic method to 'psychoanalysis' (SE 3: 282).

16 For the first occurrence of the term 'unconscious', see SE 2: 45n.

17 This is the first mention of resistance according to Strachey (SE 2: 154 n. 1).

18 See 'Negation' (1925), where Freud writes that 'negation is a way of taking cognizance of what is repressed' (SE 19: 235).

19 Börne's piece is reproduced in J. E. Gedo and G. H. Pollock (eds), *Freud: The Fusion of Science and Humanism: The Intellectual History of Psychoanalysis* (New York: International Universities Press, 1976): pp.253–4.

20 In 1908, Freud embarked upon 'a general methodology of psychoanalysis', which he later abandoned (Marinelli and Mayer 2005: 14). The 'technical writings' in Volume 12 of the *Standard Edition* belong to that

incomplete project. Wilhelm Stekel's book on nervous anxiety states and their treatment (1908) was one of the first technical manuals written to the attention of practitioners (Marinelli and Mayer 2005 [2003]: 41–3).

2. THE JUXTAPOSITION OF STORIES AND MECHANISMS

1 See 'On Transience' (1916 [1915]; SE 14: 305–7), for a reflection on mourning which develops in a pastoral set-up.
2 'The basis for repression itself can only be a feeling of unpleasure, the incompatibility between the single idea that is to be repressed and the dominant mass of ideas constituting the ego. *The repressed idea takes its revenge, however, by becoming pathogenic*' (SE 2: 116, our emphasis).
3 In view of the way in which incompatible ideas come up against 'ethical standards', it is not surprising that Freud later proposes an interpretation of the progress of civilization in terms of the opposition between the drives and 'ethical standards'. The application of psychoanalytic theses to the development of civilization plays a fundamental role in the elaboration of psychoanalysis.
4 The giving up of hypnosis is gradual: at first, Freud tells his patients to 'concentrate', in a gesture reminiscent of hypnosis. One step includes 'mere insistence' (SE 2: 268).
5 Freud described the tendency in 1892 thus: '*The nervous system endeavours to keep constant something in its functional relations that we may describe as the "sum of excitations". It puts this precondition of health into effect by disposing associatively of every sensible accretion of excitation or by discharging it by an appropriate motor reaction*' (Freud's emphasis, SE 1: 154). Freud had presented that hypothesis privately to Fliess and Breuer during the late 1890s, and mentioned it in subsequent writings, but he discussed it fully only in *Beyond the Pleasure Principle* (1920): 'The mental apparatus endeavours to keep the quantity of excitation present in it as low as possible or at least to keep it constant' (SE 18: 9, quoted in Editor's Introduction SE 2: xx).
6 The expression of emotions is linked with symbolization in *Studies on Hysteria*. See SE 2: 180 on Darwin's *The Expression of the Emotions* (1872), Chapter 1, n. 11 above and Chapter 4 below.
7 Freud specifies in 'Fetishism' (1927) two concepts for the pushing away of the affect and of the idea. Repression [*Verdrängung*] applies to the affect, and disavowal [*Verleugnung*] to the idea (SE 21: 153).
8 In view of the idea of primary defence, the cure (the analysis of resistances as means of defence) was developed as though in order to mirror the pathological mechanisms (there is a homology between the formation of symptoms and the means to free the patient of them).
9 On sexuality and the comic, Freud writes: 'the spheres of sexuality and obscenity offer the amplest occasions for obtaining comic pleasure alongside pleasurable sexual excitement; for they can show human beings in their dependence on bodily needs (degradation) or they can reveal the psychical demands lying behind the claim of mental love

(unmasking)' (SE 8: 222). See on the comic the way in which primary processes are comic (SE 14: 186).

10 See Silberer 1914, on how the concept 'sexual' might have been submitted to 'an error of superimposition' (SE 16: 304).

11 De Lafayette 1992: 128.

12 When do the forces develop? See SE 7: 162 n. 2 on phylogenesis.

13 Freud stated that the motif of civilization is in the end 'economic': 'since it does not possess enough provisions to keep its members alive unless they work, it must restrict the number of its members and divert their energies from sexual activity to work' (SE 16: 312). See SE 15: 22–3 required by civilization the original sacrifice.

14 That neuroses retain the imprint of the development of the libido and of the ego is stated among other places in SE 12: 59–79.

3. DREAMS

1 A patient declares, when telling the analyst about his 'forgotten' memories during the cure: 'As a matter of fact I've always known it: only I've never thought of it' (SE 12: 148).

2 In obsessional neurosis, 'the poor ego feels itself responsible for all sorts of evil impulses of which it knows nothing, impulses which are brought up against it in consciousness but which it is unable to acknowledge' (SE 19: 133–4).

3 It is possible to read *The Interpretation of Dreams* as it was actually published in a recent translation of the text by Joyce Crick in Freud 1999. For a study exploring further the multifarious natures of the book, see Marcus 1999.

4 The book is a historical document for the historian of psychoanalysis, but it also contains echoes of Austrian, and especially Viennese, social and political life at the turn of the century. Freud's dreams often involved political figures or events (notably in so far as he lived through the period of the gradual exclusion of Jewish people from public office and life).

5 In 1914, Freud added references to contemporary anthropological works on the meaning of dreams in prehistoric times (SE 4: 2).

6 See *Psychopathology of Everyday Life* ([1901] SE 6: 147) about the stratification of the mental apparatus.

7 Jane Austen provides an interesting dynamic picture of memory in *Mansfield Park*: 'If any one faculty of our nature may be called *more* wonderful than the rest, I do think it is memory. There seems something more speakingly incomprehensible in the powers, the failures, the inequalities of memory than in any other of our intelligences. The memory is sometimes so retentive, so serviceable, so obedient – at others, so bewildered and so weak – and at others again, so tyrannic, so beyond control! – We are to be sure a miracle every way – but our powers of recollecting and of forgetting, do seem peculiarly past finding out' (Austen 2003 [1814]: 163).

8 Dreams have to do with the future as popular belief knew all along, except that 'the future which the dream shows us is not the one which

will occur but the one which we should *like* to occur' (Freud's emphasis, SE 5: 674).

9　See 'A Disturbance of Memory on the Acropolis' ([1936] SE 22: 239).

10　See Freud 2006: 589–92.

11　Weber 2002: 102.

12　This is particularly the case around the 'Irma injection dream'. See, for example, Mehlman 1976 and Sprengnether 2003.

13　The series of alarm-clock dreams is particularly telling. Here is one of Freud's such dreams: 'I always found it difficult to wake early. I used then to have a dream of being out of bed and standing by the washing-stand; after a while I was no longer able to disguise from myself the fact that I was really still in bed, but in the meantime I had had a little more sleep' (SE 4: 125).

14　Some linguistic symbols that are dreamt, and which are unknown to the dreamer 'probably originate from earlier phases in the development of speech' (SE 23: 166).

15　This recalls the way in which 'sexual aberrations' *analyse* the variable relation between the sexual aim and object, prior to their being obscured in the 'normal picture' of sexuality. See Chapter 2.

16　See Derrida 1967 on the primary and secondary processes.

17　The essay 'From the History of an Infantile Neurosis (The 'Wolf Man') (1918 [1914]) shows that not all children's dreams are as transparent as that of the young Anna Freud (see SE 17: 3).

18　See Foucault and Binswanger 1986, for a discussion of Freud's emphasis of the semantic side of dreams. Foucault's introduction to Binswanger's *Dream and Existence* is a good place to pursue the study of Binswanger's criticism of Freud.

19　Sontag 1990: 6–7.

20　Freud related his discovery of early affective wishes towards one's parents to the plays *Oedipus Rex* and *Hamlet*. The plays demonstrate according to Freud that these wishes are 'universal', against the views of modern anthropologists, who argue that Freud's theories are based on one particular family structure – the Viennese bourgeois one – and cannot be extended to 'everyone'. For an examination of the nineteenth-century literary context in which Freud's interest in and use of the Oedipus myth lie, see 'Freud's Classical Mythologies' in Bowlby 2007.

21　One of the famous criticisms of the notion of censorship, elaborated by Jean-Paul Sartre in *Being and Nothingness* (1943), was that, in order to have censorship, it was necessary to have some form of awareness of both the censoring agency and the censored material, that is, to have a third overlooking consciousness. See Gardner 1987.

22　See Gilman 1993.

4. AFFECT AND REPRESENTATION

1　Freud maintained that hypothesis in his understanding of anxiety in 1932. It is possible to give an accurate account of anxiety 'if we separate what happens to the idea that has to be repressed from what happens to the quota of libido attaching to it'. The idea is distorted, repressed and becomes unrecognizable, while the quota of affect may be transformed into anxiety (SE 22: 83).

2 For an account of the importance of language in psychoanalysis see Forrester 1980 and Chapters 3 above and 5 below.

3 Jonathan Lear writes: 'The value of treating an emotion as being a quantity of energy, the discharge of that quantity or the subjective appreciation of that discharge is that it holds open the possibility of explaining mental life in quantitative terms. And, of course, a quantitative treatment conforms to Freud's scientific image: it allows Freud to believe that he is approaching the subject of his study from an objective, third-personal point of view and that he is providing a mechanistic explanation of the phenomena. The cost of a quantitative treatment, though, is that it prevents him from seeing that what is at issue is an orientation to the world' (Lear 1990: 52).

4 See Wollheim 1971: 62–3, for a defence of Freud's economic conceptions. Criticism of the economic account comes from the fact that commentators 'usually dwell exclusively upon the distortions to which it is supposed to give rise as far as our view of human actions are concerned . . . they concentrate upon that part of the theory which concerns the discharge of energy or the eruption of it from the system'. They leave aside the other part that concerns 'shifts or transfers of energy within the system'.

5 See Kitcher 1992.

6 See 'On the History of the Psycho-Analytic Movement' (1914), where Freud discussed briefly the disagreement with C. G. Jung about the drives, given that the latter's modification of the theory 'loosens the connection of the phenomena with instinctual life' (SE 14: 60, and 60–6).

7 For Strachey 'even in his profoundest psychological speculations little or no discussion is to be found upon some of the *most* fundamental of the concepts of which he makes use: such concepts, for instance, as "mental energy", "sum of excitations", "cathexis", "quantity", "quality", "intensity", and so on' (Strachey's emphasis, SE 4: xvi).

8 Freud discussed memory-traces in terms of inheritance in *Moses and Monotheism: Three Essays* (1939 [1937–39]; SE 23). Phylogenesis refers to the countless accumulation of experiences. See Surprenant 2003, especially Chapter 4.

9 Freud elaborated the notion of introjection, among other places, in that essay, which has been developed by Abraham and Torok 1994.

10 Guilt plays an important role in the process of civilization. See Freud's account of the origin of society in *Totem and Taboo* (1912–13; SE 13).

11 See Whitebook 2004: 56–7, and Bergo 2004: 343–5.

12 Jocelyn Benoist's exploration of the ontological status of the drive suggested that it is not necessary to reject Freud's physicalist and biologistic explanations. For Benoist, the concept of the drive shows that the body (or the somatic) remains a cause, even if Freud has established, through his study of hysteria, the hermeneutic dimension of the relation between the body and the psyche. Psychical transformations are

not solely a matter of translation, expression of meaning (see Benoist 2006).

13 See Jones 1953.

14 The place of biology in Freud is dealt with in Sulloway 1979, Laplanche 1976 and Kitcher 1992, among others. See Bowie 1991 for a subtle presentation of how the rejection of biology motivated to a large extent Jacques Lacan's 'return to Freud'.

15 Herman Helmholtz applied the law of conservation of energy in physiology (1847) after Robert Mayer had introduced it in physics (1842) (Assoun 1981: 158). He worked on the speed of nervous influx, on vision and hearing. See Freud's brief discussion of his first scientific work in neurology under Brücke's direction, which pertained to 'the origin of the posterior nerve-roots in the spinal cord of small fish of very archaic structure' (SE 16: 340).

16 See Kitcher 1992.

17 Freud specified in the section on psychopathology of the 'Project' that the term 'excessively intense' is a quantitative term (SE 1: 350). It is possible to explain the formation of a symptom, whereby an excessively intense idea A 'forces its way into consciousness' and 'gives rise to weeping'. It is absurd to weep at A, but not at B. It is as though A had taken the place of B, or it had become 'a *symbol* for B'. In mathematical terms: 'Something has been added to A which has been subtracted from B. The pathological process is one of *displacement*, such as we have come to know in dreams – a primary process therefore' (SE 1: 350). The displacement of psychical energy (and more generally, the process of symbol-formation) can be rendered into an equation: 'We can at once recognize this resistance against B, the amount of the *compulsion* exercised by A' (SE 1: 351).

18 Among other abbreviations, Freud used Q to refer to quantity 'in general, or of the order of magnitude in the external world'; $Q\eta$ to refer to quantity 'of the intercellular order of magnitude'. There are three systems of neurones, the system of permeable neurones designated by ϕ; the system of impemeable neurones by ψ, and the system of perceptual neurones designated by ω (SE 1: 294). For an insightful reflection on that model, see Derrida 1967.

19 See the introduction in Gill and Pribram 1976: 14–22.

20 See Derrida 1980 for an analysis of the relation between the pleasure principle, the reality principle, biology and Freud's figurative language.

5. METAPSYCHOLOGY AND ECONOMICS

1 Only five of these papers were published. Seven of them were written and never published. Ilse Grubrich-Simitis discovered a 1915 draft of the twelfth one entitled *A Phylogenetic Fantasy. Overview of the Transference Neuroses*, ed. Ilse Grubrich-Simitis, trans. A. and P. Hoffer (Cambridge, MA: Harvard University Press, 1987).

2 On Freud's illustrations, including those he produced as a neurologist, see Borck 1998.

3 The extension of sexuality relates to Freud's reclassification of the drives into two classes: 'those which seek to preserve and unite – which we call "erotic", exactly in the sense in which Plato uses the word "Eros" in his *Symposium*, or "sexual", with a deliberate extension of the popular extension of "sexuality" – and those which seek to destroy and kill and which we group together as the aggressive or destructive instinct' (SE 22: 209). 'The concept of "sexuality", and at the same time of the sexual instincts, had, it is true, to be extended so as to cover many things which could not be classed under the reproductive function; and this caused no little hubbub in an austere, respectable or merely hypocritical world' (SE 18: 51).

4 Jean Laplanche and Jean-Bertrand Pontalis hint at such an extension of the meaning of economy towards a non-economic point of view when they discuss the economic point of view in the *Language of Psychoanalysis*: The economic point of view opens the way to phenomenological analyses (and not the less mechanistic aspects of Freud's work). In the subject's personal world, objects and ideas are affected by certain *values* which organise the fields of perception and behaviour. Now, in the first place these values may appear to differ qualitatively among themselves to such an extent that it becomes difficult to imagine equivalences or substitutions between them . . . There is thus a temptation to abandon the economic terminology and to translate the Freudian conception of cathexis into a language inspired by phenomenological thinking and based on such concepts as intentionality and value object. . . . [in some places] cathexis seems to mean less a measurable load of libidinal energy than qualitatively differentiated emotional intentions' (Laplanche and Pontalis 1973: 64–5).

5 See Bowie 1991 on Lacan's return to Freud.

6 Note that 'topicality' is sometimes a necessary component of jokes (SE 8: 122–3).

7 'Saving' and pleasure would seem also to be inspired by domestic imperatives. Freud compared the economy involved in jokes to that of housewives (SE 8: 44), as well as to that of a business (SE 8: 156–57).

8 Exploring Freud's theory of jokes poses acute problems of translation, as does the theory of dreams and other 'psychopathologies of everyday life', all of which show the mode of functioning of the primary processes as plays on language. Suffice it here to say that a question arises as to whether one should find an equivalent wordplay in the target language or whether one should aim at translating as literally as possible the wordplay into the target language.

9 See SE 8: 110–11 for a more elaborated account of the value of Jewish jokes.

10 See 'Creative Writers and Day-Dreaming' ([1908] (1907) SE 9: 143–53).

11 The connection with sexuality is not anodyne. Freud was writing the two books at the same time, and elaborating the notion of 'fore-pleasure' with reference both to the comic and sexuality. See Nancy 1993.

12 Freud referred to Spencer 1860 [1901].
13 In other words, 'jokes . . . seek to gain a small yield of pleasure from the mere activity, untrammelled by needs, of our mental apparatus' (SE 8: 179). Jokes are partly a disinterested kind of pleasure.
14 Children, 'a man from the common people, or a member of certain races', when narrating stories, express their subject matter with 'expressive movements' (SE 8: 192).
15 See also SE 10: 233. See Bowlby 2006 for an examination of psychoanalytic theory in the light of modern reproductive technologies.

BIBLIOGRAPHY

WORKS BY FREUD

All references to Freud's writings in *Freud: A Guide for the Perplexed* are to *The Standard Edition of the Complete Psychological Works of Sigmund Freud*, vols 1–24, ed. J. Strachey in collaboration with A. Freud, A. Strachey and A. Tyson, assisted by A. Richards (London: Hogarth Press and the Institute of Psychoanalysis, 1953–74; the 24 volumes of the *Standard Edition* were also published by Vintage, 2001). References are abbreviated as SE, followed by the volume and page number, and appear in brackets in the text after the quotation.

SE 1
(1892–3) 'A Case of Successful Treatment by Hypnosis', 115–32
(1940–1 [1892]) 'Sketches for the "Preliminary Communication" of 1893', 145–54
(1950 [1895]) 'Project for a Scientific Psychology', 283–391
(1950 [1892–9]) 'Extracts from the Fliess Papers', 175–280
(1956 [1886]) 'Report on My Studies in Paris and Berlin', 5–15

SE 2
(1893–5) *Studies on Hysteria*, 1–305

SE 3
(1893) 'Charcot', 9–23
(1894) 'The Neuro-Psychoses of Defence', 43–61
(1893) 'On the Psychical Mechanism of Hysterical Phenomena: A Lecture', 25–39
(1896) 'The Aetiology of Hysteria', 189–221
(1896a) 'Further remarks on the Neuro-Psychoses of Defence', 159–85
(1898) 'The Psychical Mechanisms of Forgetfulness', 288–97

SE 4
(1900) *The Interpretation of Dreams*, 1–338

SE 5

(1900) *The Interpretation of Dreams*, 339–621
(1901) 'On Dreams', 631–86

SE 6

(1901) *The Psychopathology of Everyday Life*, 1–279

SE 7

(1904 [1903]) 'Freud's Psychoanalytic Procedure', 249–54
(1905 [1901]) 'Fragment of an Analysis of a Case of Hysteria', 3–122
(1905a [1904]) 'On Psychotherapy', 257–68
(1905b) *Three Essays on The Theory of Sexuality*, 125–243
(1906 [1905]) 'My Views on the Part Played by Sexuality in the Aetiology of the Neuroses' 271–9

SE 8

(1905c) *Jokes and their Relation to the Unconscious*, 3–236

SE 9

(1907 [1906]) *Delusions and Dreams in Jensen's* Gradiva, 3–95
(1908 [1907]) 'Creative Writers and Day-Dreaming', 143–53

SE 10

(1909) 'Analysis of a Phobia in a Five-Year-Old Boy' ('Little Hans'), 3–149
(1909a) 'Notes upon a Case of Obsessional Neurosis', 153–318

SE 11

(1910 [1909]) *Five Lectures on Psycho-Analysis*, 3–55
(1910a) 'The Psycho-analytic View of Psychogenic Disturbance of Vision', 209–18
(1910b) 'The Future Prospects of Psycho-Analytic Therapy', 140–51

SE 12

(1911) 'Formulations on the Two Principles of Mental Functioning', 213–26
(1912) 'A Note on the Unconscious in Psychoanalysis', 257–66
(1913 [1911]) 'On Psycho-Analysis', 207–11
(1914) 'Remembering, Repeating and Working-Through', 147–56

SE 13

(1913a [1912–13]) *Totem and Taboo*, 1–161
(1913b) 'The Claims of Psycho-Analysis to Scientific Interest', 165–90

SE 14

(1914) 'On the History of the Psycho-Analytic Movement', 3–66
(1914a) 'On Narcissism: An Introduction', 67–107
(1915) 'Instincts and their Vicissitudes', 111–40

(1915a) 'Repression', 143–58
(1915b) 'The Unconscious', 161–215
(1917 [1915]) 'A Metapsychological Supplement to the Theory of Dreams', 219–35
(1917a) 'Mourning and Melancholia', 243–58
(1916 [1915]) 'On Transience', 305–7

SE 15 and 16

(1916–17 [1915–17]) *Introductory Lectures on Psycho-Analysis*, Parts I–II 3–339, Part III 243–463

SE 17

(1918 [1914]) 'From the History of An Infantile Neurosis' (The 'Wolf Man'), 3–122
(1919) 'The "Uncanny" ', 217–52

SE 18

(1920) *Beyond the Pleasure Principle*, 3–64
(1920) 'A Note on the Prehistory of the Technique of Analysis', 263–5
(1921) *Group-Psychology and the Analysis of the Ego*, 67–143
(1923 [1922]) 'Two Encyclopaedia Articles', 235–59

SE 19

(1923) *The Ego and the Id*, 3–59
(1924) 'The Economic Problem of Masochism', 157–70
(1925 [1924]) 'A Note upon the "Mystic-Writing Pad" ', 227–32
(1925) 'Negation', 235–9
(1925a) 'The Resistance to Psychoanalysis', 213–22
(1923 [1922]) 'Remarks on the Theory and Practice of Dream-Interpretation', 109–38

SE 20

(1926) 'The Question of Lay Analysis', 183–258
(1926 [1925]) 'Psycho-Analysis', 261–70

SE 21

(1927) *The Future of an Illusion*, 3–56
(1927a) 'Humour', 160–6
(1927b) 'Fetishism', 152–7
(1930 [1929]) *Civilization and its Discontents*, 64–107

SE 22

(1933 [1932]) *New Introductory Lectures on Psycho-Analysis*, 3–182

SE 23

(1937) 'Analysis Terminable and Interminable', 216–53
(1937a) 'Constructions in Analysis', 257–69

(1939 [1934–8]) *Moses and Monotheism: Three Essays*, 7–137
(1940 [1938]) *An Outline of Psycho-Analysis*, 144–207
(1940a [1938]) 'Some Elementary Lessons in Psycho-Analysis', 281–6

Other works by Freud

Freud, S. (1985), *The Complete Letters of Sigmund Freud to Wilhelm Fliess, 1887–1904*. Cambridge, MA and London: Belknap Press of Harvard University Press.
——(1987), *A Phylogenetic Fantasy. Overview of the Transference Neuroses*, ed. Ilse Grubrich-Simitis, trans. A. and P. Hoffer. Cambridge, MA: Harvard University Press.
——(1995), *Sigmund Freud Ludwig Binswanger. Correspondance 1908–1938*. Paris: Calmann-Lévy.
——(1999), *The Interpretation of Dreams*, trans. J. Crick. Oxford: Oxford University Press.
——(2006), *Lettres à Wilhelm Fließ 1887–1904*, ed. J. M. Masson and M. Schröter, transcription by G. Fichtner, trans. from German by F. Kahn and F. Robert. Paris: Presses Universitaires de France.
Meyer-Palmedo, I. and Fichtner, G. (1999), *Freud-Bibliographie mit Werkkonkordanz*. Frankfurt am Main: S. Fisher Verlag. (This bibliography provides a concordance between *The Standard Edition* and two editions of Freud's work in German, notably *Gesammelten Werke*, eds A. Freud, E. Bibring, W. Hoffer, E. Kris and O. Isakower. Frankfurt am Main: S. Fisher Verlag, 1960–87.)

SECONDARY LITERATURE ON FREUD AND OTHER CITED WORKS

Abraham, M. and Torok, N. (1994), *The Shell and the Kernel: Renewals of Psychoanalysis*. N. Rand (trans., ed. and with an introduction). Chicago: Chicago University Press.
Appignesi, L. and Forrester, J. (1992), *Freud's Women*. London: Virago.
Assoun, P.-L. (1976), *Freud, la philosophie et les philosophes*. Paris: Presses Universitaires de France.
——(1981), *Introduction à l'épistémologie freudienne*. Paris: Payot.
——(1997), *Psychanalyse*. Paris: Presses universitaires de France.
Austen, J. (2003 [1814]), *Mansfield Park*. Oxford: Oxford University Press.
Benoist, J. (2006), 'Pulsion, cause et raison chez Freud' in *La Pulsion*. J.-C. Goddard (ed.). Paris: Éditions Vrin. 113–38.
Bergo, B. (2004), 'Psychoanalytic Models. Freud's Debts to Philosophy and His Copernican Revolution' in *The Philosophy of Psychiatry: A Companion*, ed. J. Radden. Oxford: Oxford University Press.
Bernheimer, C. and Kahane, C. (eds) (1985), *In Dora's Case: Freud, Hysteria, Feminism*. London: Virago.
Binswanger, L. (1970 [1936]), 'La Conception freudienne de l'homme à la lumière de l'anthropologie [Freuds Auffassung des Menschen im Lichte der Anthropologie]' in *Discours, parcours et Freud*, trans. R. Lewinter. Paris: Gallimard. 201–307.

Borch-Jacobsen, M. (1996), *Remembering Anna O. A Century of Psychoanalytic Mystification*, trans. K. Olson, X. Callahan and the author. New York: Routledge.

Borck, C. (1998), 'The Rhetoric of Freud's Illustrations' in *Freud and the Neuro-Sciences. From Brain Research to the Unconscious*, eds G. Guttman and I. Scholz-Strasser. Vienna: Verlag der Österreichischen Akademie der Wissenschaften.

Börne, L. (1823), 'The Art of Becoming an Original Writer in Three Days' in J. E. Gedo and G. H. Pollock (eds) (1976), *Freud: The Fusion of Science and Humanism: The Intellectual History of Psychoanalysis*. New York: International Universities Press: 253–4.

Bowie, M. (1991), *Lacan*. London: Harvard University Press.

Bowlby, R. (2006), 'Family Realisms: Freud and Greek Tragedy' in *Essays in Criticism* LVI.2: 111–38.

——(2007), *Freudian Mythologies*. Oxford: Oxford University Press.

Dalbiez, R. (1936), *La Méthode Psychanalytique et la Doctrine freudienne*. 2 vols. Paris: Desclée de Brouwer.

Darwin, C. (1872), *The Expression of the Emotions in Man and in Animals*. London: John Murray.

Derrida, J. (1967), 'Freud and the Scene of Writing' in *Writing and Difference*, trans. A. Bass. Chicago: Chicago University Press.

——(1980), *The Postcard: From Socrates to Freud and Beyond*, trans. A. Bass. Chicago, London: Chicago University Press.

——(1996), *Resistances of Psychoanalysis*, trans. P. Kamuf, P. A. Brault and M. Naas. Stanford: Stanford University Press.

Erwin, E. (1997), 'Psychoanalysis, Past, Present, and Future' in *Philosophy and Phenomenological Research* LVII.3 (1997): 671–96.

Forrester, J. (1980), *Language and the Origins of Psychoanalysis*. London: Macmillan.

——(1997), *Dispatches from the Freud Wars: Psychoanalysis and its Passions*. Cambridge, MA: Harvard University Press.

Foucault, M. and Binswanger, L. (1986), *Dream and Existence*, ed. K. Hoeller. Seattle: Review of Existential Psychology and Psychiatry.

Freeman, L. (1994), *The Story of Anna O*. Northvale, NJ; London: Jason Aronson.

Gardner, S. (1987), *Sartre's Critique of Freud*. Cambridge: Cambridge University Press.

Gill, M. M. and Pribram, K. H. (1976), *Freud's Project Re-Assessed*. New York: Basic Books.

Gilman, S. (1993), *The Case of Sigmund Freud: Medicine and Identity at the Fin-de-Siècle*. Baltimore, London: Johns Hopkins University Press.

Green, A. (1986), 'Conceptions of Affect' in *On Private Madness*. Madison, CT: International University Press, 174–213.

Henry, M. (1985), *Généalogie de la psychanalyse*. Paris: Presses universitaires de France.

Hesnard, A. (1960), *L'Oeuvre de Freud et son importance pour le monde moderne*. Preface by M. Merleau-Ponty. Paris: Payot.

Husserl, E. (1970), *Crisis of the European Sciences and Transcendental Phenomenology*, trans. D. Carr. Evanston: North Western University Press.

Jones, E. (1953–7), *Sigmund Freud: Life and Work*. London: Hogarth Press.

Kitcher, P. (1992), *Freud's Dream. A Complete Interdisciplinary Science of the Mind*. Cambridge, MA; London: The MIT Press.

de Lafayette, Madame (1992), *The Princesse de Clèves*, trans. Terence Cave. Oxford University Press.

Laplanche, J. (1976), *Life and Death in Psychoanalysis*, trans. J. Mehlman. Baltimore, London: Johns Hopkins University Press.

Laplanche, J. and Pontalis, J.-B. (1973), *The Language of Psychoanalysis*, trans. D. Nicholson-Smith. London: The Hogarth Press.

Lear, J. (1990 [1998]), *Love and its Place in Nature: A Philosophical Interpretation of Freudian Psychoanalysis*. New Haven and London: Yale University Press.

——(2006 [2005]), *Freud*. London and New York: Routledge.

Macintyre, A. (1997 [1958]), *The Unconscious: A Conceptual Analysis*. Bristol: Thoemmes Press.

Marcus, L. (ed.) (1999), *Sigmund Freud's* The Interpretation of Dreams: *New Interdisciplinary Essays*. Manchester: Manchester University Press.

Marinelli, L. and Mayer, A. (2005 [2003]), *Dreaming by the Book. Freud's* Interpretation of Dreams *and the History of the Psychoanalytic Movement*, trans. S. Fairfield. New York: Other Press.

Mehlman, J. (1976), 'Trimethylamin: Notes on Freud's Specimen Dream'. *Diacritics* 6.1 (Spring), 42–5.

Mills, J. (ed.) (2004), *Rereading Freud: Psychoanalysis Through Philosophy*. Albany: State University of New York Press.

Nancy, J.-L. (1993), 'In Statu Nascendi' in *The Birth to Presence*. Stanford: Stanford University Press.

Neu, J. (ed.) (1991), *The Cambridge Companion to Freud*. Cambridge: Cambridge University Press.

Ornston, D. (ed.) (1992), *Translating Freud*. New Haven: Yale University Press.

Rand, N. 'The Hidden Soul: The Growth of the Unconscious in Philosophy, Psychology, Medicine, and Literature, 1750–1900'. *American Imago* 61.3 (2004): 257–89.

Ricoeur, P. (1970 [1965]), *Freud and Philosophy: An Essay on Interpretation*, trans. D. Savage. New Haven and London: Yale University Press.

——(1969), *Le Conflit des interprétations*. Paris: Seuil.

Schopenhauer, A. (1958 [1819]), *The World as Will and Representation*, trans. E. F. J. Payne. New York: Dover Publications, Inc.

Schreber, D. P. (1955 [1903]), *Memoirs of My Nervous Illness*, trans. I. Macalpine and R. A. Hunter. London: William Dawson and Sons.

Silberer, H. (1914), *Problems of Mysticism and its Symbolism*. New York: Moffat, Yard & Co.

Sontag, S. (1990 [1968]), *Against Interpretation and Other Essays*. New York, London: Anchor Books, Doubleday.

Spencer, H. (1901 [1860]), 'The Physiology of Laughter' in *Essays* 2. London: Williams & Norgate.

Sprengnether, M. (2003), 'Mouth to Mouth: Freud, Irma, and the Dream of Psychoanalysis'. *American Imago* 60.3 (Fall).

Sulloway, F. (1979), *Freud's Biologist of the Mind: Beyond the Psychoanalytic Legend*. New York: Basic Books.

Surprenant, C. (2003), *Freud's Mass Psychology: A Question of Scale*. London: Palgrave.

Thurschwell, P. (2000), *Sigmund Freud*. New York and London: Routledge.

Weber, S. (2002), *The Legend of Freud*. Stanford: Stanford University Press.

Whitebook, J. (2004), 'Weighty Objects. On Adorno's Kant–Freud Interpretation' in T. Huhn (ed.), *The Cambridge Companion to Adorno*. Cambridge: Cambridge University Press.

Wollheim, R. (1971), *Freud*. London: Fontana.

——(1991), 'Supplementary Preface (1990)' in *Freud*, 2nd Edition. London: Fontana.

Wollheim, R. and Hopkins, J. (1982), *Philosophical Essays on Freud*. Cambridge: Cambridge University Press.

Wundt, W. (1904 [1874]), *Principles of Physiological Psychology*, trans. E. B. Titchener. London: Swan Sonnenschein & Co.

INDEX

Groddeck, George 117
guilt (sense of) 42, 103

Heine, Heinrich 147
helplessness (*Hilflosigkeit*) 158, 159
Herbart Johann Friedrich 122
'Heredity and the Aetiology of the
	Neuroses' 2
Hildebrandt F.W. 71
history of psychoanalysis 9, 32, 68,
	121
'History of the Psycho-Analytic
	Movement, On' 27, 48, 161,
	168
Hoffmann, E.T. A. *The Sandman*
	12
homosexuality 74, 78
'Humour' 144, 151, 156
hypotheses 10, 12, 15, 19, 30, 47,
	52, 68, 104, 125, 134, 135
hypnosis 21, 23, 24, 25, 26, 32, 33
hysteria 20, 121, 125, 113

Ibsen Henrik 91
id 3, 104, 107, 116–19, 120, 138
ideas 7, 21, 33, 47–55, 57, 69, 76,
	85, 93, 94, 99, 101–7, 109, 112,
	122, 133, 139, 142, 168
	erotic 44, 53; incompatible 43,
	55, 49, 163; involuntary 34, 37,
	76, 77, 151; repressed 33, 85,
	86, 101, 113; traumatic 52;
	unconscious 32, 35, 86;
	excessively intense 42, 127,
	167; unpleasurable 52
ideational content 42, 101 (*see*
	representation, idea)
ideational mimetics 153
ignorance 23, 47, 67
incentive bonus (*see* fore-pleasure;
	yield of pleasure) 146, 147
infantile
	amnesia 64; mental life 79; origin
	of symptoms 36; sexuality 29,
	55, 62, 63, 64, 68, 133, 144;
	traumatic events 162;
'Instincts and their Vicissitudes'
	109, 110, 136, 162

instinctual 107, 109, 116, 132, 159
	demands, 48, 120, 158; impulses
	49, 108, 141; life 109, 166;
	needs 110, 117; processes 41;
	satisfaction 118
instincts (*see* drives) 59, 62, 64, 107,
	108, 109, 110, 112–15, 117,
	119, 142, 168
interpretation (*see* dream-
	interpretation) 10, 14, 18, 20,
	33, 36, 37, 38, 39, 40, 41, 46,
	50, 68, 72, 73, 75, 77, 84, 87,
	99, 144, 160
Interpretation of Dreams. The 4, 10,
	14, 19, 36, 40, 55, 57, 68,
	70–77, 87–100, 102, 117, 123,
	137, 145, 147, 156, 162, 164
*Introductory Lectures on Psycho-
	Analysis* 6, 17, 72, 75–78, 116,
	132, 134

Janet, Pierre 54
Jung Carl Gustav 9, 166
*Jokes and their relation to the
	Unconscious* 1–2, 8, 11, 61, 92,
	123, 133, 136, 138, 146, 153,
	157
jokes (*see Witz*) 1, 46, 61, 92, 125,
	136, 139, 146, 147–55, 157,
	168, 169
joke-techniques 148, 149, 151
joke-work 148
Jones, Ernest 121, 167

Kant, Immanuel 147, 161

Lacan, Jacques 145, 167, 168
language 15, 44, 69, 81, 94, 105,
	129, 140, 148, 149, 151, 155,
	166, 167, 168
Laplanche Jean 120, 167, 168
latency 61, 64, 65
laughter 1, 2, 6, 123, 153, 156
Lear Jonathan 3, 7, 15, 36, 88, 97,
	140
	Love and its Place in Nature
	140
libidinal economy 139

libido 58, 111, 113, 114, 115, 120, 142, 143, 164, 166
Lipps, Theodor 147

Mach, Ernst 122
Madame de Lafayette, *Princesse of Clèves* 60
masochism 113, 119
Maury, Alfred 71
meaning 10, 44, 69, 71, 92, 99, 105, 121, 161, 167
measurement of mental phenomena 122, 141
megalomania 115, 144
memory 18, 22–27, 29, 36, 45, 49, 50, 51, 52, 53, 55, 56, 57, 58, 63, 69, 74, 77, 79, 84, 88, 92, 99, 101, 102, 105, 130, 131, 132, 133, 154, 164, 165, 166
  pathogenic effect of 27, 32; as gaps 32; stinks 46; accumulation of 27; of early childhood 28; in dreams 71
memories (*see* memory)
memory trace 50, 51, 82, 105, 154, 166
mental
  apparatus 52, 71, 73, 79, 87, 95, 99, 101, 109, 139, 149, 151, 163, 164, 169; forces 61, 109, 121, 152
Merleau-Ponty Maurice 7
metapsychology 11, 73 107, 135–37, 138, 140, 143, 156
metapsychological point of view 8, 11. 51
morality 46, 49, 61, 64, 85
moral
  conscience 118, 127; feelings 114; sense 33, 50
Moses and Monotheism: Three Essays 12, 135, 157, 159
'Moses of Michelangelo, The' 147
mourning 102, 111, 163
'Mourning and Melancholia' 111

Narcissism 115, 144, 159
'Nature of Q, On' 123

natural sciences 4, 5, 7, 11, 121, 123, 132, 160
'Negation, On' 96, 130, 162
'Neuro-Psychoses of Defence, The' 2, 42, 48, 55, 101, 104, 123, 160
neuroses 62
  traumatic origin of 29, 53, theory of 57; and dreams 85;
neurosis 8, 23, 29, 31, 50, 53, 54, 55, 56, 57, 62, 85, 99, 110, 114, 115, 120, 121,125, 143, 144, 156, 162, 164
  artificial 31; choice of 119, 158; hysterical; obsessional 113, 127, 161; collective or mass neurosis 159
neuroses (*see* neurosis)
neurology 124–34, 167
New Introductory Lectures 116, 132
Nietzsche, Friedrich 93, 117
'Note on the Unconscious in Psychoanalysis, A' 47, 160

Oedipus complex 56, 61, 64, 98
observations 7, 10, 13–14, 15, 16, 37, 42, 61, 125, 133, 137, 143
omnipotence of thought 115
'Outline of Psycho-analysis. An' 16, 19, 106, 116

pan-sexualism 1, 141
'Papers on Technique' 19
perversions 57, 58, 59, 60, 62, 63, 110
phantasy 8, 19, 22, 27, 28, 29, 30, 31, 56, 65, 69, 80, 114, 144, 162
phantasies (*see* phantasy)
phylogenesis 117, 144, 164, 166, 167
phylogenetic inheritance 117
physiology 26, 121–22, 123, 132–33,
pictorial arrangement of psychical material 94–5
Plato 141, 168
play 15, 60, 149, 150, 151, 168